D0421559

Translation and Web Localization

Web localization is a cognitive, textual, communicative and technological process by which interactive web texts are modified to be used by audiences in different sociolinguistic contexts.

Translation and Web Localization provides an in-depth and comprehensive overview of this emerging field of study. The book covers the key areas and main theoretical and practical approaches of the subject, rather than a step by step practical guide. Topics covered include the often controversial definition of localization, how the process develops, what constitutes a text in this process, digital genre theory and its implications, and how to conduct research or training in this field.

The book concludes with a look into the dynamic nature of web localization and the forces, such as crowdsourcing, that are reshaping web localization and translation as we know it.

In the light of the deep changes brought by the Internet, *Translation and Web Localization* is an indispensable book for researchers, postgraduate and advanced undergraduate students of translation studies, as well as practitioners and researchers in related fields such as computational linguistics, applied linguistics, Internet linguistics, digital genre theory and web development.

Miguel A. Jiménez-Crespo holds a PhD in Translation and Interpreting Studies from the University of Granada, Spain, and is the director of the MA and BA programme in Translation and Interpretation at Rutgers University, USA.

Translation and Web Localization

Miguel A. Jiménez-Crespo

Routledge
Taylor & Francis Group

LONDON AND NEW YORK

First published 2013
by Routledge
2 Park Square, Milton Park, Abingdon, Oxon OX14 4RN

Simultaneously published in the USA and Canada
by Routledge
711 Third Avenue, New York, NY 10017

Routledge is an imprint of the Taylor & Francis Group, an informa business

© 2013 Miguel Jiménez-Crespo

British Library Cataloguing in Publication Data
A catalogue record for this book is available from the British Library

Library of Congress Cataloging in Publication Data
Jiménez-Crespo, Miguel A.
Translation and web localization / Miguel A. Jiménez-Crespo.
    pages cm
  1. Translating and interpreting (Social aspects).   2. Translating and interpreting (Philosophy).   3. Communication and technology.   4. Intercultural communication.   5. Sociolinguistics.
  I. Title.
  P306.97.S63J56 2013
  418'.020285 – dc23

2012043801

ISBN: 978-0-415-64316-0 (hbk)
ISBN: 978-0-415-64318-4 (pbk)
ISBN: 978-0-203-52002-8 (ebk)

Typeset in Sabon and Scala
by RefineCatch Limited, Bungay, Suffolk

Printed and bound by CPI Group (UK) Ltd, Croydon, CR0 4YY

Contents

ILLUSTRATIONS

FIGURES

TABLES

ACKNOWLEDGEMENTS

I would like to thank the following copyright-holders for permission to reproduce the figures and tables listed: Frank Austermühl for Figure 4.2, Mariana Orozco for Figure 6.3, the PACTE group for Figure 7.1, JOSTRANS for the Table 4.1.

I would also like to thank Ignacio García and the Department of Foreign Languages at the University of Western Sydney, Australia, for having inviting me as a Visiting Professor to write this book. I am extremely grateful to my colleagues who graciously reviewed portions of this manuscript: S.E. Wright, I. García Izquierdo, A. Alcina, M. Orozco, M. Tercedor, P. Zatlin, J. Ritzdorf and I. García.

My thanks go to my family in Spain, to Dr Maribel Tercedor at the University of Granada, A. Cadogan for the inspiration for the cover and especially to the new family I found in Sydney: Harris K., Allan D., Allan J., Alan C., Cath M. and many others. I could not have imagined a more engaging and exciting environment in which to write this book. Your love and friendship made me feel the happiest and most fortunate man on this planet. This book is dedicated to you all.

Last but not least, I would like to thank Sophie Jaques and Louisa Semlyen at Routledge for all of their help and assistance in the preparation of this manuscript.

ABBREVIATIONS

CAT	Computer-Assisted Translation
CMS	Content Management System
G11n	Globalization
GALA	Globalization and Localization Association
GMS	Global Management System
I18n	Internationalization
ISO	International Standard Association
L10n	Localization
LIS	Localization Industry Standards
LISA	Localization Industry Standards Association
LS	Localization Studies
MT	Machine Translation
QA	Quality Assurance
ST	Source Text
TM	Translation Memory
TS	Translation Studies
TT	Target Text
W3C	World Wide Web Consortium
WAI	Web Accessibility Initiative
WWW	World Wide Web

INTRODUCTION

Since the emergence of the World Wide Web, we have witnessed the unprecedented growth of web localization, a communicative, technological, textual and cognitive process by which interactive digital texts are modified for use by audiences around the world other than those originally targeted. The success of websites as global platforms for communicating, sharing information or selling goods and services has hinged on the development of localization processes, bridging the gap between Internet users from different socio-cultural and linguistic contexts. The economic importance of this phenomenon is continually increasing, and its significance is attested by the increasing body of research devoted to localization, the specialized conferences and the number of institutions offering courses at both graduate and undergraduate levels. However, despite its significance in Translation Studies and in modern societies, this process has yet to receive the attention it deserves from a scholarly perspective. This is partly due to a lack of comprehensive theoretical and methodological foundations on which research in the area can build.

This book intends to make good this shortcoming by providing the first comprehensive interdisciplinary overview of web localization. It departs from a translation-studies perspective and goes beyond the most common approach used in previous publications: procedural descriptions of best professional practices. It draws different perspectives and disciplines together to provide a solid foundation for scholars and students searching for, or attempting to get involved in, research on this fascinating area. The main connecting thread is examining how the 'technological turn' (O'Hagan 2012a; Cronin 2010, 2013) is reshaping theorizations and the practice of translation in general, and of localization in particular. Currently, classic (if much debated) notions such as text, culture, quality, genre, adaptation, professionalization, transla-tion competence-skills or the individualistic character of translation are constantly being redefined and negotiated, and they pose daunting methodological and theoretical challenges to those embarking on research in the area. To introduce readers to localization, key concepts, models, approaches and methodologies are here critically analyzed and explored, and a new interdisciplinary approach that embraces cognitive, pragmatic, discourse, communicative and technological perspectives is presented.

GUIDE TO CHAPTERS

This book is divided into three distinct parts that follow a progression from conceptual to analytical. The first part identifies the conceptual and epistemological middle ground between the diverse perspectives and views on localization. Part II reviews the most pressing issues for the development of research in web localization: from basic notions such as 'text', 'digital genre', 'research methodologies' and avenues for empirical research, to concepts related to textual reception such as 'quality'. The third part examines future possible developments in the ever-evolving and unpredictable field of localization, such as crowdsourcing, post-editing machine translation or localization training. Finally, the volume offers a detailed bibliography of web localization.

Each chapter offers an end-of-chapter summary and suggestions for further reading for those interested in expanding their knowledge of any of the main topics covered in each chapter. An attempt has been made to refer to publications that are readily available.

The chapters are organized as follows.

Chapter 1 charts the origins of localization within the evolution of the Internet and the World Wide Web. It reviews different perspectives and approaches of the last two decades, focusing on the industry-based attempts to establish this modality as a different process from 'standard' translation. It provides a critical, comprehensive summary of the conceptualizations, metaphorizations and metalanguage of localization from different approaches, as well as how scholars and industry experts have struggled to define localization. The metalanguage of web localization is clarified, and a new definition is presented.

Chapter 2 provides a concise description of localization processes in the context of a global GILT cycle. It attempts to describe the different factors and constraints to be taken into account while studying localization, such as the GILT cycle (Globalization, Internationalization, Localization and Translation), the agents in the process, cultural adaptations, localization levels and web usability. Careful consideration of the global holistic cycle is needed for research focusing both on the process and the products, as these intertwined processes impose specific constraints that inevitably have an impact on product and process research.

Chapter 3 revisits the notion of 'text' in a digital era, a core concept in Translation Studies (TS). Since its inception, single stable texts upon which translation tasks are based have been a constant in the discipline. Nevertheless, the emergence of new forms of hypertextuality, textual segmentation and reuse has challenged existing conceptualizations. Digital hypertexts have radically changed the ways in which digital texts are produced and received by translators and end users, changing the cognitive and communicative context of reception and production in translation and reception environments. From an interdisciplinary perspective this chapter offers a critical review of the evolution of the notion of text in TS, projecting existing work into the complex digital environment in which localization occurs. Hypertext and hypertextual approaches to textual analysis are explored, and the essential notions such as cohesion and coherence in these new non-linear texts are explored with regard to the localization process.

Chapter 4 focuses on the expanding number of emerging digital genres, such as corporate websites or social networking sites. The dynamic nature of digital genres and how research into them has been applied in scholarly disciplines is of the utmost importance for scholars and students focusing on web localization. This chapter departs from the increasing amount of theoretical and empirical TS research produced using models and methods borrowed from Discourse Analysis, Language Service Providers (LSP) and Contrastive Studies. It argues that genre analysis represents a solid foundation for research and training efforts in software and web localization. This is because the genres in different localization types show different degrees of fixation and 'genre embedding' – web genres can potentially incorporate a wide array of other genres within their structures, from contact forms to contracts or personal narratives. The chapter reviews existing research on digital genre theory and the evolution of these conventionalized forms of texts; a model for digital genre analysis, as well as the complex interrelation of textual super, macro and microstructures in digital genres, is presented. It ends with a proposed classification of web genres for categorization and research purposes.

Chapter 5 brings together industry and TS approaches to translation quality and analyses how both ends of the debate can benefit from each other's developments while understanding quality as a time – and resource – finite process. It reviews existing theoretical and practical implemented models and analyses the main issues, such as the problems with error-based approaches, error-assessment issues, standards in the industry, and the introduction of holistic and corpus-based approaches to quality evaluation. The chapter ends with a novel proposal for a framework for assessing web localization that can be customized, depending on the evaluation context.

Chapter 6 focuses on empirical research and provides a concise introduction for those scholars and students interested in developing research projects in web localization. It provides a summary of the interdisciplinary nature of web localization research and maps the different branches proposed by Holmes (1988) and Toury (1995) into a map of 'Localization Studies', a sub-discipline in its own right (Munday 2012). It reviews how to apply existing research models and paradigms, provides a guide to how to plan research methodologies and research design through comprehensive examples of existing published research. The chapter ends with a concise review of the main challenges that researchers face in this novel area.

Chapter 7 departs from the assumption that dealing with web-based texts will be a core competence for future translators due to the shift towards web-based information. The chapter proceeds from intensive research on translation competence during the last decade to review the evolving and unclear status of professional localizers, localization engineers and managers in relation to the status of translators. It introduces a model of 'localization competence' – the knowledge and skills assumed to be possessed by expert localizers that other bilinguals or translators do not have. This model accounts for the two possible pathways to localization expertise: from translation trainees to localizers, and from localization engineers and experts to localizers.

Chapter 8 projects this phenomenon towards what may potentially shape the future of localization. The issues discussed are professionalization and the boom in crowdsourcing practices facilitated by the Internet, the future of translation in light of machine-translation post-editing practices, and how the impact of technological developments on modern societies and communication practices will continue to reshape theorizations, professional practices and the way training is structured in this field.

Part I

TECHNOLOGY, LOCALIZATION AND TRANSLATION: EVOLVING CONCEPTUALIZATIONS

1

THE EMERGENCE OF LOCALIZATION

This chapter charts the origins of localization and the different perspectives and views of the last two decades. It provides a critical comprehensive summary of the conceptualizations, metaphorizations and metalanguage of localization from both Translation Studies (TS) and industry sides, and of how both have struggled to define localization either as a distinct process or as a technological extension of translation-related phenomena. We will explore issues related to the evolution of localization, definitions from industry and academic perspectives and also industry-based attempts to differentiate from 'standard' translation. We will also review how TS have incorporated web localization within the discipline, and we will discuss whether localization represents a new paradigm within TS (Pym 2010).

TECHNOLOGY AND THE EMERGENCE OF LOCALIZATION

During the last two decades we have witnessed a continued growth of the Internet that now permeates all aspects of our modern lives. The Internet gave rise to the World Wide Web, and both have been revolutionizing human communication and helping interconnect the world in ways never seen before (Folaron 2010). The possibilities afforded by the Internet have opened new forms of digital communication and, consequently, different types of new translation-mediated practices. Among these we find 'localization', a global cycle of processes that makes digital texts available to different sociolinguistic communities around the world. Localization as we know it started in the late 1970s when US computer companies brought their products to major markets such as France, Germany and Japan. These initial attempts resulted in the emergence of the now consolidated 'localization industry', the fastest-growing sector in translation. By the 1980s and 1990s, this industry had expanded to cover all sorts of digital texts that billions around the world use daily, from websites and videogames to smartphones and MP3 players. Web localization brought the largest expansion to this industry, a market that currently amounts to over $3 billion worldwide. The growth in this sector is hardly surprising considering the over 2000 billion Internet users (Internet World Stats 2012) and the almost 700 billion active websites in June 2012.[1] Over the years, localization has been consolidated as (1) a separate and attractive market niche, (2) a specific specialization within the translation industry and (3) an exciting new field of inquiry that is evolving into the emerging so-called 'Localization Studies' (Ramael 2010; Munday 2012). Localization has also opened up a fascinating field of inquiry for many interrelated disciplines, such as Computational Linguistics, Communication Studies, International Business Management, Software and Web Development, Web Usability, Digital Genre Theory and Translation Studies.

Digital technologies play a key role in localization. Since the early days, the rapid pace at which these technologies develop forced the industry to continually adapt to new innovations and the challenges they posed. Since the first stumbling blocks faced were technological problems related to the integration of translation in software products, conceptualizations of localization often bypassed mainstream translation types to stress the technological component as the main distinguishing feature. These issues still dominate discussions about localization, even though it has become the object of study in a number of disciplines. This first chapter is devoted to an analysis of the evolution of localization and a review of the different conceptualizations and discourses that have arisen over the years, attempting to build bridges between practical and academic approaches.

THE ORIGINS OF LOCALIZATION

The origins of localization can be traced back to the emergence of personal computing and software in the late 1970s and early 1980s. Such technologies started to become popular among users who did not possess programming skills, and as a result many US computing companies set out to address their needs in a comprehensive manner (Esselink 2006). Once companies such as Sun Microsystems, Oracle or Microsoft had succeeded in popularizing their products in the US, they turned their eyes towards international markets; the initial targets were Japan and the so-called FIGS countries (France, Italy, Germany and Spain). Economic reasons are therefore easily identifiable as the main driver for the emergence and evolution of localization. Emerging originally in the United States, localization processes initially flowed from English into other languages (Uren *et al.* 1993). However, with the emergence of the WWW localizations started to flow in the opposite direction, with a constant stream of websites being localized into English around the world. Nowadays, it is commonplace across the planet to find websites localized into that international *lingua franca* in order to address global audiences.

Developers initially attempted to introduce established translation practices, hiring experienced 'linguists' to help with the translation of textual strings. The first attempts at localization entailed developers finishing the programming of a software product and handing down the extracted textual strings in resource files with the supporting documentation to linguists. Once the translations were completed, developers would try to reintegrate them later. All interested parties soon discovered that separating the development from the translation stages was impractical for a variety of reasons. For example, translated segments were normally longer than source texts and could not be fitted in the space allotted for them; frequently, textual strings would include code (the so called 'hard-coded strings') that could not be translated when target locales required specific number, gender or declension agreements; dealing with these types of textual strings required a basic understanding of programming, etc. With time, the realization that localization had to be collaboratively conceived from the start of the development cycle resulted in what is now known as the GILT process or Globalization, Internationalization, Localization and Translation (see Chapter 2), in which developers, managers, localization engineers, localizers and/or translators actively collaborate to ensure the global localization process, normally working side by side (Dunne 2006a; Gouadec 2007).

From the business point of view, companies initially relied both on in-house translation teams (Microsoft or Oracle) or outsourced their translation-related tasks to translation vendors, mostly rebranded translation companies. The 1980s and 1990s saw the emergence of world localization hubs, such as Ireland, where companies established their localization headquarters thanks to government tax incentives and a very positive and competitive labour market environment (Esselink 2006). Although by the 1990s the localization service industry was clearly consolidated, companies soon found it unprofitable to maintain ever-growing localization departments within each organization (Mazur 2007), and Multi-Language Vendors (MLV) that normally worked with large multi-language projects thus emerged. Often, new target languages were offered and requested, and these constant expansions meant that MLV often had to depend on Single Language Vendors (SLV) to meet the need for an ever-expanding range of locales or languages. The 1990s and 2000s also saw a wave of mergers and acquisitions reshape the localization industry. Currently, new companies are emerging online in a push to offer quicker and more economic services by combining professional translators, post-editing machine translation and volunteer communities on the web (see Chapter 8).

Web localization emerged after years of successful efforts in software products. Initially, processes developed for software localization were modelled to the specifics of digital hypertexts (Yunker 2003, 2010; Dunne

2006a). Web localization surpassed the market share of software localization in the early 2000s (LISA 2004; Schäler 2005),[2] resulting in a 'lucrative, dynamic and interprofessional field, often involving marketing, design, software engineering, as well as linguistic processes' (Pym and Windle 2011a: 410). It also started to become a specific translation modality that required specific skills from translators and a lower degree of technological competence than software localization (Esselink 2006). Thus web localization has been open from the beginning to a wider range of translation professionals. The complexity of maintaining multilingual dynamic websites led to the creation of new technologies to author, manage, store and publish web content, such as the Content Management Systems (CMS) or Global Management Systems (GMS) (Yunker 2003: 355; LISA 2006). These technologies emerged from translation memory systems and are used to handle the dynamism of multilingual web projects in which content is continually updated and published. These technologies have helped tremendously to simplify these types of multilingual projects and keep costs down for the industry (Lynch 2006).

New technological developments, such as adding software functionalities, the move to the 'cloud'[3] with Software as service (Saas)[4] models, apps or widgets, are now blurring the boundaries between the more technical expertise required for software localization and the more content-oriented nature of web localization.[5] The present and future of web localization therefore seems more and more complex, with the Internet merging platform and content, and therefore, one could argue that software and web localization may quite possibly merge in the future.

THE INTERNET, THE WWW AND WEB LOCALIZATION

Web localization needs to be conceptualized in relation to the Internet, the most important development in communication since Gutenberg invented the printing press in the fifteenth century (Lockwood and Scott 2000). This global communicative platform has promoted the emergence of new business practices and models (LISA 2007: 5), revolutionizing translation practices globally and leading to the emergence of the subject of this volume. The Internet represents an essential medium of communication in a globalized world, with ever-increasing user counts and penetration rates. According to Internet World Stats,[6] the number of users world-wide was around two billion in 2012, reaching 30.2% of the total population. In North America or Europe the percentage of the population using the Internet is 78.2% and 58.2% respectively. In this context, the presence of businesses on the web is currently a prerequisite for competing in a globalized market. It has also meant that most organizations, collectives and individuals also have a web presence through websites or profiles in different social or directory websites.

In the 1980s, Tim Berners-Lee created what we call today the World Wide Web (WWW), defined by him as 'the universe of network-accessible information, an embodiment of human knowledge' (Berners-Lee *et al.* 1992: 52). This definition stresses the most important characteristics of the WWW, its hypertextual and networked nature. The terms 'Internet' and 'WWW' are often confused and interchanged, even when the WWW is merely one of the many communicative situations enabled by the Internet (O'Hagan and Ashworth 2003), such as chats, videoconferencing and new online SMS apps in smartphones. The WWW was possible thanks to the emergence in 1991 of the Hypertext Markup Language (HTML), as well as to later technical innovations, such as the Extensive Hypertext Markup Language in 2005. The Web 2.0 and beyond continues to expand the meteoric rise of web localization processes (Fernández Costales 2011), mostly due to the collaboration of users who are creating and translating massive amounts of content. Berneers-Lee highlighted from the start the social nature of the WWW: 'The web is more a social creation than a technical one' (Berners-Lee 2000: 113), thus forecasting the boom of the social network era. The ReadWriteWeb, as Berners-Lee refers to the Web 2.0, has brought new collaboration capabilities, resulting in alternative localization practices for existing business models: localization of open-source software, subtitling of online videos or volunteer localization of websites (see Chapter 8).

DEFINING LOCALIZATION

Localization has been with us for almost three decades, but the set of phenomena grouped under this term still represents a somewhat fuzzy area. As with any object of study, its definition and delimitation represents an initial step towards the foundation of theoretical or empirical studies (Chesterman 2004). No matter whether the perspective is academic or professional, definitions contain models that frame discourses and discussions on the nature of what is being investigated or analysed. These models not only guide how we talk or justify our decisions, arguments or actions, but they also lay the groundwork for framing related issues, such as the different ways of organizing the localization process or setting parameters for quality evaluation. In this section we will review different conceptualizations and definitions of localization from its origins, in order to understand current gaps and synergies among the different parties with an interest in its definition: developers, management and business agents, industry experts, professional translators and localizers, translation scholars, computational linguistics researchers, researchers from a myriad of disciplines (international marketing, technical writing, usability, etc.). This multiplicity of approaches currently means that so far 'definitions of localization tend to be contextually bound, reflecting the perspectives of those who formulate them' (Folaron 2006: 197). In general, the term 'localization' stems from the notion of 'locale', the combination of a sociocultural region and a language in industrial setting. It refers both to the processes by which digital texts are modified to be used by audiences in different sociolinguistic regions and to the products of these processes themselves. An array of publications, for example, discuss how to make 'localization' more efficient, while users interact with an Italian 'localization' of a website or a Canadian French version for Quebec. When the process refers to interactive digital texts on the Web, the term most often used is 'website localization' (Yunker 2003; Jiménez-Crespo 2009a; Pym and Windle 2011a), even though other scholars and industry experts have coined other terms, such as 'e-localization' (Schäler 2001: 22–26; Cronin 2003: 14), 'web-content localization' (Esselink 2006), 'website translation' (Williams and Chesterman 2002: 14) or 'translation of web products' (Hurtado 2001).

Before attempting to define localization, we should mention that even the definition of translation is a highly contentious issue today, a reflection of the multiplicity of perspectives that make up current Translation Studies (i.e. Halverson 2010). Obviously, any attempt to define localization will first encounter a stumbling block in defining what model of translation it includes. Often, simplistic and dated translation models that revert to natural equivalence relationships are mentioned. We will review this issue later in this chapter. The two groups with the greatest interest in finding a definition for the localization phenomenon are industry experts and TS scholars. The following sections review their perspectives.

Industry definitions of localization

Definitions of localization in industry publications date back to the late 1980s and early 1990s (Uren et al. 1993; Microsoft Press 1994).[7] By then, software localization was commonplace in the industry and the foundations of the GILT process were established. As already mentioned, the term localization itself derives from the industrial notion of 'locale', defined as 'coinciding linguistic and cultural options: not just a language, but usually a particular variety of a language, plus local conventions regarding currency, date, [etc.]' (Pym 2004a: 2). The term emerged to distinguish between countries/regions within mono- or multilingual countries and the notion of language itself. It also arises out of the business notion of markets rather than monolithic countries. Early definitions of locale stressed the adaptations necessary in software products, such as date, time or currency formats, and keyboard layouts, etc.[8] They also included cultural conventions as the most important aspect to consider beyond language, 'locales usually provide more information about cultural conventions than about languages' (Microsoft Corporation 2003: 7).[9] More recent definitions of 'locale', such as the one in the European Quality Standard EN 15038, include linguistic, cultural, technical and geographical conventions. A locale is expressed by the combination of the language code included in the international standard ISO 639,[10] followed by the country code as stated in the standard ISO 3166.[11] As an example, the locale code for French used in Quebec, Canada, would be Fr-Ca, and the Spanish from Chile would be Es-Cl.[12]

As for localization, the most popular definition was released by the now defunct Localization Industry Standard Association (LISA):[13]

> Localization involves taking a product and making it linguistically and culturally appropriate to the target locale (country/region and language) where it will be used and sold.
>
> (LISA 2003: 13)

This definition incorporated the basic common denominators found in most previous definitions:

1. The objects that are processed in localization are 'products' and not 'texts'.
2. The process incorporates both a linguistic and a cultural component, even when languages are culturally situated and both cannot be separated (Bassnett and Lefevere 1990). The industry has consistently insisted on the separation of culture and language, even to the point of maintaining that translation does not deal with culture (Microsoft Corporation 2003).
3. The localized product moves from a source to a target 'locale', the most common term found in industry definitions, even when in some cases the target is substituted by 'markets' (Sprung 2000; Schäler 2001; Lingo 2004; Gouadec 2007; Schmitz 2007), or 'languages' (Chandler 2005).
4. The term 'translation' is avoided in order to imply its distinct nature (i.e. LISA 2003, 2007; O'Hagan and Ashworth 2003). Very few cases do include the term translation as such (i.e. Chandler 2005: 1).

Despite the widespread popularity of this definition, LISA was aware of its limitations and offered different ones in subsequent primers (LISA 2004, 2007). These modifications were intended to expand the scope of the definition from software to websites and to a large range of services:

> Localization is the process of modifying products or services to account for differences in distinct markets [. . .].
>
> (LISA 2007: 11)

To complement this definition, the goals of the process were disaggregated into four essential components: linguistic, content-cultural, physical[14] and technical. The new definition stressed the importance of globalization and internationalization, as it included both products and services, and it adopted the notion of market instead of locale. After all, the notion of locale is part of the industry-centred discourse, and it is clearly influenced by the size or economic significance of market forces in each region (Pym 2004a: 40).

Another common denominator in the many definitions found in industry publications is the fact that localized texts need to have the 'look and feel' of locally made products. In other words, the objective should be to produce products that are received by target users as locally made. According to Globalization and Localization Association (GALA 2011), '[t]he goal is to provide a product with the look and feel of having been created for the target market to eliminate or minimize local sensitivities'. From a translation perspective, this goal characterizes industry practices in terms of an extreme 'domestication' strategy (Venuti 1995), according to which the users are not supposed to perceive any of the potential 'foreignness' of the text they interact with.

If seen in the light of TS, the most interesting trend is the attempt to define translation as a simple linguistic process within a more complex global cycle. This explains, for example, the initial emphasis on technological and cultural adaptations to separate localization from 'general translation', a more generic and 'lower-cost' process. Translation was understood in terms of the archaic natural equivalence paradigm that prevailed before the emergence of the modern-day discipline in the 1970s. Translation was also regarded as a less complex stage (Quirion 2003; Gouadec 2007; Austermühl 2007), pointing to the fact that the industry consolidated without relying on the body of knowledge of TS. However, all these definitions saw the need to define localization precisely by reference to translation, mostly trying to highlight additional components that translation supposedly did not cover. A range of metaphorizations of translation thus emerged: a key aspect that sheds light on industrial discourses on localization.

Metaphors of translation within localization: from 'texts' to 'adaptations'

The seminal work on metaphor by linguists Lakoff and Johnson indicated that, 'the essence of metaphor is understanding and experiencing one kind of thing in terms of another' (Lakoff and Johnson 1980). The early days of localization, like those of any novel phenomenon, saw the emergence of metaphorical constructs seeking to explain the challenging nature of a process 'that goes beyond translation' (GALA 2011). A trend then appeared that defined localization through underlying metaphors of translation. For our purposes these conceptualizations provide an interesting insight into its development. These metaphors mostly targeted what 'translation' was or did, rather than defining localization, and they were normally reductionist in scope. In a sense they were simply attempting both to stress the added-value component of the services offered by localization vendors, and to distinguish localization as a process 'more sophisticated than translation' (Pym 2004a: 25). This resulted in definitions of localization that essentially contrasted it with several metaphorizations.

The first metaphor can be referred to as the 'language' metaphor. Translation was 'just a language problem' (Brooks 2000), while localization addressed a number of complex and exciting additional issues. LISA, for example indicated 'localization needs to go beyond language questions to address issues of content and look and feel' (LISA 2004: 11). We will call the next metaphor the 'text' metaphor. This shows the same reductionist approach, and it can be traced back to the common practice of extracting textual strings from software products for translation. Translators handled textual strings, while localization experts handled other cross-cultural aspects. For example, Robert Sprung (2000: 10) indicated that translation was 'the core skill of converting text from one language to another, whether on hard copy or electronically'. In other publications, localization 'generally addresses significant, non-textual components of products or services in addition to strict translation' (LISA 2007: 11). Nevertheless, and as indicated in the same publication, the translation of text 'generally constitutes the bulk of a localization project'. In this metaphor we perceive the interest in placing the technical and management issues at the heart of localization. It goes without saying that the notion of text was atheoretical and did not correspond with linguistics or TS approaches of the time. In Chapter 3 we will review how current linguistic and translation approaches to 'text' incorporate not only running text, but also the images, formatting, sound and interactivity that are part of a holistic global unit (Göpferich 1995a). This multimodal textual approach implies that translation operates in any and all of these different 'components' (Gambier and Gottliev 2004). In line with this metaphor, another recurrent conceptualization describes translation as the part of the wider localization process that handles 'words'; it is therefore seen as the part of the cycle that deals with the 'translation of words' (Esselink 2006: 28) and is 'focused on communicating the meanings and messages of words' (LISA 2007: 7). Obviously, this metaphor implies that localization deals with much larger and wider ventures.

Without doubt, the 'adaptation' metaphor is the most pervasive in both TS and industry definitions. Adaptations are seen as the additional component that localization provides, as opposed to the textual or wordly nature of 'translation'. The term 'adaptation' is typically used to indicate the performative action of the localization process. Normally, it is the process of adapting a program for a local market (Microsoft Corporation 2003), the 'linguistic and cultural adaptation of digital content' (Schäler 2010: 209), or the 'the adaptation of any good or service' (Sprung 2000: xviii). The object of the adaptations is normally the product itself (Schäler 2001; Müller 2005;

Gibb and Matthaiakis 2007; GALA 2011) or the linguistic and cultural elements within it (ÖNORM 1200 2000). Rarely are the technological aspects or the deep or invisible coding structure of these products mentioned, even when performing such technical adaptations as calendar formats, measuring conventions, spelling, etc., which represents one of the main issues in software or web localization when compared to other translation modalities (Wright and Budin 2001). Thus, it is surprising that this techno-logical aspect is rarely mentioned as the main adaptation that separates localization from other translation modalities and types.

Taking this later conceptualization as its starting point, the most common model to appear is 'translation plus adaptation'. Normally, definitions distinguish translation clearly from the adaptation stage (Ørsted 2001; Microsoft Corporation 2003; Dunne 2006a; Schäler 2010). This distinction appears in several definitions, such as Esselink (2000: 2) – 'localization is the translation and adaptation of a software or web product' – or that on the GALA website:

> Translation is one of several services that form the localization process. So in addi-
> tion to translation, the localization process may also include adapting graphics to
> the target markets, modifying content layout to fit the translated text, converting to
> local currencies, using of proper formats for dates, addresses, and phone numbers,
> addressing local regulations and more.
>
> (GALA 2011)

In this definition we find the adaptations are mostly technical in nature and, as already mentioned, we certainly agree that technical adaptations are a defining feature of localization, even if some of those mentioned here, such as dates, phone numbers, etc., are common to most translation pro-cesses, especially technical translation. For example, in technical translation it is common to add different phone numbers or eliminate sections of instruction manuals aimed at specific countries (Gamero 2001). In audio-visual translation, humour is often adapted in subtitles and other types of audiovisual (Díaz Cintas and Remael 2007), theatre (Zatlin 2005) or adver-tising translation (Torresi 2010). Thus, apart from technological adapta-tions, most others are shared with many other translation modalities and types and could not be considered defining traits of localization. For example, cultural, linguistic, text type or genre adaptations have been considered a central notion in linguistic, communicative and functionalist approaches since the 1960s (i.e. Bastin 2008). As Quirion (2003: 547) indi-cates, these types of adaptations have always been part of the translation process, even if scholars continue to question how they can change the way we perceive translation (O'Hagan 2012a). We thus find two specific components that are not shared with other translation modalities: active co-operation between translators-localizers and development engineers, and the need for a comprehensive understanding of technological issues on the part of translators.

TS definitions of localization

In the more academic perspective of TS, two trends can be clearly distinguished. The first argues that localization belongs under the umbrella of translation-related phenomena, insisting that localization is no more than a translation modality shaped by specific technological and project-based features (Wright and Budin 2001; Hurtado 2001; Gouadec 2007). The other trend follows the professional approach and mostly focuses on work descriptive of industrial practices (i.e. Dunne 2006a; Schäler 2010; Dunne and Dunne 2011). The latter has been the more productive in the last decade, partly due to the arrival of industry experts in institutions of higher learning to incorporate localization in translation programs. Most published definitions have, therefore, adopted some industry models, distinguishing a linguistic and a cultural component and including adaptation as a key feature, or focusing on the significance of management in multilingual projects (Schäler 2008a, 2010).

Of the definitions found in TS publications, the most complete and comprehensive could be that proposed by Dunne:

> The processes by which digital content and products developed in one locale (defined in terms of geographical area, language and culture) are adapted for sale and use in another locale. Localization involves: (a) translation of textual content into the language and textual conventions of the target language, (b), adaptation of non-textual content (from colors, icons and bitmaps, to packaging, form factors, etc.) as well as input, output and delivery mechanisms to take into account the cultural, technical and regulatory requirements of that locale. In sum, localization is not so much about specific tasks as much as it is about the processes by which products are adapted.
>
> Moreover, localization is but one of a number of interdependent processes and cannot be fully (or correctly) understood without being contextualized in reference to them. These processes are referred to collectively by the acronym GILT.
>
> (Dunne 2006a: 4)

The principles laid out in this definition are somewhat similar to those advocated in this book. It separates a translation stage from a technical adaptation stage. It also stresses the existence of a series of interrelated processes that, obviously, require different agents for their completion. However, it does not adequately distinguish textual and non-textual elements: contemporary approaches include visual, graphical and typographic components as intrinsic parts of the text in translation (see Chapter 3). It can also be argued that this could have a detrimental impact on the status of translators, as it could reduce their task to processing 'textual strings'.

The emphasis on localization as a common global project is shared by Gouadec (2007: 29 and 319). His definition focuses on the project-based nature of localization, including a list of what can be subject to adaptations, such as cultural, physical, technical, linguistic, ethic, religious, philosophical, commercial or marketing elements. In his breakdown of all localization-related tasks, the author separates those shared with other 'common' translation processes (ibid: 37–43): out of twenty-nine steps, ten are shared with other mainstream translation types, such as researching the terminology and phraseology or performing a quality analysis. Schäler also stresses the importance of the project-management nature of localization practices, and early on indicated that 'localization is being redefined as the provision of services and technologies for the management of multilinguality across the global information flow' (Schäler 2002: 21). In his entry in the *Handbook of Translation Studies* (Schäler 2010), he precisely underscores that what makes his definition different from others is putting the management of multilingual content at the core of localization. Nevertheless, translation and localization management, in general, are a core component of the global translation industry (Dunne and Dunne 2011). As an example, projects ranging from multilingual technical translation to audiovisual translation routinely incorporate managing multilingual projects in their cycle. Defining the localization prototype on the premise of multilingual management might, however, exclude a wide array of localization practices, such as small non-profit website localization, that can occur without any dedicated management being involved.

Analysis of other TS definitions shows that the two common denominators are the separation of the cultural and linguistic stages, and the adequacy or appropriateness of the target product to the receiving sociocultural contexts. The former shows the clear influence of the industry discourse in the discipline and is even more common in TS than in industry-based definitions (Wright and Budin 2001; Gouadec 2007; Schmitz 2007; Schäler 2010). To some extent, this separation is surprising, given that cultural adaptation is part of all translation processes. As for the latter, this follows industry definitions that focus on adapting the 'look and feel' of non-translated products so that they are accepted as local productions by users. In most cases the product needs to be made linguistically and culturally 'appropriate' (Wright and Budin 2001; Schmitz 2007), or it needs to be adapted to the 'requirements' of a target market or audience (Schäler 2010; Mazur 2007). Localization is therefore conceptualized as a target-oriented translation type and, in line with the functionalist notion of adequacy, emphasizes users' expectations and achieving the communicative purpose for which the localization was commissioned, rather than equivalence relationships to source texts (STs).

Even though web localization is often included in the general definition of localization, a handful of scholars have also attempted to define it separately (i.e. Gouadec 2007; Sandrini 2008; Pym and Windle 2011a; Jiménez-Crespo 2009a, 2011a). As an example, Gouadec defined web localization as the:

> Adaptation of the contents and functionalities of a Web Site for a group of users who share a number of specific cultural and linguistic features different from those for whom the website was originally designed.
>
> (Gouadec 2007: 297)

This conceptualization of web localization is quite similar to the approach to localization in general; Sandrini (2005: 175), though, includes the web notions of accessibility and usability in his definition of web localization: 'a process of modifying an existing website to make it accessible, usable and culturally suitable to a target audience.' In an earlier publication he rightly indicates the similarities between the industry approach to the web localization phenomenon and functionalist approaches to translation, focusing mostly on the role of the translation brief or instructions provided by the client: 'a process of modifying a website for a specific locale according to the goals outlined by the client' (Sandrini 2005: 3). In general, these approaches inspired by functionalist theories can be considered as the prevailing approach in TS literature; mostly from the 'purpose-plus-loyalty' model proposed by Nord (1997). In this model, the overriding role of the function or 'skopos' in earlier functionalist proposals is somewhat modified by a compromise or 'loyalty' requirement towards the clients or commissioners. In some cases, web localization is defined by identifying features that differentiate it from 'straight' translation, as in the case of Pym and Windle 2011a. They offer a brief introductory definition in which web localization is the translation and adaptation of content to specific local markets, then later present a more comprehensive definition in which web localization is compared and contrasted to non-hypertextual[15] translation. The following specific features are offered in lieu of a straight definition:

(a) The project-based nature of web localization
(b) How translatable elements are identified
(c) The tools needed to render them
(d) The non-linearity of the texts processed
(e) The way in which the translation process is prepared and coordinated and,
(f) The extent of the changes that might be introduced.

In a sense, the approach taken resembles the project-based perspective advocated by Gouadec (2007), in which translation is no more nor less than a step in a global economic and social cycle of production and distribution of translations. This review illustrates that, despite the fact that software and website localization represent distinctively different phenomena (Austermühl 2006), most definitions resemble those previously proposed for software localization: 'products' or 'content' are translated and adapted for a target market or locale.

Proposal for a holistic definition of localization

In previous publications I have offered a definition of web localization departing from a pragmatic-cognitive translation perspective as 'a complex communicative, cognitive, textual and technological process by which inter-active digital texts are modified to be used in different linguistic and socio-cultural contexts, guided by the expectations of the target audience and the specifications and degree requested by initiators.' Web localization is seen here in the light of recent perspectives within TS in which translation represents a linguistic, communicative, cognitive and textual process (Hurtado 2001). This definition adds the dependency on technology that both led to its emergence and, at the same time, represents a tool necessary to carry out all localization processes. The role of user expectations is included because of the interactive nature of digital texts and the distinct cognitive environment of reception. Web localization is identified as a salient example of target-oriented translation types, such as instrumental (Nord 1997) or covert ones (House 1997). In this context, localized websites are not 'called on to represent any previous texts' (Pym 2004a: 6) but, rather, serve a purpose effortlessly and efficiently. Finally, web localization also depends heavily on the social and economic context in which it functions, and therefore any definition should account for these gravitational forces. This definition thus introduces the sociocultural dimension of translation, an emerging area in TS that accounts for the complex interplay of agents, technologies, market forces and processes that shape localization practices (Wolf 2010).

LOCALIZATION WITHIN TRANSLATION STUDIES

As with most technology-related phenomena (O'Hagan 2012b), the incorporation of web localization into TS has been a slow process. It first appeared as a new modality as early as the late 1990s (Mayoral 1997) and now is clearly consolidated into the discipline, as witness its inclusion in all encyclopedias (Baker and Saldanha 2008), Translation Studies handbooks (Munday 2008; Gambier and van Doorslaer 2010; Malmkjaer and Windle 2011), and all comprehensive monographs on translation theory (Pym 2010; Munday 2012). In early attempts at approaching localization, most scholarly publications adopted the industry-based discourse while attempting to bridge the gap between the industry and academia. The tendency was to focus on describing consolidated industry processes and pay less attention to TS concepts, notions or theoretical approaches. This trend was mostly led by industry experts who had moved across to academic environments. The main drive behind these efforts was to provide an understanding of a relatively complex phenomenon and provide a foundation for both training and research efforts. Some of these descriptive volumes from academic presses were entirely the work of professionals (Sprung 2000; Esselink 2001); others were edited by scholars but included work by both academics and industry experts (Reinke 2005; Dunne 2006a). The second trend was characterized by scholars maintaining that localization is nothing more than what translators have always been doing (Quirion 2003; Wright and Budin 2001). Some scholars attempted to bridge the gap between industry and academia, such as Pym (2003b) in his seminal paper 'What localization models can learn from Translation Theory'. He can be considered the first scholar to attempt to open a dialogue with the industry while at the same time denouncing the potentially dehumanizing nature of their approaches (2004a: 198). In a later publication Pym argued that localization opened up a new paradigm within TS due to the appearance of a new type of culturally-neutral internationalized text and internationalization-based equivalence. In this new type of equivalence STs are prepared from inception as neutral texts, and localization needs to be thought of from the 'very beginning, and planned for at every stage of the product development' (2010: 125). These texts are subsequently localized into multiple locales. He argues that localization should rather be called 'delocalization', as it attempts to erase all traces of the local from STs.

Another initial debate within TS focused on where localization fitted into the discipline. Originally it tended to be included within the emerging notion of 'multimedia translation', and the term 'multimedia localization' was even coined (Hurtado 2001; Gambier and Gottlieb 2004). There was a brief attempt to place localization within the booming field of audiovisual or screen translation, and subsequently the continuous blending of media and digital forms of communication has led audiovisual translation scholars to theorize on a blurring of lines between the translation of audiovisual digital products and localization (Remael 2010). Over the last decade, several attempts have been made to bring localization under the wider umbrella of TS, the first by Hurtado (2001), who proposed a classification of translation phenomena using types and modalities. Translation types are those related to specific professional fields, such as legal, medical or religious translation. The classification by modes, such as dubbing, simultaneous interpreting or sight translation, leads to distinct translation modalities. According to Hurtado, the classification by modes is important, as any source text can be translated following different modes – e.g. any text can be translated or sight translated. Software and multimedia localization were categorized as translation phenomena defined by their modality, and even in 2001 this indicated the relative lack of research on this area, despite its significance. In Vandepitte's (2008) proposed ontology of TS, software and web localization are placed within the branch of studies defined by type and, more specifically, within the studies of translation and translation technology. Obviously, localization can be studied and can be the focus of innumerable cross-categories within this ontology. The researcher acknowledges this fact precisely by suggesting the example of localization.

The debate about whether localization is a completely distinct phenomenon due to technological, management or globalization issues, or whether it is another translation modality is still going on. The 'technological' (O'Hagan 2012b; Cronin 2010) or 'audiovisual' turns (Remael 2010) in TS are fuelling the debate within the discipline about whether translation can be expanded to incorporate the multiplicity of new emerging textual production modes (Cronin 2013). However, if we stop for a second and look at localization in the context of the fast-developing field of audiovisual translation, it would be hard to justify web localization as a process separate from translation just because it includes 'multilingual management' (Schäler 2010), large 'projects' (Gouadec 2007) or distinctive procedural features (Pym and Windle 2011a). Rather, it is better to suggest viewing it as an expansion of translation at its point of junction with technological advances and business forces. As Remael indicates,

> It is difficult to predict if the trend towards expanding the concept of translation to encompass this diversification will prevail over the opposite trend, that of introducing new terms (such as localization, technical communication and multimedia localization) that aims to reduce translation to one link within a larger communication chain.
>
> (Remael 2010: 15)

Ramael rightly points out that the decision about the future direction is not just up to scholars and institutions of higher learning, but also depends on politico-economic developments that determine the translation market. A move towards a prototypical understanding of translation or translation-related phenomena (Halverson 1999, 2010) would be beneficial to the integration of localization phenomena as a new translation modality. This would allow for placing at the core of translation and localization common cross-cultural and cross-linguistic communication practices, and to identify areas at the core and the periphery that overlap. In doing so, localization can be easily conceptualized as a technology-based translation modality that requires the collaboration of a number of agents in addition to translators.

SUMMARY

This chapter has charted the origins of localization and has placed web localization within the paradigm of localization phenomena since the 1980s. We have outlined the different definitions of localization from both industry and TS perspectives, and analysed the initial gap between the localization industry and academia. It is argued that efforts at definition entailed contrasting localization with a dated conceptualization of translation. It has also been argued that the differentiating criteria chosen – adaptation, management, culture – have always formed part of modern approaches to translation (Wright and Budin 2001; Pym 2004a). We have conceptualized web localization as a specific translation modality marked by its technological dependence and the co-operation between different agents. And we have presented a definition that includes a textual, linguistic, cognitive, communicative, technological, sociological and target-oriented perspective. The chapter ended with a review of localization's place within TS.

FURTHER READING

There are a large number of publications related to general localization. For a general descriptive overview of the localization process, see Esselink (2001) for general localization, Yunker (2003) for website localization or Chandler and O'Malley (2011) for game localization. Dunne's (2006a) edited volume on localization includes both academic and industry perspectives. Although the Localization Industry Standards Association no longer exists, its LISA primers are still easy to find and represent an outstanding source for understanding industrial discourse on localization (LISA 2003, 2004, 2007). Another source of professional perspectives on localization are the *Multilingual* guides (http://www.multilingual.com/guides.php) and publications focused on localization (http://www.multilingual.com/downloads/coreFocus131). For a historical overview of the evolution of localization, see Esselink (2006). For a general overview of localization from a TS perspective, see Pym (2003b, 2004a, 2010: 221–242), Mazur (2007), Schäler (2008a, 2010), Dunne (2006a) or Folaron (2006). For a theoretical approach to web localization within TS, see Pym and Windle (2011a), Jiménez-Crespo (2011a), the functionalist approach of Sandrini (2008) and Sandra Neuert (2007). See Fernández Costales (2011) for the impact of the Web 2.0 on translation and localization, O'Hagan (2012a) for a review of the notion of 'adaptation' in localization, and Folaron (2010) for an overview of translation and the WWW.

2

THE WEB LOCALIZATION PROCESS
From GILT to web usability

To provide both a sound understanding of localization and a solid foundation for research in the area, this chapter offers a description of the global cycle of web localization. The different factors and constraints that need to be taken into account while studying or analysing localization processes and products are described, such as the GILT cycle, agents in the process, the use of translation technology, cultural adaptation, localization levels and web usability. Careful consideration of the global cycle is needed for research, as these intertwined processes impose specific constraints that inevitably have an impact on product and process-based research.

THE LOCALIZATION PROCESS AND GILT

In industrial settings localization does not exist in isolation but forms part of a much wider complex of interrelated processes known as GILT (Globalization, Internationalization, Localization and Translation). This places localization within the wider paradigm of market globalization and requires companies entering foreign markets to go beyond translation: it demands a global and radical adaptation of business structures to prepare for localization from the early stages of product development. Each component addresses different needs that emerged within market globalization.

Globalization, or G11n, represents the broader processes in the cycle and focuses primarily on organizational issues. It arose out of the need to adapt business organizations to the demands of localization: for example, making sure that if the line 'Email for further information' is localized into Chinese, then mechanisms for responding in that language will be put in place. According to LISA, globalization can be defined by its goals:

> Globalization . . . refers to all of the business decisions and activities required to make an organization truly international in scope and outlook. Globalization is the transformation of business and processes to support customers around the world, in whatever language, country, or culture they require.
>
> (LISA 2007:1).

This notion entails organizations adapting to the demands of conducting business or offering services globally, and the adaptations cover aspects such as 'technical, financial, managerial, personnel, marketing, and other enterprise decisions' (LISA 2004: 14). According to GALA, globalization is focused primarily on business issues and entails 'the revision of business processes, management procedures and even the adaptation of marketing tools' (GALA 2011). Globalization, as opposed to internationalization, is a cyclical process that occurs not only before the localization process, but also during distribution and the subsequent multilingual customer support. The goals of this process range from supporting the localization process to setting up mechanisms to handle a multiplicity of bilateral or multilingual interactions.

Internationalization occurs primarily during the development stages of any digital product. In general, it can be described as the set of processes that guarantee that:

(1) source digital products are not tied to any particular culture
(2) they are independent of whichever language they have been developed in, normally English (LISA 2007: 28)
(3) technical adaptations of any kind will be avoided once the localization process begins

One of the most concise definitions appears in the last LISA primer, as 'the process of enabling a product at a technical level for localization' (2007: 17). Other previous definitions offer an interesting insight into the goals for this process, such as avoiding future 'redesign' during the localization process (GALA 2011; LISA 2003), or the abstraction of the functionality of the product:

> . . . [internationalization] primarily consists of abstracting the functionality of a product away from any particular language so that language support can be added back in simply, without worry that language-specific features will pose a problem when the product is localized.
>
> (LISA 2004: 14)

This abstraction effort is intended to guarantee that the website is not technically, culturally or linguistically limited, creating what has been called an 'internationalized text' (Pym 2004a).[1] From a translation perspective, this type of text seeks to facilitate the 'internationalization-based equivalence',[2] that is, making sure that the text can be easily rendered into as many languages as possible without complications. Effective application of these two interrelated processes results in a marked reduction in the time and resources needed to successfully localize any digital product into multiple languages.

The next step in the GILT cycle is the actual localization process (this is also often the starting point for web localization in small-scope localization projects). In the GILT model the localization stage mostly refers to preparing, managing, engineering and quality testing the websites or software products. Translation is often outsourced and considered as a separate stage within the industry (Quah 2006: 114). It is understood as the actual transfer of textual material, and considered as one of the steps performed by translators-localizers, whereas a range of other engineering and management tasks are usually performed by others (Sikes 2011). For example, the integration of translated text can be performed either by localization engineers or directly by translators-localizers assisted by translation/localization technologies. The separation of translation from the industry conceptualization of the localization process, focused mostly on engineering and management, is apparent from the fact that normally up to 80% of the volume of text is outsourced to freelance translators. Translation or localization vendors perform only tasks related to management, quality control and business issues (Dunne and Dunne 2011). This separation of profiles between freelance translators, managers, engineers and Quality Assurance (QA) operators is more significant in software localization; a wider range of variation appears in web localization, with the combination of job profiles depending on the scope and size of the project (Sykes 2011). However, the current expansion of web localization to cover an ever-increasing number of locales, content and technologies (PHP, Javascript, Flash, Ruby on Rails, video, Flex, etc.)[3] has led to a marked increase in the complexity of managing web localization projects.

The GILT process represents a collaborative endeavour and is considered an interactive bottom-up and top-down process. Even when globalization and internationalization occur before the later translation stage, translators as intercultural communicators inform management or development teams of the cultural or linguistic issues that need to be taken into account. Many decisions are agreed upon together with all agents in the different stages of the cycle.

Figure 2.1 proposes a global interdependence and interaction model for the so-called global GILT cycle, taking into consideration that, depending on many variables, one or many of the higher stages might not be present.

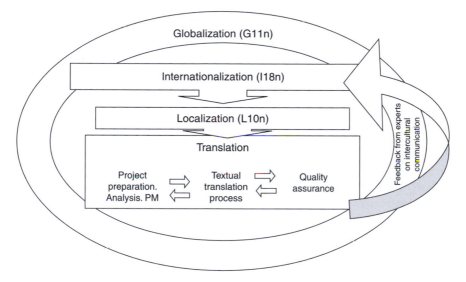

Figure 2.1 Interdependence of all stages in the global GILT cycle

One should note that in the 1980s and 1990s awareness of the inter-related nature of these processes developed from the bottom up, starting with attempts to translate extracted textual segments and developing the other processes as problems and issues arose (Dunne 2006a). Given the wider set of processes that globalization incorporates, Anthony Pym (2004a: 30) indicates that this could be conceptualized within a single process: he refers to globalization as internationalization, while localization is part of globalization strategies. Other proposals for the GILT cycle offer different variations on this same process (LISA 2007: 9). Microsoft offered one of the first proposals for a modified GILT cycle that refers to globalization as 'internationalization', while the internationalization stage is divided into 'globalization' plus 'localization enablement' (Cadieux and Esselink 2002). Other proposals from a TS perspective have proposed referring to the global cycle as 'glocalization' (Mazur 2007), as, no matter how deep the transla-tion and/or localization process might be, products always retain certain globalized features that cannot be adapted to any target locale.

From the TS perspective, the global GILT process offers an insight into the actual forces that shape a wide range of features of final localized websites. The presence or absence of any stage can, for example, configure the translation task itself and impose specific constraints or freedoms upon localizers. For example, it is common to identify localization errors that, even when the organization might be aware of them, are often not fixed (Jiménez-Crespo 2011a).[4]

LOCALIZATION TYPES: SOFTWARE, WEB, VIDEOGAME AND SMALL DEVICE LOCALIZATION

Nowadays, localization has expanded from its origins in software products for personal computing in the 1980s to a wider array of digitally mediated communications, such as software (Esselink 2001), web (Yunker 2003), videogames (O'Hagan and Mangiron 2013; Mangiron and O'Hagan 2006; Chandler and O'Malley 2011), smart phone apps, small device localization (Börjel 2007; Musale 2001), and web search engine marketing (SEM). During the 2000s the different localization types consolidated into distinctive categories that required specific translation and technical skills from the agents involved, and, although the basic localization types still exist, new emerging modalities are now blending these types and continue to redefine them. For example, cloud computing software applications are directly accessed online via the browser – the so-called 'web-based applications'. This combines traits of web and software localization into a single process. This combination also appears in small device localization, such as cell phones or MP3 players: smart phones have recently been endowed with the ability to include games and different kinds of applications via web connectivity. Figure 2.2. shows the basic types of localization organized according to the global economic impact.

Most localization processes share several characteristics, such as the digital nature of the text, the presentation on screen, the interactive nature of texts or the necessary collaboration between translator-localizers, localization engineers and developers to produce the final target product. Nevertheless, there are stark differences in the way the actual textual segments are stored, the programming or mark-up languages used and, most importantly, the possible variation in textual types and genres (Jiménez-Crespo 2008d). As an example, most software products entail a relatively standardized textual genre. Videogame localization also deals with a limited number of genres (Mangiron and O'Hagan 2006). Nevertheless, most digital or web genres are 'complex genres' (see Chapter 4), that is, genres that can incorporate within their structure other genres (e.g. e-commerce

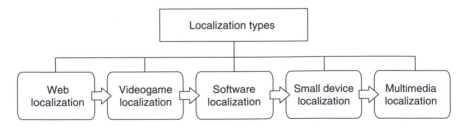

Figure 2.2 Different localization types arranged by volume of business

websites can incorporate a purchase contract). In our opinion software and website localization should not be lumped together as 'just the same kind of localization' (Austermühl 2006: 70), but should nowadays be considered as different phenomena, because of their completely different production and life cycles, textual features and types of genres. The same can be said of the emerging market of smartphone app localization.

THE WEB LOCALIZATION PROCESS

The web localization process involves a series of steps (Gouadec 2007: 40–43) in which a wide range of professionals can collaborate, such as localization engineers, managers, terminologists, QA operators and localizers-translators. In the industry setting the notion of process differs from that of workflow in that the latter is automated. Normally, industry descriptions of processes and workflows can be considered as prototypes within an organization with large resources devoted to web localization. However, in reality this process varies considerably depending on the nature of the project (marketing website, web-based application, e-commerce site, etc.), the technologies involved, the resources available or even the type of translation procedure. Currently, four main distinct web localization processes can be identified: large corporations, medium and small ones, volunteer-crowdsourcing (see Chapter 9), and individual localization in which a single agent performs all the tasks. As an example, crowdsourcing approaches require careful planning but the overall configuration of the rest of the project would be quite different from the list below (DePalma and Kelly 2011). This is the workflow model for online volunteer translations by the Center for Next Generation Localization, in which the chunking of texts to accommodate large numbers of volunteers plays a key role. The most commonly described web localization process found in the industry can be subdivided into:

(a) Initial project preparation, project acceptance (performed by localization managers, engineers)
    1. Definition of the scope of localization project with clients. Scope requirement collection (including whether or not the site has been properly internationalized, so that l10n can begin).
    2. Setting up the localization environment and managing the process (Dunne and Dunne 2011).
    3. Retrieving the site contents and architecture.
    4. Analysing the website functions and operation. Website analysis for errors or functionality problems (broken links, missing graphics, lack of uniformity, wrong addresses, etc.).
    5. Analysis of third-party components, such as shopping carts, e-commerce platforms, etc.

6. Identifying the adaptations required for the target market according to the localization level. Organizing work specifications and the overall planning of the project.
7. Breaking down the website into the different components.
8. Depending on the localization level, the future architecture of the localized site is defined. Often, not all of the source website is localized (Jiménez-Crespo 2012a). Also, the international site structure might be defined, including domain choices.
9. The content that will be translated is identified, processed and analysed for estimates. This is often done with automatic systems. Text can be extracted or translated directly on the HTML structure.
10. The overall distribution of tasks and time estimates is carried out by localization managers (Dunne and Dunne 2011).
11. The localization pack is created with all the necessary files (images, specifications, instructions, proprietary software, etc.), instructions and deliverables.
12. A mirror or clone of the future website structure is created. Folders and files are set up for each new language, and the source files are transferred under their new (local) names.
13. Creating the global gateway. Links are readdressed into the HTML or JavaScript or other files.
14. Similar components are assembled into homogeneous packs consisting of: text, scripts, frames, bars, 'pop-ups' (which appear only in the source for the pages – as tool tips and legends), titles of web pages, sound files, images and images with embedded texts, and other types (runtimes, databases, etc.).
15. A testing plan is created for the localized website.
16. All the components are set up to be sent to translators (tagging, conversions, formatting, setting up into localization environment, etc.).

(b) Performed by localization specialists or freelance translators:

17. A glossary or termbase with the essential terminology and phraseology is prepared. This step can be assigned to a specialized terminologist (Karsch 2009).
18. The textual components of the websites are localized, including videos, presentations, etc. This represents the most significant component of localization. As LISA indicated, processing texts is 'the bulk of the localization process' (LISA 2007: 11).
19. Any component that has to be made from scratch or fully adapted for the target locale and is not present in the source website is created and tested. (This is often prepared by the requester of the localization project. A localization or internationalization engineer might be subcontracted to handle the coding work.)
20. All graphics are analysed, adapted as necessary and reprocessed.

21. A new set of keywords and/or description might be prepared to allow for properly indexing the site in the target locale. This is often referred to as Search Engine Marketing (SEM) and requires a different set of agents.

(c) QA and Integration. Performed by QA specialists, engineers or localization specialists

22. The translation is proofread and checked.
23. The localized components, such as translated text, are reintegrated into the website structure, changing the links (including links to images) within the localized files.
24. All components that were created or fully adapted are integrated and functional quality tested.
25. Functional quality tests are performed.
26. Cosmetic testing is performed.
27. Staged Quality Control. Websites are 'staged' for testing before they go live. Functionality tests are carried out in as many formats and screen and navigator configurations as possible.
28. Any changes are made, and these changes are confirmed and documented.
29. A Web-ready version is created.
30. Cultural acceptability and efficiency is tested. Often an in-country review is performed.
31. Online Quality Control and validation are carried out.
32. Delivery of website to client/posting online.

As seen in this list, the number of agents involved in the process can vary, from a single person responsible for the entire process to a multiplicity of agents in large organizations: business managers, localization managers, localization engineers, terminologists, localizers, QA operators, freelance translators, etc.

WEB LOCALIZATION AND CULTURAL ADAPTATION

As we saw in Chapter 1, the critical role of culture and cultural adaptations has been brought to the fore since the early days of localization (Esselink 2001; LISA 2007: 14). This type of adaptation that often appears in localization discourse was nothing new to TS (i.e. Katan 2009), particularly since the emergence of communicative or target-oriented approaches in translation theory. Originally, the emphasis on cultural adaptations revolved around specific basic issues such as colours, icons/graphics, perception, dates, number and measurement formats, etc. – types of adaptation shared by many other translation types, such as adverting or technical translations. Many other culture-dependent issues were never mentioned explicitly, such as textual structure (Neubert and Shreve 1992), pragmatic differences or genre-specific conventions (Jiménez-Crespo 2009a). This initial emphasis on cultural adaptation soon led to one of the most interesting contradictions in the localization industry, because cost-efficiency considerations favoured a trend running counter to cultural adaptation: the internationalization discourse seeks to neutralize culture-specific features so as to make localization easier, often mentioning the goal of achieving the maximum possible cultural neutrality (Cronin 2003: 18). This has also been referred to as 'reverse localization' (Schäler 2008c).

Apart from prescriptive and practical publications, this cultural dimension has been the object of a number of studies both from TS (McDonough 2006a; Tercedor 2005; Schäler 2002) and international marketing perspectives (Singh and Pereira 2005; Singh et al. 2004). Scholars have indicated that the goal of the cultural adaptation is not to 'mislead' the user into believing that the website is a local production, but rather, to perceive that the company is conscious and respectful of the receiving culture (McDonough 2006a; Yunker 2003: 18). According to the pragmatic-textual and cognitive perspective of Tercedor (2005: 153), four cultural elements are the subject of adaptation:

- Linguistic-textual aspects, such as intertextuality, register or macrotext
- Visual-iconic aspects
- Technical aspects
- Cognitive aspects, such as navigation, metaphors, mental models or interaction.

These elements relate to a range of culture-determined issues, from cognitive aspects to the visual-iconic ones that are the most commonly found in industry literature. Empirical studies on cultural adaptations have shown that higher degrees of adaptation relate improvements in navigation, interaction and rating of websites. This is because a culturally adapted site requires a lower cognitive effort, and the interaction environment is more efficient and clear (Singh et al. 2004).

The role of culture in web localization has been studied from several perspectives. The approach with the highest impact is the international marketing approach of Singh and Pereira. These scholars have extensively researched the role of culture in localization using the dimensions of anthropological psychologist Hofstede (1991). In this model, perception, symbolism and behaviour are the key elements that define any culture, and they help establish shared values and structured patterns of behaviour. Their major contribution consists in establishing a framework for studying cultural values that differ between countries, identifying specific website features related to these dimensions that can be quantitatively measured and compared. The variables used in website design relate to Hofstede's behaviour dimension:[5]

- Individualism-Collectivism: Related to self-perception as an individual or as part of a group or collective.

- Power distance: Related to the acceptance and expectations of unequal distribution of power.
- Uncertainty Avoidance: The importance of predictability, structure and order versus the willingness to take risks and accept ambiguity and limited structure.
- Masculinity-Femininity: The importance of achievements versus personal relationships.
- Low-High Context: The importance each culture assigns to the context as opposed to the message.[6]

These five dimensions are identified and linked to certain elements in websites that, used as quantifiable variables, allow comparisons of cultural differences between websites from different regions or countries. As expected, stark differences in these values emerge. For example, the United States and Australia rank high on the individualism-collectivism dimension, while most Latin American countries or Indonesia rank very low. The cultural adaptations that the authors recommend in high-collectivism cases are to enhance community relations, chats, add family themes; in the opposite case good privacy policies or personalization might be more effective. In the case of uncertainty avoidance, Greece, Portugal or Japan rank high, while Singapore, Sweden or the United States rank very low. In this case, uncertainty avoidance can be controlled with customer service, guided navigation and testimonials.

The studies carried out by Singh use two possible methodologies: comparing original sites in every country and comparing degrees of adaptation in web localization to the specific values of the target countries. Using these cultural dimensions to quantify the degree to which websites are adapted in localization, the scholars proposed the notion of 'localization level', a notion clearly related to the monetary and time resources that are or can be devoted to any localization project.

LOCALIZATION LEVELS AND CULTURAL ADAPTATIONS

Localization is clearly constrained by limited time, human and economic resources. Hence the localization level, or the extent to which the website is adapted to the receiving culture, normally depends on the importance or size of the local market or audience (Brooks 2000). The notion of localization level was defined in the context of software localization as:

> The amount of translation and customization necessary to create different language editions. The levels, which are determined by balancing risk and return, range from translating nothing to shipping a completely translated product with customized features.

> (Microsoft Corporation 2003: 15)

In a market environment such as localization, decisions about the localization level normally depend on Return on Investment (ROI) issues: whether the potential benefits of the localization process outweigh the initial investment needed to produce the localized version(s). It is up to commissioners or initiators to request a specific localization level that can be set out in the localization commission or brief. The overall localization process therefore depends on, and is constrained by, the resources and guidelines laid out by the commissioners. In practice, web localization processes vary widely, from simply translating a small text box with contact info right up to a fully localized website.

The first mention of localization levels can be attributed to Microsoft (Brooks 2000: 49–50) and distinguished three distinct levels upon which Windows operating systems were localized:

1. Enabled products: those in which users can write and use their own language and scripts, but the software and the accompanying help and guides appear in a different language.
2. Localized products: those in which the user interface and all help files are localized, but some language-specific tools such as spell-checkers and dictionaries are not available.
3. Adapted products: those in which all linguistic tools, functionalities and content are fully adapted to the target language/locale.

Initially, this classification was also applied to web localization processes, although only the second and third levels were applicable to web environments. The differences between software products and websites soon led scholars to propose different categorizations based on industry approaches (Yunker 2003), cultural studies applied to web design (Singh and Pereira 2005: 10–15) or Translation Studies (Jiménez-Crespo 2012a, 2012b). These three different proposals could be considered complementary, as they can offer different bases for empirical studies of the strategies surrounding localization practices. The categorization proposed by Singh and Pereira (2005), primarily based on the role of cultural adaptations, distinguishes five distinct levels:

1. Standardized websites: in which a multinational company simply offers a site in one language for all countries/markets.
2. Semi-localized websites: in which the only locale/specific content is a contact page in the target language with information about local branches, contacts, etc.
3. Localized websites: in which most content and pages are localized, but the original functionalities and back end are not modified.
4. Extensively localized websites: in which there is a global localization and all content and site structure/functionalities are fully adapted to the target locale.

5. Culturally adapted websites. This is the most advanced level of localization, the one that the authors advocate, and in which there is a total immersion in the target locale. Sites are adapted to the levels of cultural descriptions proposed by Hofstede (1991): perception, symbolism and behaviour.

These different levels of adaptation entail different degrees of re-engineering of the deep structure of the website, the hidden structure that contains the programming and tagging. Normally, web localization operates on the structure that the user sees, the visual (Mata 2005), front-end (Cronin 2003) or surface structure (Kersten *et al.* 2002), while higher localization levels also require adaptations and re-engineering in the underlying structure or deep structure. Lower localization levels only require the translation of the surface structure by means of replacing the textual strings in the website. Often, websites are not fully adapted to the receiving culture due to cost considerations, and hence, as Singh and Pereira (2005) point out, very few websites are fully localized to the highest level; the only example close to this level of adaptation was the IKEA website. Their categorization has been widely used for research studies into web localization. However, it cannot cover all possible cases, such as some localization processes undertaken from non-economic motives (volunteer translation, crowdsourcing, non-profit websites, self localization of personal websites, for instance). In Jiménez-Crespo (2012a, 2012b), I proposed a localization-level model derived from studying the web presence of almost 2000 non-profit organizations in the US and their web strategies for disseminating information. These websites cannot be strictly understood in terms of resources available for localization or ROI issues, and, obviously, the localization strategies of non-profit organizations diverge considerably from corporate websites. The proposed categorization includes a 0 level for websites that included localized documents in .pdf or .doc format as well as machine translation, given that the organization does at least acknowledge the need for translation, even if this cannot be considered localization. This appears as a recurrent option for disseminating information (Gaspari 2007) in cases of economic or human-resource constraints within which these organizations operate. The categorization can be described as follows:

1. Level 0: Website offers translated .pdf documents or MT engine links.
2. Level 1: Website offers a paragraph or page in a different language. Normally it is a brief description of the organization and basic contact information.
3. Level 2: Several localized web pages appear. All navigation menus are in English.

4. Level 3: Website offers several localized web pages with at least one navigation menu in the target language.
5. Level 4: Fully localized mirror website.

In any case, it should be mentioned that levels 0 and 1 might not be considered web localization *per se*, as they might not be cases of localized web content, but rather the posting of printed translations, or else simply writing the contact information from scratch. In these levels, translators might not work directly with any source texts or even adapted ones.

Finally, another interesting strategy that determines the localization level in business scenarios is the centralized/decentralized model (Yunker 2003; O'Hagan and Ashworth 2003: 74). In centralized models the web localization process is controlled from a central location and stored in a common repository. The decentralized model implies offering a common 'shell' or visual structure for the sites, with the actual local websites controlled and produced in each country, often mixing localized and local content, but also creating a new full website from scratch.[7]

LOCALIZATION AND WEB USABILITY

The target-oriented perspective of web localization is closely related to the objectives of web usability, which examines the reception of websites by means of empirical studies whose findings result in guidelines for web development. These guidelines are intended to improve user interaction, leading to higher user satisfaction and quality perception. Research focuses, from a cognitive perspective, on the basic patterns of interaction that guide relationships between users and websites and how websites are processed (Nielsen and Pernice 2010; Nielsen and Loranger 2006; Nielsen and Tahir 2002; Adkisson 2002; Brinck *et al.* 2002; Krug 2006). This type of research emerged from the challenges that new interactive on-screen hypertexts posed for developers and web users. Usability in general can be defined as 'a quality attribute that assesses how easy user interfaces are to use . . . [it] also refers to methods for improving ease-of-use during the design process' (Nielsen 2003).[8] It comprises five main dimensions: learnability, efficiency, memorability, errors and user satisfaction.

The main basic premise behind usability is that on-screen texts are processed differently from printed ones. Research has shown that reading slows down by 25% to 50%, and users do not read web texts but rather scan the pages in search of the information that might draw their attention (Nielsen 2001: 101). If they find an item of interest, they focus on it and process it further. Since patterns of cognitive interaction with these on-screen multimodal texts are different, one of the goals of usability is therefore to research how best to adapt online texts to the new medium and screen presentation.

One important contribution of usability is to shift the focus from the static concept of readers as passive recipients of information[9] to 'users' who actively engage and interact with texts, charting their own reading path. This is one of the main differences between interactive digital texts and printed texts; the latter being supposedly 'read' but not necessarily 'used'. In eye-tracking usability studies it is interesting to observe how users visually interact with a web page (Nielsen and Pernice 2010). The implications for web design are manifold, but the most critical is the fact that website success is measured by its so called 'stickiness':

> [O]ne key benchmark of Web success is stickiness, the ability to attract new and repeat visitors and keep them on a site.
>
> (LISA 2004: 35)

In web environments, users normally leave a web page or websites if some elements – texts, design, interaction – are too complex to process cognitively, moving on to search for similar information somewhere else (Nielsen and Loranger 2006).[10] The implications for web localization are clear: localized sites should be as clear, concise and efficient as possible.

The significance of web usability has been acknowledged in web localization research (Pym and Windle 2011a; Jiménez-Crespo 2009a). For example, Pym and Windle (2011a) remind us that, as users scan pages, texts should be separated during localization according to their degree of risk within the site. Recently industry practices have been adopting this approach, for example differentiating texts within localization according to 'user sentiment' (O'Brien 2012) or creative segments that might require a different treatment. Pym focuses mostly on the significance of structural and design elements in usability research. However, despite the significance of these elements, translators are normally not in charge of any usability changes in the design or visual components. Usability publications, however, do offer guidelines on web writing styles that increase the usability of the site (Jiménez-Crespo 2011e), encouraging clear, concise and unambiguous text writing. The significance of good web writing style was recognized in usability from the start:

> Plain text is the foundation of most web information.
>
> (Nielsen and Tahir 2002: 48)

> Effective content writing in one of the most critical aspects of all web design.
>
> (Nielsen and Tahir 2002: 14)

With these statements, usability guru Nielsen rated the importance of text production on a par with other elements of websites. Localizers are directly responsible for text production, so a sound knowledge of writing styles for on-screen reading is part of what has been called 'professional localization competence' (Jiménez-Crespo and Tercedor 2010). Web style guidelines developed by usability researchers therefore represent a key element for anyone involved in web localization (Jiménez-Crespo 2011e).

Another aspect that relates translation theories and usability research is the role of conventions. Functionalist approaches to translation (Reiss and Vermeer 1984; Nord 1997) highlight the replacement of source cultural conventions with target cultural conventions in instrumental translation as a key element of quality in translation. Similarly, the commonest mantra in usability publications is to follow established conventions at all levels, and some publications focus exclusively on this issue, for example Krug (2006). Users approach new websites, original or localized, with a conventional generic model that guides the interaction whenever they encounter anything new in the digital genre:

> by the time a user arrives at your homepage for the first time, that user will already be carrying a large load of mental baggage, accumulated from prior visits to thousands of other homepages . . . by this time, users have accumulated a generic mental model of the way homepages are supposed to work, based on their experiences on these other sites.
>
> (Nielsen and Tahir 2002: 37)

This generic mental model represents the matrix of expectations that guides the cognitive processing of the text, as happens with any other reading process. The underlying premise here is that users of websites have a lower tolerance of uncertainty, and presenting familiar or conventional features reduces the cognitive load needed to process web information (Nielsen and Loranger 2006; Spyridakis 2000). Some empirical studies have confirmed that following conventions has a clear effect on users' interactions with websites, and it has been proved that following structural, textual, lexical and pragmatic conventions improves comprehension, usability, recall, satisfaction and navigation (Vaughan and Dillon 2006). However, different empirical studies have shown that professionally localized sites tend to not comply with the conventions found in spontaneously translated or non-translated websites (i.e. Jiménez-Crespo 2009a).

SUMMARY

This chapter has outlined the global cycle of web localization within the larger GILT (Globalization, Internationalization, Localization and Translation) paradigm. A prototypical approach was adopted, as not all website localization processes follow the mainstream approach of large corporations (i.e. a small non-profit website). The overall web localization process was broken down into its constituents, and the main issues affecting the web localization process were discussed, such as localization levels, cultural adaptation, the communicative process and web usability.

FURTHER READING

For an overview of the GILT cycle see Dunne (2006a) or Cadieux and Esselink (2002). Jiménez-Crespo (2010b) provides a critical overview of the impact of internationalization strategies. All the previously mentioned descriptive professional manuals on localization provide a breakdown of tasks during localization (Esselink 2001; Yunker 2003), as well as in Gouadec (2007: 38–45). For cultural adaptation in localization see Tercedor (2005), McDonough (2006a), Schäler (2002) and Singh and Pereira (2005). For localization levels and strategies see Brooks (2000), Singh and Pereira (2005: 10–15) and Jiménez-Crespo (2012a). See Karsch (2009) for a typical terminology process within localization or Sikes (2011) for the role of localization managers. For the communicative context in which websites operate, see Janoschka (2003) and O'Hagan and Ashworth (2003). There is a massive amount of publications on web usability, some basic ones are Nielsen (2001), Nielsen and Loranger (2006), Nielsen and Pernice (2010) and Krug (2006). Jacob Nielsen's website www.useit.com is an excellent resource for all types of web usability research.

Part II

CURRENT ISSUES IN LOCALIZATION RESEARCH

3

WEB LOCALIZATION AND TEXT

The notion of 'text' has always been at the core of Translation Studies (Neubert and Shreve 1992). The existence of single stable texts upon which translation tasks are based has been a constant in the discipline. Nevertheless, the technological revolution and the emergence of new forms of hypertextuality, textual segmentation and reuse have challenged these existing conceptualizations. These new forms of hypertextuality and multimodality have changed the cognitive and communicative context of production, distribution and reception in both translator and end-user environments. This chapter reviews the evolution of the notion of 'text' in Translation Studies from an interdisciplinary perspective that includes Text Linguistics, Applied Linguistics and Translation Studies. Furthermore, it revisits the definition of 'text' in light of the new hypertextual model that dominates web localization. This analysis is long overdue, as the lack of a theoretical textual approach in localization has most likely hindered the development of further research. We will review the evolution of 'classic' types of texts into hypertexts, as well as their different types and structures as a core distinguishing feature between localization and other modalities and types. We will also explore hypertextual approaches to textual analysis and key notions in hypertext theory, such as cohesion and coherence. The chapter will end with a review of the implications of the hypertextual model for localization processes.

LOCALIZATION, TRANSLATION AND TEXT

Contemporary theories understand translation as a communicative, cognitive and textual process (Hurtado 2001: 40). As a textual operation, source texts (STs) situated in a socio-cultural context are the starting point for all translation activities. They are seen as unitary, stable entities that undergo a transformation through the cognitive and communicative act of translation, metaphorically moved from one context to another. Stable STs that exist prior to the act of translation are precisely one of the principles most unchallenged since early theorizations in the discipline. For some theories the notion of text is so relevant that it has even been brought to the forefront, as in the case of Text Linguistics perspectives (Neubert and Shreve 1992). In this approach, texts represent 'the central defining issue in translation. Texts and their situations define the translation process' (Neubert and Shreve 1992: 5). The emergence of new forms of hypertextuality, textual segmentation and reuse have nevertheless challenged the stable nature of these STs, dramatically changing the way texts are produced, distributed and received by users and translators (Bowker 2006; Jiménez-Crespo 2009b; Pym 2010). This novel life cycle also defines web localization, as hypertexts are the main objects processed.

Assumptions about the nature of texts necessarily influence the outcome of any research or practical efforts. So sound theoretical foundations are required to proceed with localization research that involves descriptive product-based studies, experimental cognitive studies on localization or corpus-based approaches (see Chapter 7). These implications go beyond translation research (i.e. how do translators cognitively process the understanding of a segment of a hypertext if no textual boundaries are identified?), but also for industrial processes such as quality assurance (QA): how can coherence and cohesion be evaluated in translated 'material' or 'content'? Does translation quality originate from a segmental level or does it operate at higher macrostructural ones?

Compared to printed texts, web texts represent new forms of textuality with truly distinctive features. First of all, the boundaries of web texts are apparently harder to identify. As a result, readers may suffer from what is known as the 'informational short-sightedness' effect (Conklin 1987: 40): readers might be disoriented due to the impossibility of identifying textual limits. Translators are often presented with hypertexts in a non-linear fashion that is quite different from how end users receive them. Hypertexts are authored by collectives, rather than individuals, and are translated by a multiplicity of agents (Pym 2004a). They are also less stable or concrete, due to technological advances in textual development, distribution and localization (Mossop 2006; Biau and Pym 2006).

LINGUISTICS AND THE DEFINITION OF TEXT

If we go back to the linguistic notion of 'text', which is a relatively recent concept as opposed to theorizations in literary studies, we see that it has been evolving in different paradigms and schools of thought during the last century. In the 1960s structuralists focused on structural features of texts originating from the work of Saussure (1916) or Chomsky (1965). Then criticism of the lack of attention to semantic relations and the relationship between texts and their surrounding context opened up a new approach focused on communicative aspects; this described texts according to functionalist features of the communicative situation, incorporating senders and receivers as key players in the production and understanding of texts. These communicative and dynamic approaches, such as applied linguistics, discourse analysis and text linguistics, are the most influential in the introduction of the notion of text in TS.

Without doubt, the most influential definition from text linguistics originated in the work of de Beaugrande and Dressler, in which a text is:

> A COMMUNICATIVE OCCURRENCE which meets seven standards of TEXTUALITY. If any of these standards is not considered to have been satisfied, the text will be non-communicative. Hence, non-communicative texts are treated as non-texts.
>
> (de Beaugrande and Dressler 1981: 3)

In their view, texts are regarded as communicative occurrences, highlighting the communicative function of all texts. However, only those that fulfil the seven 'standards of textuality' – cohesion, coherence, intentionality, acceptability, informativity, situationality and intertextuality – can be considered as texts (a definition of these standards is offered in Table 3.1). These standards as a whole embody what is called 'textuality': the existence of an inherent nature of any text that is expressed through all these standards combined. Out of them, two – cohesion and coherence – are text-centred; the other five focus on pragmatic-communicative aspects of the text relating to the relationship between the sender and the receiver.

Translation scholars have suggested that not all standards of textuality are equally relevant in all contexts, but coherence and intentionality

Table 3.1 Definitions of the seven standards of textuality according to de Beaugrande and Dressler (1981)

Standard of textuality	Definition:
	Property of a text when it. . .
Cohesion	. . . is continuous on the syntactic level.
Coherence	. . . has continuity of sense at the level of meaning.
Intentionality	. . . is intentionally produced and has a purpose.
Acceptability	. . . is relevant or meaningful to whoever receives it.
Informativity	. . . includes new information.
Situationality	. . . makes sense in regard to the situation in which it is presented.
Intertextuality	. . . depends on other previous texts for reference.

(purposefulness) are normally considered the most significant for translation (Göpferich 1995b; Hatim and Mason 1997). As will be explored later, the role of coherence is highlighted in digital texts due to certain characteristics of the ways hypertexts are processed (Janoschka 2003: 165–7).

DEFINING TEXT IN TS

Translation Studies initially incorporated different linguistic approaches to the study of text, such as de Beaugrande and Dressler's text linguistics models (Neubert and Shreve 1992), or Hallidayian systemic-functionalist approaches to the study of text (i.e. Hatim and Mason 1990, 1997; Baker 2011). Great theoretical efforts have been directed towards defining texts, as they represent the operative unit upon which translation activities are based. They also embody the minimal unit in didactic, evaluative or research efforts (Hurtado 2001).[1]

Among the several approaches that have had an impact on subsequent TS research, Hatim and Mason define text from a Discourse Analysis perspective as:

> a coherent and cohesive unit, realized by one or more than one sequence of mutually relevant elements, and serving some overall rhetorical purpose.
>
> (Hatim and Mason 1990: 178)

The communicative nature of texts is thus highlighted and brought to the fore, with texts possessing a main textual function. For Hatim and Mason texts can be multifunctional, with a combination of a primary and secondary functions. For example, a web infomercial has a main exhortative or appellative function to convince users to buy the product, with a secondary, expository one that provides the necessary information. In the case of multifunctional texts such as websites, the possibility of a related set of functions represents a key element in understanding them.

From the point of view of hypertext localization, the work of Hatim and Mason can help us draw attention to specific key issues, such as the importance of textual boundaries or the fact that texts are the largest unit of discourse. In their own words: 'it is of vital importance for translators to identify text boundaries' (1990: 178). The identification of textual boundaries is essential during translation tasks to process the ST, assisting in the identification of coherence and cohesion relationships in comprehension processes, and also to produce appropriate cohesive target texts (TTs). As will be explored later, the use of translation memory tools and content management systems has slowly forced translators to work with textual segments in which the limits might be unknown, leading to specific problems in the configuration and subsequent reception of TTs. They also indicate that in translation there is no significant operative unit 'beyond the level of the text, [and] it is difficult to perceive any regularly occurring patterns which would enable us to identify a unit of discourse' (*ibid.*).

Writing from a functionalist perspective and deeply rooted in communicative and pragmatic approaches, Nord interrelates internal and external factors and defines a text as 'the totality of communicative signals used in a communicative interaction' (1991: 14). A text therefore is not merely expressed by linguistic means, but rather, 'a text is a communicative action which can be realized by a combination of verbal and non-verbal means' (Nord 1991: 15). This widening of the definition of text to all signals used in a communicative situation is key to approaching text in audiovisual and multimodal models, and intrinsically incorporates visual, sound, interactive or typographic aspects into the definition.

Definitions of text for technical translation also provide insight for our purposes, partly because most localization types can be considered as technical translation. The definition offered by Susanne Göpferich departs from a functionalist and communicative approach and implicitly incorporates the significance of visual elements:

> A text is a coherent whole made up by linguistic or graphic-linguistic elements that presents a textual and/or functional orientation. It was created with a specific purpose, the communicative purpose, it fulfils an identifiable communicative function . . . and represents a thematic and functional unit.
>
> (Göpferich 1995a: 57)

It is easy to see how websites as source texts for localization can fit within this definition, especially in the merging of linguistic and graphic elements to serve an identifiable communicative function.

Turning specifically to localization, we find very few attempts in this direction. Pym offered a simple definition for software localization as 'a text is quite simply whatever unit is distributed as a unit' (2004a: 17). In his approach one of the most salient features of texts in localization is therefore their dependence on their distribution process and the gradual disappearance of the source text:

> The localized text is not called on to represent any previous texts, it is instead part of one and the same process of constant material distribution, which starts in one culture and may continue in many others.
>
> (Pym 2004a: 6)

Although he explicitly extends this notion of a textual distribution model to websites in later publications (2010; Pym and Windle 2011a), it can be argued that hypertexts can be rather defined as units of production, information and storage, or as units that are developed and presented to the user as such.[2]

The following list reviews the main shared principles in previous definitions of text from different perspectives in order to shed light on an operative definition of text for web localization.

1. First of all, a text represents a 'unit'. This is the most widely repeated principle from all perspectives and paradigms. As an example, from a systemic-functionalist approach, this notion is understood as an essential property of a text, a 'unified whole' (Halliday and Hasan 1976: 1). From a text-linguistic approach, they represent a single 'communicative occurrence' (de Beaugrande and Dressler 1981), or the fundamental unit of language from a communicative perspective. In TS, and proceeding from these systemic-functionalist, Text Linguistic or Discourse Approaches, a text is a 'coherent and cohesive unit' (Hatim and Mason 1990), a 'coherent whole' (Göpferich 1995a) or simply, 'a unit' (Pym 2004a). Websites represent cohesive and coherent units of information that can, nevertheless, continually be enlarged by means of adding more content.

2. The unitary character of any text is represented in its inherent nature, referred to as 'textuality' (de Beaugrande and Dressler 1981: 3). This nature combines semantic and linguistic aspects (close to structuralist and generativist linguistic theories), as well as pragmatic ones (adopting the perspective that highlights the important role of extralinguistic aspects). Textuality, as the global essence of any text is related to the notion of 'texture' (Hatim and Mason 1997), defined as the property of any text by virtue of which it has a conceptual and linguistic consistency, that is, it has a continuity both in its sense (coherent) and in its surface elements (cohesive), and also possesses a clearly articulated thematic progression (Hurtado 2001: 415).

3. A text is 'situated', that is, it is only considered as such through the 'actualization' that a specific receiver carries out in a specific reception situation (Reiss and Vermeer 1984: 90). This implies that there could be as many instances of texts as potential receivers (Nord 1997). This dependence on the context of reception in 'actualizing' a text makes reading a unique act that depends on this reception situation. According to de Beaugrande, reading is 'a process subject to the particular contextual constraints of the occasion, just as much as the production of the texts is' (de Beaugrande 1978: 30). From Neubert's (1996) text-linguistic approach, the fact that any translation depends on the unique reading and comprehension process of a translator has been referred to as 'translational relativity'. This notion is of interest in web localization for two reasons. First, this unique actualization process can differ considerably between end user's reading processes and translators'; the latter often work with the internal technology-based organization of the text and not necessarily the final communicative structure, so, the

distinct comprehension process during translation can lack certain communicative cues that often reflect the configuration and features of localized TTs (Jiménez-Crespo 2009b).

4. Texts are defined in a broader sense as not only based on linguistic or verbal aspects, but also on non-verbal ones, such as graphic, typographic and visual (Nord 1991; Göpferich 1995a), as well as multimedia or audiovisual elements (Remael 2010). This global entity represents a unitary whole whose value is higher than the sheer sum of its verbal and non-verbal elements (Snell-Hornby 1996: 55). As such, the reception of a global website by a user entails interaction with a text that is perceived as a whole (and not just the sum of parts that do not make up a whole – as, for example, with search engine results). Additionally, it should be mentioned that texts in localization incorporate interactivity and specific sequencing of events that resemble dialogic exchanges (e.g. error messages that pop up when something is done incorrectly), and there-fore, interactivity is an integral part of the text. This is represented through HTML, XML or other tags (Santini 2007), Cascading Style Sheets (CSS or XSL) and scripts (Kennedy and Shepherd 2005).

5. All texts possess a specific textual configuration or structure that is deter-mined by its communicative purpose. Texts as such cannot exist without this communicative purpose (Göpferich 1995a: 40). Digital texts in localization possess highly conventionalized textual structures. This is true both in web texts (Adkisson 2002; Nielsen and Loranger 2006; Jiménez-Crespo 2009a, 2010a, 2011c), software products (Austermühl 2006) and videogames (O'Hagan and Mangiron 2013). The textual structure is multilinear (Fritz 1998), and it is organized around a global superstructure that users expect (Askehave and Nielsen 2005).

6. Texts can be classified as 'simple' and 'complex' (Reiss and Vermeer 1984). 'Complex texts' can incorporate other instances of texts in their open structure. This distinction between simple and complex is highly productive for the purposes of web localization, as most websites can incorporate instances of simple texts in their structures. For example, users can expect the instructions for a product as a .pdf document uploaded in a corporate or product website. Reiss and Vermeer also proposed the notion of 'complementary texts': those that depend on the existence of prior texts, such as a book review. It is easy to identify how search engines can easily fit within this category.

Towards an operative definition of text in web localization

In most studies in localization, both from industrial and TS perspectives, the notion of text is hardly defined (no surprise, given the theoretical challenge posed by the nature of texts in complex, interconnected, hypertextual cyberspace). As a result, STs are often referred to as: 'material' (Esselink 2001), 'content' (Dunne 2006a; Schäler 2008a), 'documents' (Shreve 2006b) or 'information elements' (Lockwood 2000). This illustrates the range of perspectives, among which, interestingly, the influence of Information Management predominates. In this approach, the most important issue is how textual segments of varying lengths, and other types of audiovisual, multimedia or iconic element in a number of targeted languages, are carefully managed and assembled automatically for distribution in web environments. Localization Studies have so far reached out to other areas to support research efforts that include digital texts, such as technical translation (Göpferich 1995a, 1995b; Gamero 2001), audiovisual translation (Zabalbeascoa 2008), multimodality (Gambier and Gottliev 2004; Pedrola 2009), and functionalist approaches to text analysis (Nord 1991, 1997). Web localization is a new development within TS, and so it is productive to look to other newly established fields, such as audiovisual translation, that have devoted great efforts to defining the audiovisual 'text'. These new multimodal forms of texts have required the characterization and delimitation of the object of study, the audiovisual text, and the obvious incorporation of visual, sound, musical and textual elements into its overall configuration (Remael 2010).

In our search for a definition of text in web localization, the two main issues to take into consideration are:

(1) the fact that texts represent a coherent whole or unit with a communicative purpose, and
(2) that this communicative purpose can be achieved through textual, visual, aural, typographic or interactive means.

In web localization, and from a textual and cognitive perspective, a complete hypertext or website represents the minimal textual unit (though in certain cases it might be just made up of one single page). In the early days of localization scholars often identified the single web pages as the main operative unit of analysis and translation. This was partly due to the fact that the WWW was metaphorically conceptualized as a collection of 'pages' that anyone could easily browse, search or bookmark, while hypertexts were divided into hyperconnected 'nodes' (see below). Nevertheless, web pages are the units of storage, information, and presentation simply because of the constraints imposed by screen presentation, forcing hypertext producers to subdivide hypertexts into discrete textual subunits. These pages cannot be considered as complete texts in themselves, but rather as subtexts within global hypertexts. For our purpose, it should be kept in mind that any page is cognitively processed within the frame of reference of the global hypertext, and inferences and global coherence are built upon that underlying structure. Even in the case of documents uploaded or linked to a website, users approach and process them within the framework provided by the global website: i.e. we read the same piece of news differently if we find it on the *New York Times* website or in a satirical online paper such as *The Onion*.

In light of the previous review, the notion of text in all localization types will be defined as: 'a digital interactive entity that is coherently developed as a unit and presented to users as such'. Additionally, and in order to account for the minimal operative textual unit with identifiable textual limits in which global coherence resides, the notion of text in web localization is:

> A digital interactive entity that is developed and presented to the user as a unit in the WWW and is coherent within itself. It represents a thematic and functional unit that has a hyperlinked multilineal structure made up of subtexts. It comprises linguistic, graphic, visual, typographic, aural and interactive components.

This definition also incorporates the so-called 'accompanying subtexts' (Göpferich 1995b), defined as those texts that end users will not read or interact with but that, nevertheless, are key to fulfilling the communicative function of the text. The case of legal terms in most websites can serve as a case in point. These legal texts are rarely read by end users (Jiménez-Crespo 2011c), even when these sections are required from a user-credibility perspective.

TEXTS, SEGMENTATION AND TRANSLATION TECHNOLOGY

Over the last three decades, innumerable studies have focused on the impact of technologies on translation and, more specifically, on how technologies have changed the ways texts are produced, translated and distributed. The 1990s saw the emergence and wide adoption of translation memory tools (TM) based on the principle of subdividing the text into segments, presenting them to the translators, and subsequently storing them in pairs in order to enable future reuse (Macklovitch and Russell 2000; Bowker 2002; Hartley 2009). Translation memories revolutionized the translation industry, speeding translation processes and leading to higher productivity and faster turnaround. However, scholars warned early on about the potential negative impact of reuse in translation processes, as translators gradually shifted from working on unitary texts to smaller segmental units. To some extent, scholars warned of the perils of conceptualizing the notion of translator as a simple *traducteur de phrases* or 'sentence translator' (Bédard 2000). This shift was also taken further with the emergence in the 2000s of Content Management Systems (CMS) and Global Management Systems (GMS), another translation technology widely used in web localization and now mostly web-based. CMS and GMS were built upon TM technology with the objective of handling an ever-increasing number of language versions of websites or multilingual documentation. These systems combine the previous textual segmentation capabilities and functionalities of translation memories and dynamically manage the translation of updates or changes into multiple languages (Budin 2008). GMS facilitate the localization process by identifying and feeding to translators precisely the textual segments or 'chunks' that have been modified or added. This process provides the ability to maintain and update large websites in multiple locales or languages. GMS force translators to work in 'batch mode' (Bowker 2002) or 'pretranslation' mode (Wallis 2008), that is, a process in which an automatized system compares the source text to the database of previous translations and feeds translators only those segments that do not have an exact match. Nowadays, almost all localization processes are carried out using one or both of these technologies, in part due to the need to protect the programming or deep structure of the website (Kersten *et al.* 2001; Mata 2005). The text that users see is embedded in programming structure, and TM and GMS tools provide safe platforms to access the text that is visible without accidentally changing the programming structure behind it. New online cloud technologies have also been developed to manage localization processes and workflows. This means that translators frequently interact with just the translatable textual segments, while the programming structure is kept intact.

Since the introduction of these technologies, scholars have researched and theorized on the potential disappearance of the notion of 'source text' and the move towards segmented dynamic textual entities upon which translators carry out translation tasks (Bowker 2006; Mossop 2006; Pym 2010, 2011a). As is often pointed out, translators no longer work with complete source texts, rather, their work is reduced to processing decontextualized textual segments. This trend has been taken to the extreme with new crowdsourcing approaches, in which volunteers are often presented with discrete textual segments to translate or evaluate. It was inevitable that the introduction of TM systems would change the nature of translation-related tasks (Bowker 2006; Heyn 1998), mostly through the introduction of non-linear modes of text production and translation. A great deal of research has been devoted to the effect of translation memory tools on the products translated (texts), or on the process, either from a technological or cognitive perspective. Publications have therefore explored:

1. the way texts are processed by the translator in light of cognitive and communicative constraints that segmentation imposes on comprehension, and/or
2. the effect of using these technologies on the products, the translated texts themselves (Bowker 2006; Jiménez-Crespo 2009b).[3]

What has not been discussed is the nature of the source text as a global cohesive single unit of production and reception, except for the fact that source texts can be produced using Controlled Language software, limiting the style, structure and lexical variation (Lockwood 2000; Pym 2011a). From a process or cognitive perspective, in localization tasks 'the very notion of document is [often] lost' (Macklovitch and Russell 2000: 140), thus forcing translators to work with disaggregated textual units that are not necessarily 'the totality of communicative signals used in a communicative interaction' (Nord 1991: 14). Instead, translators gradually process sub-textual units that are part of a complete text that is sometimes unavailable (Mossop 2006). This has clear implications in terms of cohesion, coherence and contextual cues during source text comprehension and the subsequent textual production stage, as, communicatively speaking, only a global unitary text can constitute the minimal unit of translation (Neubert and Shreve 1992; Nord 1997).

In respect of the product-based perspective, the body of empirical literature on the effects of TM tools on translated texts shows that they often lack uniformity in style and tone, due to the combination of multiple authoring and the insertion of pretranslated segments by both human and machine translation engines. This common effect has been referred to as 'sentence salad' (Bédard 2000), 'train wrecks' (Bowker 2006), or 'collage texts' (Mossop 2006). Unfortunately, this often characterizes a great many localized websites. Web texts that are supposed to show higher levels of coherence and cohesion due to the benefits of TM tools have been proved to show lower levels of terminological coherence than naturally produced ones (Jiménez-Crespo 2009b).[4] Translated web texts also tend to replicate the textual structure of source texts, the more so in cases where the translator works exclusively on textual updates (Jiménez-Crespo 2011c). This affects their potential naturalness and quality, as texts maintain the same order and number of sentences in the target text (Bowker 2002: 117). Finally, translated texts are less cohesive and readable, as translators might formulate texts in a way to maximize their future reuse with TM, avoiding anaphoric or cataphoric references. This is what Heyn (1998: 135) refers to as 'peephole translations', or the result of translators focusing on microstructures without a clear global macrostructural and superstructural guiding model. All these effects due to TM use regularly appear in localized texts, resulting in:

> a text that is inherently less cohesive or coherent, less readable, and of a lesser overall quality. It may be grammatically correct, but it risks containing oversimplified syntax, monotonous rhythm, and a lack of diversity.
>
> (Bowker 2006: 180)

According to some of my own empirical studies (Jiménez-Crespo 2009b; Jiménez-Crespo 2010a), if we compare localized to non-localized websites, the latter are in fact less terminologically and orthotypographically coherent.

THE DEATH OF THE SOURCE TEXT?

Pym (2010: 123–4) argues that the combination of translation technologies plus the novel hypertextual non-linear model have resulted in the gradual disappearance of the 'traditional' notion of STs. In localization the traditional dual move from a ST to a target text is replaced by a move from a source text to an intermediary version called an 'internationalized version' as we have seen. This intermediate version is intentionally 'delocalized' or 'internationalized' as the industry attempts to remove all traces of features that are language- and culture-dependent, in order to facilitate the subsequent translation process. As a result, translators do not work directly on the source text, but rather, with a hybrid middle version.

The question of whether the notion of source texts is disappearing may be complex, but in general and from a cognitive perspective, translation cannot successfully proceed without global cohesive and cohesion cues that help the translator understand the ST (Hatim and Mason 1990). Even the intermediary versions proposed by Pym, from the point of view of the translation process, still represent the ST as such. Translators, through prior accumulated experience with similar texts or by constructing a mental model of what the texts might be, consciously or unconsciously possess a model of the global text that compensates for the potential lack of communicative context or co-text. Where the translator's inferences might be inadequate, errors or inadequacies occur, but then the global localization cycle incorporates an enhanced quality-assurance stage precisely in order to deal with these potential pitfalls. Additionally, if source text and target text end users do interact with global hypertexts, the source text, *per se*, does exist, even when at specific moments (maybe less often than researchers argue) translators might not have access to the global text. To sum up briefly, source texts might not exist in a traditional stable manner, but rather in a dynamic fashion. Translators might be simply adapting to a new hypertextual model that requires the skills to infer a coherence mechanism in hypertext environments (Fritz 1998). In localization, a tangible stable or highly dynamic source text that is transformed into a target text exists, as witnessed by the millions of existing localized websites. The death of the source text that is often suggested has to be understood in the context of process and cognitive approaches to translation, that is, the source text during translation tasks, and not necessarily a product-based one. As already mentioned, this new model might simply require sharing the responsibility of producing a final coherent and cohesive text to a greater extent between translators and an enhanced QA stage.

LOCALIZATION AND HYPERTEXT

The emergence of web localization processes needs to be set in the context of the framework of new hypertextual production and distribution models

that started in the late 1960s. Web localization operates mostly on hypertexts, and understanding their main features is essential to localizing them
and/or conducting any type of research involving these open and multilinear
forms of text. The development of the Internet, and later the WWW, made
widely available the new textual model shaped by the constraints of both
the medium and the presentation on a screen of limited dimensions. Initially,
these discrete textual units were metaphorically referred to as 'pages', the
original basic unit of presentation, information and storage (Nielsen and
Loranger 2006). Later, the building blocks that make up hypertexts were
referred to in hypertext theory as 'nodes' (Landow 1992), although,
depending on the approach, they are also referred to in literary hypertext
theory as 'lexias' (Barthes 1977), as well as by a number of other terms, such
as 'textual elements' (Fritz 1998) or 'hyperdocuments' (Crowston and
Williams 1999). These nodes or pages were part of a larger hypertext, a
larger cohesive textual unit that, nevertheless, was stored and accessed by
users in a non-linear or multilinear way. Hypertexts were not necessarily a
new development: printed hypertexts, such as phonebooks, had existed for
decades before the invention of the Internet. However, the way in which
they were digitally stored, distributed and accessed in a non-sequential way
represented a novel development.

Definition and features of hypertexts

Since the 1970s the notion of digital hypertext represents a heterogeneous
concept. Different studies refer to hypertext in diverse ways; sometimes a
hypertext is a complete web page, sometimes the different components of
pages, but more commonly it refers to complete websites. In its origins, in
what is known as Hypertext Theory, Ted Nelson who is often credited as the
creator of the notion of modern hypertext defined it as:

> non-sequential writing-text that branches and allows choices to the reader, best
> read at an interactive screen.
>
> (Nelson 1993: 2)

Hypertexts have often been defined by specific features that distance them
from printed texts with linear structures. They are read on screen and they
are interactive, requiring active reader participation. This interactive nature
means that hypertexts are accessed and read in a unique order determined
by users' preferences – a new type of reading that has been referred to as
'self-selective reading mode' (Storrer 2002). Web localizers also approach
hypertexts in a non-linear fashion, but very differently from end users: the
structures that translators work on are organized according to programming or storage criteria instead of communicative ones. These differences
imply that translators have to bear in mind the potential hypertextual

reading path of end users as part of the context or co-text of each textual segment they process.

The most important issues regarding hypertexts are:

1. the different types of hypertexts and their implication for web localization,
2. the importance of coherence and cohesion in hypertexts, and
3. that they have a different non-linear structure, with users choosing their own 'self-selected path' (Fritz 1998). This structure is 'open', as hypertexts can be constantly enlarged at any time by adding new pages, content, user-generated material or external links (Landow 1992).

These three issues – types, cohesion and coherence, and structure – will be reviewed separately below. Other features of interest are:

4. Hypertexts are also updated and modified much more often than printed texts, and temporal considerations play a key role due to immediacy and currency in Internet-mediated communications (LISA 2006: 4). This dynamism is normally controlled with GMS and CMS. Not all hypertexts are dynamic, as the origins of the WWW were marked by 'static' websites: those equally retrieved by all users at a specific point in time.[5] Nowadays professional websites are normally 'dynamic': assembled from the server side according to the user's preferences, history, etc. New examples of 'dynamic' websites are services such as MSN or Google portals, social networking sites, news aggregators, etc.
5. Hypertexts also represent multimodal texts that comprise a number of multimedia or multimodal elements, such as audio, graphics, icons, video, animations, as well as independent elements such as web advertising that does not necessarily relate to the main hypertext (Janoschka 2003).
6. That hypertexts are mostly accessed in open online environments implies that they can potentially reach a much larger audience than printed texts. Usability studies indicate that it is complex to identify the profile of the 'unique average user' (Krug 2006: 135).

Hypertexts and textual structures

Hypertexts are multilinear entities, even though they are often described as non-linear: developers do organize their overall path structures and the possibilities of interconnection by means of hyperlinks (Janoschka 2003: 173). Therefore, even though users ultimately choose a 'self-selected path' depending on their preferences or communicative needs, the initial possibilities of interaction are pre-arranged:

The hypertext designer will have to select the text elements to be interconnected by electronic links. Normally, this selection will also involve choosing a global structure for the system of nodes and links.

(Engebretsen 2000: 211)

This overall global structure is normally represented in navigation maps or sitemaps, but, contrary to what happens with a book or document users do not perceive the textual boundaries of the text. This apparently results in the previously mentioned 'informational short-sightedness' effect (Conklin 1987: 40), mitigated in web design through navigation menus, visual web maps or breadcrumb[6] navigation, which reduce the cognitive effort involved in processing hypertexts.

Hypertexts are normally arranged according to two basic structures: axial-hierarchical and networked (Landow 1992). Both types of structure are commonly combined in current websites as navigation menus and other navigation options allowing for travel in a networked way (similar to a neuronal structure) throughout the website. Modern hypertexts also provide networked navigation options, such as indexing practices by search engines, to allow travel directly to any page within a website – a mechanism known as 'deep linking' (Nielsen 2001: 179) – gradually reducing the significance of home or start pages. This means that hypertextual structures are decentralized and cannot be conceptualized as a static structure from the user's perspective.

Links or hyperlinks are without any doubt the most significant feature of hypertexts. Berners-Lee (2000: 235) defined hyperlinks as 'a unity of connection in hypertext'. Hyperlinks provide the connection between all nodes by means of overtly marked textual cues that identify a referential, interactive and functional connection. Hyperlinks are composed of two parts, the 'trigger', or element that can be activated, and the 'target', or the node that is activated (Janoschka 2003: 179). The trigger is conventionally highlighted in a different colour or indicated by the mouse pointer changing from an arrow to a hand. There are different types of hyperlinks, such as 'internal', 'external', 'intranodal' and 'implicit'. Internal hyperlinks are led to a page or node within a unitary hypertext, while external ones direct the user to a node outside the limits of the containing hypertext. Certain digital genres are mostly comprised of internal links – such as corporate web pages, where the intention is to keep users as long as possible in the web page – while others, such as search engines or certain blogs, consist mostly of external links. A variant of the internal hyperlink is the 'intranodal' one, which interconnects two areas within a single page when the page length is greater than the screen can display. Implicit links are those that contribute to the global cohesion of a hypertext, such as web maps or web indexes (Engebretsen 2000). Other authors have coined the terms 'content-related' and 'navigational' hyperlinks to refer to the same notion (Conklin 1987).

Hypertexts also have two distinctive structures within web pages due to the lack of a linear structure: interface text and content text (Price and Price 2002). Interface texts consist of all recurring segments whose function is to articulate the global hypertext, such as main or foot navigation menus, summaries of contents in right-hand columns, search functions, site maps or breadcrumb navigation trails. Content text can be defined as the unique and exclusive content in each page within a site. The title of a web page usually includes a summary and/or description of this unique content in the context of a cohesive global website. As seen in Figure 3.1, current design conventions assign content text to central columns in the structure of a page.

Types of hypertexts

It cannot be assumed that any text found online depends on the medium for its existence. The WWW has become a repository of documents of different types and in different formats (Hofmann and Menhert 2000), and texts created for any medium, such as a contract, an instruction booklet in .pdf format, a televised news broadcast, a research paper or a personal blog can be stored and retrieved in the WWW. Nevertheless, the textual, communicative, discursive and linguistic features of these texts will be the same whether they are accessed online or in printed form. The only difference will

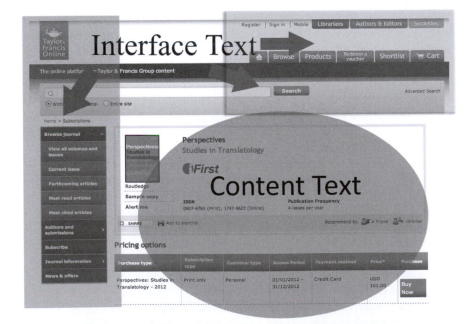

Figure 3.1 Interface text and content text in a web page (Price and Price 2002)

be their mark-up format – HTML, XML or .pdf – and the fact that they include a number of textual segments that comply with the different standards required for each page to be successfully stored and retrieved. Thus, the web page might incorporate a navigation menu, a page title, or a brief keyword description in the HTML tag <meta name='keywords' content='text'>. The WWW is also populated with web texts created exclusively for the web, such as RSS news, corporate websites, or portals.

Thus, not all text found on the Internet can therefore be identified as hypertexts, even when made available online. Following the typology proposal by Angelika Storrer (2002), we will divide texts found online into three categories: 'e-texts', 'hyperdocuments', and 'hyperwebs'.

1. 'E-texts' are sequentially organized printed documents that are simply uploaded and made available on the Net, such as a contract or a tourist brochure. The object of study of web localization or hypertext theory cannot be the processing of these documents *per se*, but rather the overall hypertextual structure that allows the embedding of this text. Nowadays, not all e-texts are copies of printed texts, as novel content types, such as RSS news or tweets, can be considered independent e-texts that can be embedded in hypertexts.
2. 'Hyperdocuments' are the new textual and communicative model that appeared exclusively on the WWW. They can be defined as networks of textual nodes and links that serve a distinct textual function and address a comprehensive, global topic. These hyperdocuments are open, because the developer can add other nodes or textual segments at any time. Hyperdocuments, such as corporate or institutional websites can be defined as the prototypical object of study of web localization (see Chapter 6).
3. 'Hyperweb' is defined as a network of different hypertexts linked on the WWW. At a larger scale, the whole WWW could be defined as a hyperweb. The digital genre 'web portal' – e.g. MSN.com or Yahoo.com – can be identified as such, as it incorporates a number of hypertexts (the individual sites included in a portal).

The implications for web localization are clear, as even when the prototypical texts that might be processed are hyperdocuments or websites, they may also include a never-ending list of e-texts of all types within their open structures, making this modality one of the most complex possible in the language industry.

Cohesion and coherence in hypertexts

Coherence and cohesion are two basic properties that depend on how the texts are sequenced. They apply to all texts, no matter the medium or mode, including hypertexts. Users make sense of hypertexts and receive them as cohesive units, even when coherence- and cohesion-building mechanisms are slightly different from that of linear printed texts. This conundrum, the fact that non-linear hypertexts are coherent and cohesive initially drew the attention of hypertext theorists (i.e. Foltz 1996; Fritz 1998; Storrer 2002; Janoschka 2003), who delved into the cognitive processing of hypertexts and the adaptations required for writing, developing and theorizing on hypertexts.

In terms of a text-linguistic approach cohesion is defined as the way in which components of the surface text are mutually connected within a sequence, and it rests upon grammatical dependencies (de Beaugrande and Dressler 1981: 3). Cohesion is therefore realized through grammatical and syntactic relations in the sequencing of textual units. Coherence, in turn, focuses on the meaning and comprehension of the text, and it emerges through the interrelation of meaning in the surface of the text and the activation of knowledge by receivers. Various viewpoints and schools of thought normally see coherence as the most important property (i.e. de Beaugrande and Dressler 1981; Hatim and Mason 1990; Neubert and Shreve 1992; Göpferich 1995a).[7] In general, the importance of coherence is related to the need for texts to make sense, and this occurs 'because there is a CONTINUITY OF SENSES among the knowledge activated by the expressions of the text . . . the foundation of COHERENCE' (de Beaugrande and Dressler 1981: 84). This notion of 'continuity of sense' depends on the active participation of the receivers through the activation of prior knowledge prompted by the proposition that is being processed. It is easy to perceive that in selective or non-linear reading modes the continuity of sense represents a key element, even when coherence relations may be fuzzier if compared to linear texts (Tyrkkö 2011). This dynamic understanding of coherence is most popular in the study of hypertexts (Jucker 2003; Janoschka 2003), and also in translation in general (Baker 2011). This approach defines coherence as a mental action (rather than a static property of texts) that is assigned by language-users in their interactions with texts and discourses (Van Dijk 1988: 62). Coherence is regarded as the necessary tool to make the 'text hang together conceptually' (Hatim and Mason 1990: 239), and it establishes the necessary continuity of senses as a 'result of the interaction between knowledge presented in the text and the reader's own knowledge and experience of the world' (Baker 2011: 219). The active participation of the user or receiver is therefore essential, as it is inferred during textual processing (*ibid.*: 222), and his/her knowledge, linguistic and non-linguistic expectations and familiarity with conventions play an essential role in coherence-building. From this perspective, coherence cannot be understood as a universal feature of texts, but rather depends on the receiver's intervention through his/her prior knowledge. This receiver intervention and the dependence on prior knowledge make coherence a relevant issue in translation and localization.

Hypertextual coherence

The *lack of linear structure* in hypertexts seems to make it impossible to create or perceive coherence (Jucker 2003). Hyperlinks also seem to produce the opposite effect to coherence; they introduce the possibility of lack of continuity of sense (Tyrkkö 2011: 94). This discontinuous text-processing is due to users needing to make constant decisions as to whether to continue reading or select from the available successor nodes, a process that reduces the attention they have available for textual comprehension. Conklin described this effect as 'cognitive overhead' (1987: 40).[8] In order to investigate this issue, researchers have focused on coherence-building mechanisms from the user's point of view, revisiting how prior linear approaches to the construction of coherence might apply. The specific case of coherence in hypertexts has been the subject of a number of studies from different perspectives (Foltz 1996; Fritz 1998; Engebretsen 2000; Jucker 2003; Storrer 2002; Bublitz 2005; Tyrkkö 2011). The reading of hypertexts to some extent involves a dialogic exchange that the writer must pre-arrange by introducing links upon which the users create their 'self-selected reading path'. The interplay between the receiver's prior knowledge and hypertexts is highlighted by Fritz when indicating that:

> Users make sense of a path or a segment of a path by seeing sequences of textual elements as realizations of sequencing patterns and by drawing inferences on the basis of their local and general knowledge.
>
> (Fritz 1998: 223)

According to Fritz, this does not mean that regular coherence-building mechanisms do not apply to hypertexts: it depends on the type of hypertext under study, as sometimes strong prototypical coherence can be found in self-guided tours and/or online newspapers. What is clear is that coherence-building in hypertext depends more on forward-looking mechanisms rather than on classical cohesive ties between textual elements. And this means that some aspects, such as thematic progression and cohesive cues or ties, are necessarily different in hypertexts.

Angelika Storrer (2002) introduced two basic notions borrowed from the process-based approaches to coherence-building in Text Linguistics, 'hypertextual global coherence' and 'local coherence'. Local coherence occurs between two continuous elements in a text, and it is established mainly by cohesive cues. In a wider context, local coherence can also be established between two consecutive semiotic elements, such as the relationship between an image and its description in the 'alt' tag in the HTML code. In hypertext theory, local coherence is identified with 'intranodal coherence', or the type of coherence that can be found within a single hypertextual node, such as a piece of news or a product description. Local coherence is also related to 'internodal coherence', the relationship between two nodes or elements that are linked through a hyperlink sequentially, such as the relationship between a hyperlink description and the node that is activated.

Internodal coherence is more flexible than the intranodal type, as it can be more freely interpreted by the user. Nevertheless, users must somehow infer some sort of relationship between the activated hyperlink and the activated node to maintain a fuzzy 'continuity of senses'. Otherwise, failure to interpret a coherence relation in this interactive sequence might lead the user to believe an error has occurred. Figure 3.2. graphically represents the negotiation of local and global coherence in hyperlink activation.

Hypertextual global coherence can be defined as the overall linkage of hypertext constituents as mediated by the general theme addressed in the text, as well as by its rhetorical function in a wider context. In this sense, global coherence plays a more important role than in linear texts, as selective and discontinuous reading modes need increased levels of global cohesion cues to mediate the comprehension process. This type of coherence has also been referred to as 'structural coherence' (Engebretsen 2000). In order to account for this type of coherence, hypertexts offer distinct coherence cues that increase the global coherence in self-selected reading paths, such as navigation menus, breadcrumb navigation maps, headings, titles or topic indicators. These global cues 'allow the user to correctly relate the currently visited node to the global theme of the corresponding hyperdocument' (Storrer 2002: 12), which helps establish a global reference frame to guide coherence-building mechanisms.

HYPERTEXT IN THE TRANSLATION PROCESS

The previous section reviewed the specific characteristics of hypertexts that separate them from printed texts. Web localization, a modality that focuses

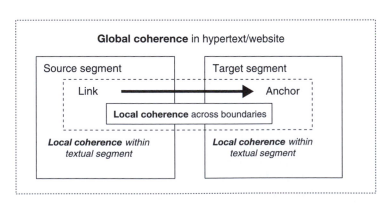

Figure 3.2 Formal schematic of hyperlinking as both local and global coherence phenomena. Adapted from Tyrkkö (2011: 98)

exclusively on hypertexts, has been inexorably shaped by the specific features mentioned above, and these have also determined the most salient characteristics of the translation process within the global localization cycle. The differences fall into two basic areas: technical considerations and cognitive issues.

The technical features of hypertextual translation processes are the recurrent topic in previous literature, either comparing them to non-hypertext translation (Pym 2011a), or to software localization (Mata 2005). From a technical process perspective, hypertext translation entails a distinct process because of differences in the identification of translatable elements, the tools needed to process them, the way in which projects are organized and managed, and the adaptation or localization levels that determine which changes might be introduced. Many of these features, as (Pym 2011a) indicates, are shared with current technical translations, which increasingly use hypertext technologies. One of the most significant differences relies on the fact that hypertexts have a multilayer structure that fulfils different communicative purposes, each of these structures contains translatable text extracted for translation by hypertext translation tools. As previously mentioned, each page contains content text and interface text, and both are included in the surface or presentation structure that is seen by end users. The process of extracting and translating content text, such as the description of a company in an 'about us' description, represents a process similar to any non-hypertextual process, but nevertheless, technological tools that protect the technical code (HTML or other) are required to protect the appearance or functionality of the web page. Additionally, the deep structure or coding structure of each page incorporates a number of textual elements that need to be translated. Some of them are included in order to index each page within the global hyperweb, such as the title, the descriptors and keywords, which appear within the heading of each web page. Some other elements are incorporated due to accessibility issues, such as alternative image, sound or audiovisual file descriptions incorporated for the benefit of users with different disabilities, such as web readers for people with visual impairments,[9] or the text within the image, animation, sound files or videos themselves. The fact that hypertexts can incorporate a wide range of audiovisual and multimodal elements also require the use of different technologies, such as subtitling software or Flash presentation translation tools.[10]

Also from a technical perspective, two characteristics of hypertexts represent challenges for translators: the openness of hypertext and its dynamic nature. Both issues are closely related, and both imply that, currently, hypertexts are open by nature, and new content is constantly added and modified. The life cycle of a hypertext, as opposed to a printed text, is highly dynamic in nature, and users expect new content in websites to keep visiting it (Nielsen and Loranger 2006). In many instances, the bulk of the translation process entails working on modifications and updates instead of localizing a complete website from scratch. As mentioned in Chapter 2, translation memories and GMS systems are widely used and enable the translations of small texts or modifications in the website to be distributed automatically to all versions of the website.

These technological issues also shape and differentiate the cognitive process that occurs during hypertext translation. The most significant issues here relate to comprehension and coherence-building mechanisms in cases in which textual segments are processed without clear context or co-text. As happens with other translation processes, the use of translation memory tools and other technologies affects the cognitive-translation process (Wallis 2008; Jiménez-Crespo 2009b), leaving marks in the final translated product. In these cases, the distinction between local and global coherence established in hypertexts can help mediate the overall comprehension process. GMS and CMS present to translators decontextualized segments that are part of either e-text or global hyperdocuments, and the rest of the text might be unavailable. The results from empirical studies on the cognitive foundations of translation expertise can be useful in order to understand how textual segments might be processed. These experimental studies have identified that experts guide their decisions while translating using strategies more at the macrostructural level than novices or bilinguals (see Chapter 7). Ideally, one would expect that experts would rely on negotiating local and global coherence mechanisms differently when processing hypertext translations than when dealing with non-hypertexts. Expert knowledge of the digital genre in question, its structure, different communicative purposes within each website, participants in the communicative situation, conventionalized structures and interaction possibilities may also guide comprehension mechanisms at the macrostructural level even while processing supposedly decontextualized segments. In a sense, despite potential cognitive challenges during the comprehension stage, experts most likely develop strategies either in a pre-translation stage (by acquiring prior knowledge of the global hypertext in question before processing any textual segment), or during the translation process (by guiding their decisions from a prototypical model of the digital genre in question and negotiating between the macro and micro structural levels) to compensate for the lack of context or the potential lack of access to the entire text.

As a final note to this section, it should be mentioned that the processing of hypertexts that determine certain common traits in the localization cycle should be understood in a prototypical fashion (Halverson 1999, 2010). Previous literature on this issue has mostly focused on certain aspects that might not necessarily represent the prototype of translation process during web localization, such as processing highly decontextualized segments. Translating hypertexts represents a wide range of potential processes, from the translation of a linear e-text such as a press release to translating a listing of textual segments that appear in a flash animation without an indication of the sequencing of events or how they relate to each other. However, the only common trait in all localization processes, perhaps, is the fact that hypertexts are embedded in code, and translation technology tools may be necessary to render them. Other specifications of the translation process vary widely, from some processes that are very similar to regular technical translation, to others with highly decontextualized segments from an update fed to translators via GMS.

SUMMARY

The new forms of hypertextual production, distribution and consumption pose a number of challenges to practitioners and translation scholars accustomed to working with printed linear texts. This chapter focused on how to redefine the notion of text in the light of new hypertextual models that are at the core of web localization, as well as the new technological environment in which source texts are pre-processed and disaggregated into decontextualized segments that are then presented to translators. Following a review of the notion of text in text linguistics, applied linguistics and TS, a proposed definition of text in web localization was offered, focusing on the unitary, interactive and multilinear nature of hypertexts. This chapter also explored the main issues in hypertext theory that are of interest for web localization: hypertextual structures, types of hypertexts and hypertextual cohesion and coherence. It ended by arguing that hypertexts and the new way they are processed during localization has radically changed the cognitive and communicative contexts of the translation process.

FURTHER READING

Text and hypertext theories represent a vast field. Neubert and Shreve (1992) offer an adaptation of text linguistics approaches to Translation Studies, mostly the seminal work of de Beaugrande and Dressler (1981). Bowker (2006), Jiménez-Crespo (2008c, 2009b) and Biau and Pym (2006) offer insights into to the changes translation experiences as a result of hypertextual segmentation. Mossop (2006) also reviews the impact of translation technology on texts. Pym in several publications also reviews issues related to the effects of textual segmentation (2011a; Biau and Pym 2006) and offers insight into the notion of internationalized texts (2004a; 2010). For a review of coherence in translation, see Baker (2011: 217–59). For general hypertextual coherence, see Fritz (1998), Storrer (2002) and Tyrkkö (2007, 2011), whereas the study by Jiménez-Crespo (2009b) focuses on the effect of segmentation on coherence in web texts.

4

WEB LOCALIZATION AND DIGITAL GENRES

The technological revolution has led to the emergence of a burgeoning number of digital genres, such as blogs, corporate or social networking sites, and the proliferation of studies and conferences on them. In this chapter we review the significance of these dynamic and digital entities for scholars and professionals who deal with their analysis or production. The chapter starts with an overview of the vast amount of theoretical and empirical research that has been produced in TS using models and methods borrowed from Discourse Analysis, Language Service Providers (LSP) (Swales 1990, 2004; Bhatia 1993, 2008) and Contrastive Studies (Hartman 1980). We will argue that genre analysis can represent a solid foundation for the practice, research, and training efforts in web localization. A model for digital genre analysis is presented in which the complex interrelation of textual super-, macro- and microstructures plays an essential role. This type of analysis can be of the utmost importance when conducting quantitative and qualitative empirical research using these genres. The chapter ends with a proposed open taxonomy of digital genres.

LOCALIZATION AND DIGITAL GENRES

During the last two decades, the rise of Internet-mediated communications has resulted in a growing number of digital genres, such as social networking sites, corporate websites or online newspapers. The very essence of localization cannot be understood without taking account of its relationship to these new conventionalized forms of texts that facilitate recurring instances of web-mediated communications. We all quickly recognize and identify websites that we encounter as instances of digital genres, prompting conceptual labels such as 'corporate website', 'personal homepage' or 'blog'.

These labels come to mind when we recognize visual and linguistic proto-typical features that are learnt through multiple encounters with instances of the genre in question. The same process would occur if we encountered a text that reads 'add a tablespoon of sugar and mix well'; we would quickly ascribe this conventionalized phrase to the genre 'recipe'. We share these acquired frameworks of expectations with other members of our discourse community, facilitating the cognitive effort during production and reception. Usually, a website that lacks key prototypical features expected by the targeted discourse community complicates its comprehension and, more importantly, reduces its credibility (Vaughan and Dillon 2006). No one would purchase anything online if the order form included typos or did not comply with the conventions expected in each culture (Jiménez-Crespo 2010a). This is one of the main reasons why the notions of genre and text type matter in localization: translators-localizers need to be know-ledgeable about the prototypical features of any given genre in the source and target contexts and be able to include whichever conventions receivers are accustomed to.

Even though digital genres are a recent phenomenon, the interest in classifying texts dates back to the works of Greek philosopher Aristotle. Since then, different disciplines such as Rhetoric, Literary Analysis, Discourse Analysis, Applied Linguistics or Documentation and Library Science have striven to produce operative classifications of texts for multiple purposes, such as storage and retrieval of texts, introducing students to the production of specialized professional genres (Swales 2004), to identify genres automatically, and for web indexing and retrieval purposes (Santini *et al.* 2011; Kennedy and Shepherd 2005). In the case of TS, the classification of texts came with the introduction of theoretical and methodological principles of Contrastive Studies, Discourse Analysis and Applied Linguistics, and textual classifications are currently widely applied to TS practice, didactics and research. The theoretical and methodological principles provided by genre theory are widely used for training and research in a number of translation modalities and types, such as medical, technical, audiovisual or legal translation (i.e. Borja 2000; Gamero 2001; Montalt and Davies 2006; García Izquierdo 2005, 2007). However, the great benefits that genre approaches can provide for advancing teaching, practice and research on localization have only just begun to be acknowledged (Folaron 2006; Jiménez-Crespo 2011c).

The next section traces the origins of the notion of genre and digital genre, clarifies the confusion surrounding the notion of text type and genre, incorporates such notions as 'complex genres' and 'genre embedding' in order to account for the open hypertextual nature of digital genres, and provides an overview of the recent research on digital genre theory.

GENRES AND TEXT TYPES: FROM INITIAL CONFUSION TO CONSOLIDATION

Genres and text types represent two complementary theoretical notions that have been used, and often confused, in order to classify recurring instances of texts (Trosborg 1997). Any specific text type or genre represents a proto-type of conventionalized forms of texts that help achieve a communicative purpose in recurring social situations. Both help reduce the cognitive load and uncertainty in communicative interactions, as they represent frames that can be followed in producing and comprehending repetitive communi-cative situations. They are different in that genres are defined by extra-textual factors, such as sociocultural, communicative and cognitive features, while text types are conventionalized in respect of their intratextual or linguistic configuration. Genres, such as a recipe or a blog, are more concrete than textual types, while text types represent more abstract categories, such as argumentation or persuasion. Moreover, genres are more dynamic constructs that appear and evolve and therefore are unlimited in nature (Miller 1984), while text types represent closed categories with limited types, such as exhortative, expositive and argumentative types (Hatim and Mason 1990). Both are culture-dependent, as their existence depends on recurring social or communicative occasions in specific sociocultural contexts, for example, a business letter, a tweet or the need to persuade someone to buy your product online.

As already mentioned, genres and text types are the result of an ongoing epistemological interest into the classification of text dating back to classical Greece. In the 1960s this interest made its way into Linguistics, and consequently into TS, resulting in a great number of proposals according to different criteria (Hurtado 2001: 451–60), such as classifications based on genres (i.e. Swales 1990; Bhatia 1993; Nwogu 1997) or on the search for differentiating criteria (i.e. Longacre 1983; Biber 1989). The multiplicity of classifications and perspectives led to a conceptual confusion that lasted several decades, witnessed by the fact that these terms were often avoided in a number of studies.[1] However, a wider consensus emerged in the 1990s and 2000s, in part due to the works of researchers such as Trosborg (1997). The volume she edited represents a great step in the dis-ambiguation of these two notions in TS. Her integrative perspective sup-ports combining text type and genre in textual analysis for research and translation purposes, fostering the development of strategies that can facilitate translation tasks:

> Text typology involving genre analysis can help the translator develop strategies that facilitate his/her work and provide awareness of various options as well as constraints.
>
> (Trosborg 1997: viii)

She also pointed out the significance of genre knowledge in translation, as inadequate translations often result from lack of knowledge of the function of genres and text types, their conventions and main intercultural differences in the expression of these conventions (Trosborg 1997: 18).

The notion of text type

The interest in classifying text according to the linguistic notion of 'text type' emerged in Linguistics and Discourse Analysis in the 1960s, promoting the development of Text Linguistics and its introduction a decade later in TS. The basic premise behind text type research was that senders and receivers consciously or subconsciously take a previously stored mental model of internal linguistic features of the text that is shared with other members of the discourse community during textual production and reception. These intralinguistic features refer to the way senders might organize persuasion or argumentation in a specific communicative situation. For example, the way English and Arabic speakers might structure an argument varies considerably (Hatim and Munday 2004; Baker 2011). The notion of text type was defined from a Discourse Analysis perspective as: 'the purpose of the text, i.e. the reason for which a text has been written. Text types are related to the producer's intention towards the receivers' (Biber 1989: 5). From this perspective, TS scholars Hatim and Mason defined this notion as 'a conceptual framework which enables us to classify texts in terms of communicative intentions serving an overall rhetorical purpose' (1990: 140). Hence the purpose of the communicative interaction is the main guiding principle that helps us classify texts according text types. Despite differences in text-type taxonomies proposed over the years, we find that they are normally divided intro three main purposes in human communication: to inform, to argue and to persuade (i.e. to seek to modify receivers' behaviour). These types are normally related to the three aspects or dimensions of language distinguished by functionalist Bühler (1965): representation, expression and appeal.

Nowadays, it is understood that any text can be multifunctional – that is, a text can serve more than one rhetorical purpose: 'multifunctionality is the rule rather than the exception, and any useful typology will have to be able to accommodate such diversity' (Hatim and Mason 1990: 138). An example of this multifunctionality could be the 'mission' or 'our values' pages that corporate websites often include. At first sight it would seem that the purpose of the text is to inform the receiver, giving objective information about the company or organization; nevertheless, these pages also represent an effort to modify the receiver's opinion, casting a positive light on the company. Therefore, it can be argued that these pages serve two rhetorical purposes at the same time, to inform and to appeal. In the words of Hatim and Mason (1997), they include a primary and a secondary 'text type focus' or purpose.

Initially, TS saw the rise of categorizations that departed from thematic or professional criteria (i.e. Kade 1968; Delisle 1980; Snell-Hornby 1996). Later, most classifications were influenced by functionalist and communicative approaches, in part due to the work of Reiss (1971, 1976; Reiss and Vermeer 1984). Reiss pioneered the adoption of typologies that could be developed exclusively for TS, so relieving the researcher of the effort of validating any classification within the wider framework of Linguistics. These functionalist and communicative typologies in TS could at the same time be divided into:

1. Functionalist typologies: based on the function of the text (Reiss 1971; Reiss and Vermeer 1984; Nord 1997) – texts are normally classified as informative, expressive, operative, multimedia[2] and phatic.
2. Rhetorical purpose typologies from a systemic-functionalist perspective (i.e. Werlich 1975; Hatim and Mason 1990, 1997; Trosborg 1997; House 1997) – texts are primarily classified as descriptive, narrative, expositive, argumentative and exhortative.

These two types of typologies do not necessarily need to be understood as competing classifications. According to Trosborg (1997: 16–17), typologies can at the same time take into account the function of the text and the rhetorical purpose of the sender. In TS the most influential proposals are those of Hatim and Mason (1990, 1997), House's (1997) framework oriented towards quality evaluation, and the functionalist proposals of Reiss (1976; Reiss and Vermeer 1984) and Nord (1997). Despite multiple approaches and criticisms, it can be argued that functionalism provides one of the best theoretical frameworks for contextualizing localization: in this interactive environment fulfilling the communicative intention of the sender remains a key factor.

Nord's functionalist typology (1997) departs from Beaugrande and Dressler's definition of text: a 'communicative occurrence' (1981: 3) that is produced in a specific contextual situation. The function of a text is understood as a pragmatic quality assigned by a receiver in a specific situation, rather than a quality inherent in a text. For example, a web ad is produced with the intention of changing receivers' behaviour and hopefully leading to a sale of products or services; some users might simply ignore it, while a researcher will read it to analyse promotional discourse on the web. Nord's typology is based on the referential, expressive and appeal functions of language proposed by Bühler (1965), combined with the phatic function of Jakobson (1960). Within these four basic functions, Nord conceptualizes this typology as an open list of subfunctions under each type:

1. Referential function: refers to the description of phenomena or objects in the world. It includes other functions such as informative, meta-linguistic, instructive and formative.

2. Expressive function: focused on the expression of emotions or opinions from the sender about specific objects or phenomena. Includes the emotive and evaluative functions.
3. Appellative function: directed towards producing a specific reaction in the receiver's behaviour through an appeal to feelings, experiences, sensitivity, etc. Includes the illustrative, persuasive, imperative, pedagogic and advertising subfunctions.
4. Phatic function: directed towards establishing, maintaining or ending the communicative interaction. Includes the salutational, small talk or peg subfunctions.

The development of this typology based on the function of the texts is subsequently used by Nord to establish two different translation types: documentary or instrumental translations. The former entails a type of translation in which the TT refers to the ST and represents it within the source culture. The TT is therefore a metatext that is received as a translation, such as a translated poem or most privacy policies within websites (Jiménez-Crespo 2011c). Instrumental translations are texts that use the ST as a model and it fulfils a purpose within the target culture as an original production. Receivers are normally not aware that the text they are interacting with is a translation, as would be the case with most localized websites, software or videogames. This type of translation therefore represents the goals of most industry publications for localized texts: to be received and accepted as original productions within the target culture (LISA 2003; GALA 2011). Nord's types roughly correspond to the 'overt' and 'covert' translation types of House (1997), although the departing point of the latter typology is the rhetorical purpose from a Hallidayian systemic-functionalist approach, rather than the textual function.

The notion of text type has also been explored in connection to web texts, mostly from a semantic-lexical computational perspective. Biber and Kurjian (2004) presented a multidimensional study of web text types through a functional and rhetorical model that computationally analyses texts according to statistical clusters. Four basic types are identified: personal, involved narration, persuasive-argumentative, advice and abstract technical discourse. Despite its novel approach, the types presented correspond broadly to the text types based on rhetorical purpose. However, certain problems can be identified in this proposal, such as the use of the web page as the unit of analysis, or the fact that only running text is analysed through the computational model, leaving aside the multimodal and visual-iconic nature of web communication.

GENRES IN APPLIED LINGUISTICS AND TRANSLATION STUDIES

According to Paltridge (1997), the first study of genre in the modern sense appeared at the end of the nineteenth century in folklore studies by the

Grimm brothers. Since then, the notion of genres has been researched within numerous disciplines, such as Linguistic Anthropology, Ethnography of Communication, Conversation Analysis, Rhetoric, Literary Theory, Sociolinguistics or Applied Linguistics. This diversity of perspectives results in a multiplicity of theoretical conceptualizations, due to the different theoretical points of departure. It was not until the 1960s that the notion of genre started to be developed in Linguistics mainly from systemic-functionalist approaches (Halliday and Martin 1993) by the North American New Rhetoric school (Miller 1984; Kress 1993; Berkenkotter and Huckin 1995), the Australian school (Martin 1985; Reid 1987) and the Applied Linguistic field of English for Specific Purposes (Swales 1990; Bhatia 1993, 2008). The introduction of genre in TS in the 1980s came mostly from German Contrastive Textology, and more importantly, from the English for Specific Purposes (ESP) approach. This was due to the fact that TS shares with ESP studies an interest in describing the most frequently used specialized genres in their specific sociocultural context, as it is necessary for anyone producing specialized genres to know their main conventions in order to produce a valid exemplar of the genre.

Despite the many theoretical approaches, several authors agree that approaches to genre share several basic principles (Paltridge 1997: 4; Swales 1990: 58; Devitt 2008: 13):

1. Genres represent social action and communicative interaction within a social and cultural context or a within a specific 'discourse community'.[3]
2. This action is typified or conventionalized and it arises from recurring communicative interactions or conditions, such as companies communicating with customers over the WWW or friends telling each other a 'joke'.
3. The structure of these conventionalized texts is essential in their description and definition. According to Swales (1990: 58): 'exemplars of a genre exhibit various patterns of similarity in terms of structure, style, content and intended audience'.
4. Genres represent open-ended categories unlike text types, as new genres emerge and develop constantly (Miller 1984).
5. These typified or conventionalized communicative instruments are mainly defined by extralinguistic aspects, even when they determine the conventions at the intralinguistic level (Jiménez-Crespo 2009a). Their conventional features help reduce the cognitive effort in both the production and the reception of any instance of a text, from greetings to contact forms, as we know what to expect in recurring communicative situations.

If we look for a concise definition of genre, US rhetorician Carolyn Miller (1984) identified genres with typifications of social and rhetorical actions:

> Genres refer to a conventional category of discourse based in large scale typifica-
> tion of rhetorical action; as action, it acquires meaning from situation and from the
> social context in which that situation arose.
>
> (Miller 1984: 37)

This typification is grounded in the social world in which we live, it being impossible to be part of a social community without a wide repertoire of social responses in recurrent situations. By these responses the author refers not only to greetings and thank yous, but everything from an acceptance speech for an Oscar, to a contact form on a website or a scientific paper (Berkenkotter and Huckin 1995: 4). Genres are therefore dynamic constructs that reduce the cognitive load via shared frames of expectations in both form and content, and this knowledge can make us part of a specific discourse community.

The trend with most impact on TS defines genres[4] through a combination of extra and intraliguistic features (i.e. Swales 1990; Trosborg 1997) rather than using mostly extralinguistic aspects, such as the North American New Rhetoric or the Australian School. Genres can differ between cultures, and this is one reason why this notion was introduced in Contrastive Studies (Hartmann 1980) and in the research and practice of translation. Hatim and Mason depart from sociolinguist Kress (1985: 19) and define genres as:

> Conventionalized forms of texts which reflect the functions and goals involved in
> particular social occasions as well as the purposes of the participants in them.
>
> (Hatim and Mason 1990: 69)

This definition sums up the most important aspects of the study of genre: formal aspects reflected in conventionalized forms of texts, cognitive features related to the purposes and expectations of the participants and sociocultural aspects. Hatim and Mason's approach to the study of genre has been the most influential in a boom in contrastive genre studies in TS, with multiple initiatives, mostly in the Germanic and Spanish contexts, focusing on the didactics and practice of translation. These studies were initially influenced by the introduction into TS of principles of German Contrastive Textology (Hartmann 1980), which contrastively analyses specialized genres with high volumes of translation in two or more cultures. The findings of these studies are normally used later as a foundation for professional translation or to familiarize students with intercultural differences in the expression of the same genre in two cultures. Research groups such as the GENTT or GITRAD[5] have produced extensive research on specialized genres such as medical, technical or legal translations using this genre framework (i.e. Gamero 2001; Agost 1999; Borja 2000; Bolaños 2004; García Izquierdo 2005, 2007).

Classification of genres: subgenres, supragenres and complex genres

Genres do not exist independently, but rather form genre networks or exist in hierarchical structures (Swales 2004). Genre analysts long ago instigated different 'supra' and 'sub' categories for grouping genres that share different features. Subgenres, normally most often discussed in genre analysis, are defined as secondary genres, as opposed to the primary genres themselves. An example would be the websites of banks as a subgenre of the corporate website genre. These subgenres or subclasses can be quite different from one another (Biber 1988: 1970). Bhatia defined them as genres that present communicative purposes and strategies for their realization different from those of the primary genres themselves; they emerged due to 'minor changes or modifications in the communicative purpose(s)' (Bhatia 1993: 14). Nowadays, the emergence of subgenres is not normally understood to depend exclusively on a single criterion, such as the different communicative purposes, but rather, scholars rely on other criteria such as 'field', 'audience' or 'level of specialization'. The emergence of subgenres on the web is often the result of the combination of media or the introduction of new functionalities – as was the case of the digital genre 'blog' (Herring *et al.* 2004; Miller and Shepherd 2004), which quickly branched out and developed the subgenre 'videoblog'.

'Supragenres' represent groupings of similar genres that do not correspond with specific concrete genres: for example homepages, in which individuals (personal homepage), corporations (corporate websites) or institutions (institutional websites) communicate with audiences globally in a process mediated by the web. The classification of genres into supragenres has been more complex and varied than that of subgenres, with multiple proposals and terminology such as 'suprageneric terms' or 'pre-genre' (Swales 1990; 2004), 'macrogenre'/'genre ecologies' (Martin 1995; Borja *et al.* 2009), 'colony of genres' (Bhatia 2002), 'systems of genres' (Bazerman 1994) or even web 'supergenres' (Lindemann and Littig 2011). Figure 4.1 shows graphically the evolution and current state of basic genres under the supragenre 'homepage' on the web; this groups the institutional, corporate, personal and non-profit website genres (Kennedy and Shepherd 2005). Some of these are currently evolving into new genres, as with the personal homepage, which has evolved into the social networking homepage.

In addition to the distinction between supra and subgenres, other genre classifications are of great interest in localization research. A case in point is the notion of 'complex genres' proposed by the Australian genre theorist Martin (1995) and Hanks (1996: 242).[6] Complex genres are those textual genres that can potentially incorporate instances of other genres within them, such as a church service that can incorporate a sermon, or a blog that can include a poem or a recipe. Martin (1995: 24) and Bhatia (1997) call this relationship between primary and secondary genres 'genre embedding', a very productive notion that can be easily applied to digital genres in

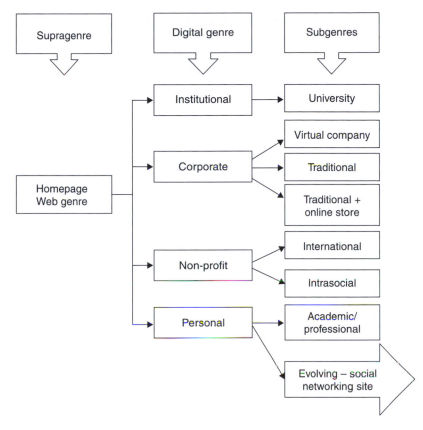

Figure 4.1 Genre ecology of the homepage genre

localization. As an example, an online store can incorporate a contact form, although a contact form cannot incorporate an online store. The hyper-textual nature of websites involves the potential inclusion of other genres within them, but nevertheless, the secondary genres embedded in them are necessarily contextualized within the wider framework of the parent complex genre. For example, the contact form will follow the politeness tone of the parent online store. This distinction between complex and secondary genres on the web can assist in the dual nature of websites as genres in themselves and as potential containers of other secondary genres, such as FAQs (Crowston and Williams 1997), Flash animations (Paolillo *et al.* 2007) or contact forms (Jiménez-Crespo 2010a). These secondary genres do not normally exist independently, i.e. a contact form does not make sense without the wider framework of the containing genre, nor FAQs without the entire website. A prime example of genre embedding in hypertexts would be the inclusion of 'e-texts' in websites.

Genres and text type confusion in localization research

As far as *localization research* is concerned, the use of the terms 'genre' and 'text type' has also suffered from the prevailing confusion in Linguistics and TS. These terms are used idiosyncratically to represent different types of textual variation (Reinke 2005; O'Hagan and Ashworth 2003; Austermühl 2006). For example, the publications on localization training by Uwe Reinke (2005) argue that:

> the notions of 'text type' . . . are rather intuitive and – depending on the . . . purpose, scope and other factors – may differ in granularity.
>
> (Reinke 2005: 15)

The only text types mentioned are web texts and interface texts, an intuitive classification of little use in localization training. For his part, Austermühl (2006) uses the notion of text type with a didactic focus in mind to refer to the different sections and subtexts within a software product. In this sense, his approach corresponds to the notion of textual genre, with its conventionalized sections and subsections (see below). The criteria used to subdivide the overall genres are heterogeneous, such as printed vs. digital texts, XML vs. HTML, etc. Figure 4.2 shows the textual typology offered by Austermühl that corresponds to the current digital genre 'software product'.

Despite the confusion surrounding these two notions in localization research, Austermühl (2006) and Folaron (2006) can be considered the first researchers to bring to the fore the potential benefits of contrastive studies of the main genres in localization:

> Scholars might want to look at and compare text types involved in website and software localization. Using a typology of software text types . . ., analyses could focus on the textual characteristics, inter- and intracultural differences or technical constraints of these specific texts . . .
>
> (Austermühl 2006: 79)

In this regard, Austermühl anticipates the potential benefits of genre analysis to the study of localization. Other scholars such as Shreve (2006b) have also proposed the introduction into localization practice one of the most defining aspects of genres, their textual structure, referred to by the author as 'document structure'. This brief review points out the confusion surrounding these two notions in localization, which is precisely why this chapter is relevant for anyone interested in localization processes and products.

THE EMERGENCE OF DIGITAL GENRES

The emergence of the Internet and the WWW quickly resulted in the adaptation of existing textual genres, such as newspapers, to the new possibilities

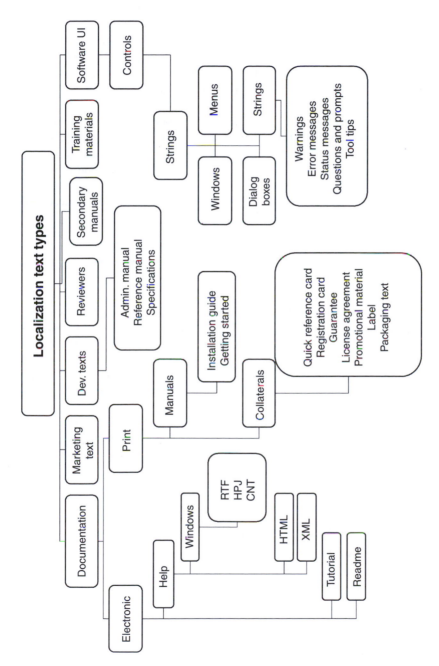

Figure 4.2 Textual typology in software localization proposed by Austermühl (2006: 8)

afforded by the medium (Yates and Orlikowski 1992). It also prompted the creation of novel digital genres, such as social networking sites, wikisites or videoblogs. This new textual universe was originally referred to as 'cyber-genres' (Shepherd and Watters 1998) or 'web genres' (Santini 2007), a supragenre category covering all genres used on the web. All these cyber-genres were initially inspired from previously existing genres, following a main feature of all genres rightly pointed out by literary theorist Todorov:

> Where do genres come from? Quite simply from other genres. A new genre is always the transformation of an earlier one, or of several: by inversion, by displacement, by combination.
>
> (Todorov 1990: 15)

In fact even the social networking site Facebook, one of the most successful websites in recent history, can be easily traced back to school yearbooks in US educational institutions. It quickly evolved to its current state thanks to a series of functionality options only available in the new medium, turning it into an everyday social communicative platform that has become ubiquitous in modern life (Singh *et al.* 2012).

In general, digital genres have also been evolving faster than other genres, due in part to the constant evolution of the functionalities on the web (Shepherd and Watters 1998). All genres are in constant evolution (Swales 1990), but digital ones are much more 'uncontrolled and unpredictable if compared to publications on paper' (Santini *et al.* 2011: 9). This also means that digital genres might not only emerge and develop, but also disappear, following the normal life cycle of any genre. According to Miller (1984: 153), 'genres change, evolve, and decay', and, in the case of digital genres, the life expectancy might be dramatically shortened. The example of the personal homepage can clearly illustrate this point. Initially, it was conceptualized as probably the first stand-alone digital genre (Dillon and Gushrowski 2000). Users from all over the world created their own personal page with personal information about their lives, education, hobbies and interests, etc. This digital genre quickly evolved into two distinctive genres, the social networking site and the subgenre professional/academic homepage. But at the same time the personal homepage genre *per se* started to decay, due to privacy concerns and diversification/specialization. However, social networking sites with different goals, professional, personal, romantic, etc., are still growing exponentially in popularity (Jiménez-Crespo 2013), while the professional or academic personal homepage subgenre still remains as a popular digital genre (Rehm 2002).

Digital genres are fluid and show a high level of hybridism (Tercedor 2005; Herring 2010). They are also characterized by their fragmentation across several nodes or subtexts, and by the impact of functionality such as hyperlinking, scripting, posting facilities, etc. (Santini and Sharoff 2009: 129). The notion of digital genres has been previously defined by the most prolific research area into digital genres, the automatic identification of digital genres from a computational perspective, starting from the social, cognitive and communication principles of applied linguistics and adding digital interactivity. For Erickson a digital genre is:

> A patterning of communication created by a combination of the individual (cognitive), social, and technical implicit in a recurring communicative situation. A genre structures communication by creating shared expectations about the form and content of the interaction, thus easing the burden of production and interpretation.
>
> (Erickson 1999: 2)

This definition is in line with the summary of previous approaches we presented above: a typification of recurrent communicative situations that are used in order to reduced the cognitive load through shared expectations. It also relates to later proposals to define digital genres not only by the interplay between content and form, but also by the three-pronged approach 'form, content and functionality' (Shepherd and Watters 1998; Shepherd *et al.* 2004), emphasising the role of the latter. Other scholars, such as Santini (2007), have offered a simple and generic definition of web genres as genres that are used on the web – although, given the open nature of the web, it would be appropriate to add that web genres are those 'exclusively' used on the web. For example, an audiovisual commercial can be used on the web, and this does not make it a web genre. In order to research these new genres, an incipient field referred to as web or digital genre theory has boomed during the last decade (Crowston 2010). This novel field uses web genres as a vital tool for applied fields such as documentation science, data mining, etc. (Santini *et al.* 2011). Another perspective on digital genre theory, although less developed, is the linguistic branch that researches digital genres with a pure ontological interest (Giltrow and Stein 2008).

Extant and novel digital genres

In order to chart the transition from paper to digital genres and the emergence of new ones, Shepherd and Watters (1998) identified two basic types: 'extant genres' and 'novel genres'. The former are those that were directly transferred to the WWW without any adaptations, or 'genres as they appear in their source media' (1998: 98). 'Novel genres' are those that do not exist in printed form or that are 'genres wholly dependent on their new medium' (1998: 99), such as search engines or videoblogs. According to the authors, the main distinguishing feature between novel and extant genres is the 'level of functionality that makes it fully dependent for its existence on the new medium' (1998: 100). Nevertheless, the functionality provided by the Internet and the demands of on-screen reading has led to a different type of language (Crystal 2001, 2011) and therefore, even when

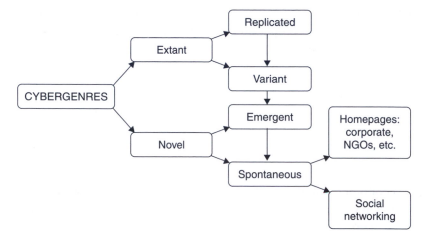

Figure 4.3 Digital genres. Adapted from Shepherd and Watters (1998) and Kennedy and Shepherd (2005)

digital genres might originally have been adapted from other mediums, they represent different genres.

The proposal by Shepherd and Watters further subdivides 'extant genres' into two categories: 'replicated' and 'variant'. Replicated digital genres are those simply made available online without any adaptations. These genres are usually unsuccessful on the web, due to their lack of adaptation to the medium (Nielsen and Loranger 2006). Variant genres show some minor adaptations, as the earlier online newspapers did. Novel genres are further subdivided into 'emergent' and 'spontaneous' genres. The former can be defined as those genres that result from the evolution of a printed genre, such as online encyclopedias that incorporate a number of functionalities provided by the Internet, and the latter are genres that appeared directly on the new medium, such as blogs or homepages. Figure 4.3 illustrates the proposal.

It should also be mentioned that the notion of digital genre has to incorporate the ephemeral nature of web texts. Shepherd and Watters also indicated that all digital genres can be either 'persistent' or 'virtual'. The former are those that exist in a static form and are not modified over time; the latter can be defined as genres that do not exist in a static form but that might change, be modified, or are created out of CMS depending on the user, time of access or preferences (and which nowadays represent the overwhelming majority of websites).

TOWARDS A FRAMEWORK FOR ANALYSING DIGITAL GENRES: FROM PRINT TO SCREEN

The notion of genre has been used in TS as a tool for analysing the most localized websites, such as corporate websites (i.e. Bolaños *et al.*

2005; Jiménez-Crespo 2008b, 2009a, 2011a; Diéguez 2008; Diéguez and Lazo 2011), non-profit websites (Jiménez-Crespo 2012a, 2012b) or social networking sites (Jiménez-Crespo 2013). In the first attempt at studying web localization, the most widely used genre framework was proposed by Shepherd and Watters (1998) and Yates and Orlikowski (1992). Departing from Documentation Science, it described cyber-genres through a three-pronged approach consisting of form, content and functionality. In this proposal, digital genres as a macrogenre constella-tion were subdivided into five basic types: homepage, brochure, resource, catalogue and search engine. For example, the genre homepage was described in terms of content as providing information about a company/person/institution; the form included an introduction, hierarchical images and animated images; and the functionality included browsing and e-mail.

The limitations of this genre model have given rise to intense debate, as it does not account for the multimodal nature of web genres and can even be misleading in classification efforts (Karlgren 2011; Santini *et al.* 2011). From an epistemological perspective, it could be argued that the working concepts, such as 'content', are not succinctly described. And, in the case of 'functionality' features, even since this proposal was developed in the 1990s, they have been extremely limited, quite intuitive, and do not fully account for possibilities of interaction made available by the Internet. Despite these limitations, this model can be recognized as the first and most popular model in this area and one that opened up the field for further research in many related disciplines, serving as the foundation for a number of contrastive studies of different genres. In the 2000s other perspectives were introduced, and this model was mostly replaced by other approaches such as the adaptation of Swales's ESP model and the hypertextual navigation modes (Askehave and Nielsen 2005) or computational approaches based on multi-level cluster analysis used in the automatic identification of web pages (Santini 2007; Santini *et al.* 2011).

In the specific case of TS, it can be argued that the most productive approach is the applied linguistic model of ESP. One of the reasons behind the adoption of this model was that the didactic perspective focused on ulti-mately training students to produce specialized genres within the ESP model, an interest which was also shared by the first translation scholars who adopted it. These models provide an empirical and didactic foundation by combining the extratextual parameters, such as function, communicative situation or functionality, with intralinguistic features that are conventional in each genre, such as terminology, specific phraseology, or recurring units of meaning associated to each section. An example of this type of recurring unit of meaning is the expressions used in each culture to invite users to fill out a form to contact a company or institution.

Parameters in genre analysis

The ESP-inspired model normally characterizes genres using five primary parameters (Göpferich 1995b; Gamero 2001; Borja *et al.* 2009):

1. conventional aspects
2. textual function
3. elements of the communicative situation
4. influence of the sociocultural context and
5. intratextual elements.

These five parameters subsume the main notions in the description of genre previously mentioned. They offer a concise framework for analysing and classifying the burgeoning network of digital genres. In the specific case of localization, it is necessary to add the interactivity or functionality of digital genres as a sixth parameter. This interaction represents a core feature and has been described as the engine that fuels their emergence and evolution (Shepherd and Watters 1998). Figure 4.4 shows the digital genre description model adapted from the proposal for technical texts from Gamero (2001: 60).

The proposed model places digital genres in the sociocultural context where they emerge and exist. This context determines their emergence, as genres only emerge if there is a communicative need within any specific sociocultural context. Web genres, at the same time, posses other characteristics that are determined by their function: the elements of their communicative situation and the interactive functionality. All these elements are considered extratextual, part of the surrounding context of the text, and they also determine other types of conventions that appear in each genre.

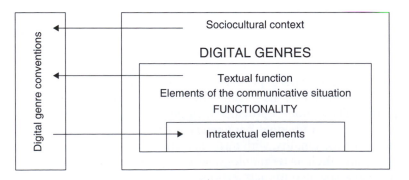

Figure 4.4 Genre description model for digital genres in translation. Adapted from the model developed for technical translation by Gamero (2001: 60)

For example, the specifics of the communicative situation determine the level of formality. Most of the conventions, but not all, are instantiated through intratextual or linguistic elements, such as syntax, lexis, speech acts, super-structure, etc. These six elements are not equally relevant in the description of all genres (Gamero 2001: 51). For example, the sociocultural context can be decisive in the widespread popularity of some digital genres if they are better suited to local customs. The case of Facebook can illustrate this point: it is the most popular social networking site with over 900 million users around the world in 2012; however, in Japan the most used social networking sites are blogging platforms such as Ameba or Livedoor, while the social networking site Mixi is more popular than Facebook. The following sections explore more in detail the characterizing features of this model.

Conventions

The *notion of convention* has been defined from a philosophical perspective as regularities in human behaviour in situations of co-operation (Lewis 1969). Conventions emerge due to the need to establish a co-ordination equilibrium between participants in recurrent communicative situations. This equilibrium leads to higher cognitive efficiency for participants in all types of recurring situation, such as greetings, writing an email or filling out a contact form. Within TS, the notion of convention has been defined as:

> Implicit or tacit non-binding regulation of behavior, based on common knowledge and the expectations of what others expect you to expect from them (etc.) to do in a certain situation.
>
> (Nord 1991: 96)

Conventions are established in a culture-dependent process. This implies that they can potentially differ between similar genres in different cultures (Nord 1997: 54). Hence they play an important role in any translation and localization process. Translators should recognize any conventional feature in STs and be capable of replacing these with existing established conventions in the target culture. Nord's definition stresses the fact that they are non-binding, an aspect that distances this notion from that of 'norm' in TS (Toury 1995).[7] In digital texts, non-compliance with a convention, such as placing the navigation menu to the right of the screen as opposed to the left, might slow down the communication process, but it will not stop it (Vaughan and Dillon 2006). Non-compliance with a norm, such as including recurring spelling errors, will produce a negative effect on the user who will associate it with a lack of quality on the part of the company that released the text (Jeney 2007). This could lead to a lack of credibility that would stop the text from achieving its communicative purpose.

Conventions appear at different levels, such as genre (Reiss and Vermeer 1984), style, non-verbal conduct or translation conventions (Nord 2003,

1997). They provide a good starting point for a number of potential research studies and applications in translation, quality management, didactics, etc. (Jiménez-Crespo 2009a). Industry publications also repeatedly refer to conventions, such as 'cultural, language, business conventions' (LISA 2007). Microsoft (2003) for example indicates that locales determine conventions such as sort order, keyboard layout, date, time, number and currency formats. In order to provide a more solid understanding of the functioning of conventions, their basic theoretical principles can be summarized as follows:

1. Conventions require alternatives and variants. Without an alternative, a convention as such cannot exist (Göpferich 1995a). An alternative consists of a linguistic form that is not conventional but that can accomplish the same communicative goal. For example, it is conventional in web pages to include a link with the lexical unit 'contact us' (Nielsen and Tahir 2002). A possible alternative could be 'get in touch with us', 'how to reach us' or 'call or email us'. Nevertheless, the former lexical unit is present in 89% of all commercial websites in English (*ibid.*), even when a wide array of lexical units could accomplish this same function. A variant is the reduced array of variation that is accepted to replace any given convention. As an example, in Spanish corporate websites the most used lexical units in this case would be *contacto, contactar, contáctenos, información adicional* or *contacte con nosotros* (Jiménez-Crespo 2009a). Any translator has to be acquainted not only with the most conventional feature in any given genre, but also with the possible variants. In fact, in most non-technical genres stylistic variation might even be required (Gamero 2001: 54).
2. Conventions are arbitrary. The process by which conventions come into existence is totally arbitrary, provided that all possible alternatives can successfully accomplish the same communicative goal (Lewis 1969: 70). The fact that they are established at random is precisely the reason why they can differ from culture to culture (Gläser 1990: 29). Normally, localized websites tend to show interference from the conventions of source texts, mostly due to the fact that during the cognitive translation process, translators' intuition might not provide a valid judgment (Nord 2003; Hurtado 2001). The quantitative approach of corpus use and genre-based corpus studies can assist in the identification of conventional linguistic features for digital genres in each culture (Jiménez-Crespo 2009a).
3. Active and passive competence of genre conventions. Active competence can be defined as the ability of speakers of a language to recognize and produce the conventional features of textual genres, such as writing a résumé or an email. Nevertheless, most speakers might not be able to produce certain textual genres, such as a patent, a purchase contract or

a privacy policy on a website. They might recognize just prototypical instances of the genres and be able to identify the possible range of variation. This is referred to as passive competence (García Izquierdo and Montalt 2002). This is precisely why they play a crucial role in professional activity and translator training (Gläser 1990: 72). In localization, most members of a discourse community have an active competence in writing emails or blogs, but the ability to produce a privacy policy or an effective homepage has to be consciously developed. Learning what is conventional in any specialized genre requires a systematic and conscious effort that allows the speaker to consciously develop an active competence (Gläser 1990: 27). The lack of active competence on any given textual genre has been referred to as 'genre deficit' or 'text type deficit' (Hatim and Mason 1997: 133).[8]

4. Conventions are flexible and evolve with time. Genre conventions are not totally stable throughout time; on the contrary, they evolve and change. So translators need to be aware of this possible evolution both in time and space (Göpferich 1995a). The evolution throughout time is of special interest due to rapid development in all technological arenas. This evolution can be due to changes in a given culture, changes in the co-ordination problem that gave rise to a specific convention (Lewis 1969), and lastly, the assimilation of certain interferences due to borrowings or mistranslations that might eventually be accepted as valid and correct. Many examples of this last instance can be found in digital texts. According to Bouffard and Caignon (2006), even when *contactez-nous* in French or *contáctenos* in Spanish could be considered borrowings, most speakers would consider these lexical units as valid choices in a website.

5. The role of conventions in localization and translation. Genre conventions play an important role in the identification and translation of most technical and localized genres (Nord 1997: 53). First of all, they function as signs that facilitate recognition of a given genre. Secondly, they activate the expectations of the reader. And finally, they are signs that co-ordinate the text comprehension process (Reiss and Vermeer 1984: 189). Therefore, given that translation entails both a textual comprehension and a textual production process, conventions also play a crucial role in it (Göpferich 1995a: 168; Nord 1997, 2003). It should be noted that, from a functionalist perspective, the substitution or adaptation of the conventions in the source text for those in the sociocultural context of reception is not automatic, but depends on the *skopos* of the translation and the norms of the target culture (Reiss and Vermeer 1984: 194). Nevertheless, it is logical to assert that most localized genres need to be functional texts in the target culture, and in principle all target texts should incorporate whichever conventions are established in the receiving locale.

6. Conventions in web usability and localization. As seen above, the facilitating role of conventions in web usability has been recognized by most researchers in the field (Nielsen and Loranger 2006; Brink *et al.* 2002). Users approach any website with a 'generic mental model' (Nielsen and Tahir 2002: 37) of a set of conventions shared by a specific discourse community for a specific genre. This model includes not only linguistic and cultural features but also typographical, graphical or functionality aspects. As an example, any web user has a generic mental model of what happens when a word is typed in a search box and the 'search', 'ok' or 'go' button is activated. Nielsen (2004) indicated that of all possible basic features in websites, 77% were conventional, and users expected them. He divided these features between 'standards' (those that appear in over 80% of websites), 'conventions' (appearing in 50 to 79% of websites) and 'confusion' (features that appear in under 49% of websites and which users do not expect).

Textual function

As with any other text, the producers of any website have an *underlying intention* (de Beaugrande and Dressler 1981: 7). This intention shapes its potential textual function. This is not a property inherent in texts, but rather, the function is assigned by the user or receiver in any given situation (Nord 1997). Depending on the discipline or approach, textual function classifications have different denominations, but if all proposals are summarized in broad terms, they all include three basic types: exhortative or persuasive, expositive and argumentative (see above). Expositive types are often subdivided into narration and description, the first priming verbal use, while the latter is more focused on nouns and adjectives. In contemporary genre theory it is assumed that text does not necessarily express just one function; rather, a text can be multifunctional, with one or two primary functions and a possible secondary function (Hatim and Mason 1997; Göpferich 1995b; Gamero 2001). In TS the multifunctionality of texts was referred to by Nord in the following terms:

> When I refer to 'function', in this context [the text], I mean function or set of functions, because texts are rarely intended for one function only. Various functions usually form a hierarchy of functions, subfunctions, etc.
>
> (Nord 1997: 9)

This set of functions can be applied to digital genres with hypertextual structures, as the different nodes can possess different functions or sets of functions. Nevertheless, they all contribute to the overall general function of the website as a complex genre (see above). For example, a promotional ad for the organization responsible for a site clearly possesses an exhortative function, even when the website *per se* might not be exhortative in principle.

Communicative situation and the Internet-mediated communication model

All genres are situated within a specific communicative situation that is determined by its senders and receivers or audience, as well as by its field (areas such as medical or legal), mode (written, spoken, audiovisual, etc.) and tenor (politeness relationship). Each of these features are key in the description of any genre, and any potential changes in them would result in a different subgenre, or a new genre altogether. For example, corporate websites normally show a more formal tone in their websites, while their Facebook or other web pages in social networking sites adopt a more informal tone, as the communication is supposedly established among equals.

Web localization, like any translation-mediated interaction, is obviously initiated with an underlying *communicative purpose* (Holtz-Mänttäri 1984). It was Ana Janoschka (2003) who argued that this *communicative process* occurs within a new paradigm opened up by the Internet's communicative capabilities, referred to as an Internet-mediated communication model. This model merges elements of interpersonal, one-on-one, and mass communication processes using the Internet as a medium, while browsers and computers serve as instruments. The Internet offers both synchronous (i.e. chats, videoconference, etc.) and asynchronous (i.e. emails, forum postings) interpersonal communication. In chats and online messages, sender and recipients participate in an interpersonal communicative process that makes them take turns being message producers and receivers. The information is exchanged in written, oral and visual form (i.e. emoticons). Emails also represent a case of asynchronous interpersonal communication, even when in some cases the longer email exchanges are shared almost in a synchronous fashion. In some new social networking websites, such as Facebook, the boundaries between chat and email exchanges have been blurred by blending both in a single platform. The synchronous and asynchronous nature of these two forms of interpersonal communication also represent different language styles (Crystal 2011), with chats being closer to 'conceptual orality' or spoken language and emails being closer to written forms of communication. The mass communication capabilities in online communication refer to the messages or texts that are digitally transferred to a larger audience via the Internet. Message senders can be either individuals or collectives, such as an organization or company. For example, all corporate website companies address their larger customer base with ready-made information about the company and products, providing a single repository of all types of information about them.

Janoschka argues that, generally, websites represent a new communication model that she refers to as the 'Interactive communicative process'. It is interactive because it allows interaction between users and senders, as well as between users and the medium. It is also a mass communication process, as it follows the principles and criteria of mass communication found in

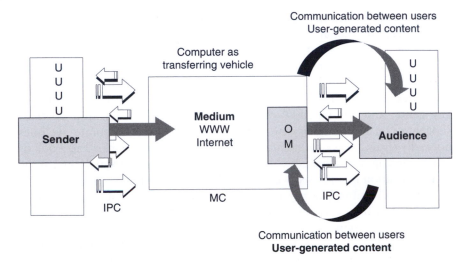

Figure 4.5 Interactive mass communication model. Adapted from Janoschka (2003: 98)

advertising or TV. In this new communicative model, the communicative flow or online message (OM) moves primarily from the sender to the audience via the Internet, but nevertheless, the communicative flow is also digitally mediated in the opposite direction, although to a lesser extent. The black arrows and the white arrows respectively represent this in Figure 4.5. The black arrows indicate the larger communicative flow that can be associated with the Mass Communication model (MC), in which the online message transfers from one to many. The communicative process also incorporates elements of interpersonal communication (IPC), or one to one, as the sender (S) and audience (A) exchange messages and information via the computer as an input and output device. They also interact with the computer and the Internet *per se*, i.e. when users hit the 'send' button, the browser indicates 'you cannot connect to the Internet right now' or when we are informed that a date format is incorrect after filling out a form.

For the purposes of web localization, it is key to separate the interaction that occurs between human participants and the different levels of human–computer interaction that happen simultaneously. Janoschka (2003: 116) coined two terms in order to differentiate between these two processes: 'interaction' and 'interactivity'. The former can be described as the communicative process established between the sender and the receiver, and it can occur through selective reading of the website, emails, chats, online contact forms, etc. Interactivity refers to the communication process between user and medium (Jucker 2003), such as search functions in websites, activation of hyperlinks, using navigation menus or any other interactive process between the user and the medium (*ibid.*: 116).

Among the several translation and interpreting processes that can occur digitally in synchronous and asynchronous fashion (O'Hagan and Ashworth 2003), website localization concerns asynchronous mass-communication communicative processes, such as websites. Localization facilitates a combination of mass-communication and interpersonal communication between companies or organizations and their audience – the interaction between users and websites. This means that the texts processed in website localization simultaneously serve two distinctive communicative processes with distinct registers, styles, etc. These two processes – sender to user and user to browser or website – can show linguistic and pragmatic differences between cultures. Localizers therefore mediate not only between websites senders and audiences, but also in the interaction between websites and users. Lately, localization is also starting to facilitate communication between users themselves through the translation of user-generated content. Finally, it should be mentioned that localizers cannot be considered participants or receivers of the messages in the interactive mass-communication process, as 'mediators are never the receivers of source texts but rather part of their audience (that is, they are not receivers but random receivers)' (Muñoz Martín 1995: 45). The web localization process thus requires careful attention to these existing simultaneous communicative processes within any website. As an example of this communicative process, NGOs disseminate both static and dynamic content in their websites. Communications flows mostly from the organization towards its audience, but websites necessarily include interactivity options, such as forms, subscriptions to newsletters, etc. Most information is normally static and does not change over time, for example, contact information or the description of the non-profit organization. The dynamic content includes all the sections that might be regularly updated, such as calendars, press releases, events or newsletters, and this type of information is often not localized due to the recurrent costs involved (Jiménez-Crespo 2012a).

Audiences in websites can be divided between primary audiences, supervisory audiences and peripheral audiences (Jeney 2007). The website specifically addresses the primary audience. The supervisory audience refers to the commissioners of the website, that is, both the organization that commissioned the website and/or the translation agency that may have been in charge of the localization process. Finally, the peripheral audience would be all those visitors who might not have been directly targeted when the website was created, but who might nevertheless visit it. Translators or localizers are not the primary audience in any mediation process, but rather part of the peripheral audience of any text. They are not the normally intended 'receivers' of any potential text to be translated (Muñoz Martín 1995).

Sociocultural context

All genres are contextualized in a specific *sociocultural environment*, and they develop due to a repeated communicative situation or need (Hatim and

Mason 1990; Berkenkotter and Huckin 1995). Even though most digital genres appear in most Western nations, there is still the possibility of genres being culturally specific, such as the Japanese *haiku*. These new genres that are culturally dependent might be circumscribed to one culture or might extend to others, such as the Japanese *Manga* or *Anime*. Sociocultural contexts where genres emerge and exist affects them in three distinctive ways:

1. All conventions are culture-specific and cannot be assumed to automatically transfer to other cultures (Nord 1997);
2. These contexts provide the breeding ground for new genres: without any specific communicative need within a society, genres will not develop;
3. They affect the evolution of any genre, as genres adapt to any changes within that society. As an example, in monolingual societies without multilingual immigrant communities, intracultural localized non-profit websites might not exist.

Intratextual aspects

Normally, genre description models favour extratextual elements over *intratextual elements*. However, it is often repeated that conventions are mostly expressed at the intratextual level, such as specific terminology, phraseology, discursive structure or textual structures. In websites, visual and functionality conventions as described in usability studies also play a key role, even when a localizer might not actively engage in their transformation. An increasing number of monolingual descriptive or contrastive studies on printed genres focus on one or more intratextual elements, such as superstructure, speech acts, syntax, lexis, thematic progression, cohesion, metacommunicative elements, visual and textual semiotic relationships, rhetorical structure, formality markers, etc. These types of studies of genre-specific intratextual elements still represent an almost unexplored territory for localization scholars. However, it should be remembered that not all intratextual elements are equally relevant in the description of these genres. Scholars widely agree that superstructure is the most important of all, given that it is generally highly conventionalized in most genres, as it helps provide the necessary global cohesion and coherence (Gamero 2001; Göpferich 1995a). Superstructures are also widely relevant, as most contrastive or descriptive textual analysis usually proceeds with a top-down analytical progression, starting at the superstructural level and later progressing to lower microstructural levels. The fact that digital genres possess a conventionalized structure can be directly witnessed by their description and the fact that a number of publications enthusiastically recommend reproducing them, such as web usability manuals (Nielsen and Loranger 2006; Nielsen and Tahir 2002), web style guides (i.e. Price and Price 2002; Bly 2002), as well as previous research on the conventional superstructure of digital genres (Liu *et al.* 1997; Bolaños *et al.* 2005; Adkisson 2002; Robbins and Stylianou 2003; Jiménez-Crespo 2012a). Given the importance of superstructural analysis in genre studies, a more in-depth treatment of this notion is required.

Digital genres and textual structure

The idea that a genre represents a *conventionalized textual structure* first appeared in folklore studies, where it became the only defining feature (Paltridge 1997). The importance of textual structures in genre studies was maintained in later commentaries from the systemic-functionalist perspective (i.e. Martin 1995; Kress 1993). The School of New Rhetoric textual structure is analysed in relation to the sociocultural context (Miller 1984), and other parameters such as rhetorical purpose or the intention behind the production of any genre emerge as the most important aspects in their definition. However, this more function-oriented approach to genre leads on to the study of genre structures becoming the primary focus. For ESP scholars, genres result from a recurrent communicative situation and are internally organized in a rhetorical structure made up of different textual sections called 'moves'[9] defined as:

> A text segment made up of a bundle of linguistic features (lexical meaning, propositional meanings, illocutionary forces, etc.) which give the segment a uniform orientation and signal the content of discourse in it.
>
> (Nwogu 1997: 122)

These textual segments or rhetorical moves articulate the discursive structure of a genre, and they can be further subdivided into 'steps' and 'substeps' (Nwogu 1997). For example, an academic research paper is broadly made up of the moves: introduction, literature review, methodology, results, discussion, conclusion and references (Swales and Feak 2000). These moves represent the conventionalized content of each part of the text and possess a specific function that contributes to the overall purpose of the text (Paltridge 1997: 111). As a whole, the moves represent the overall superstructure of any genre, and the order of the elements might be quite fixed, as happens with medical research papers (Swales 1990, 2004; Nwogu 1997) or even a recipe, in which the ingredients section is always followed by the preparation. Depending on the perspective of study, the building blocks of any genre are referred to as sections>moves>steps (Swales 1990; Nwogu 1997) or communicative blocks>communicative sections>significant units>significant subunits (Gamero 2001). Originally, Swales (1990) turned to the rhetorical function and the lexico-grammatical features in order to identify the different sections and moves, while later Bhatia (1993) described the rhetorical purpose as the main criterion for establishing a different section.

The development of genre theory was rooted in printed linear texts, and the emergence of hypertexts required this linear conception of the move-step structure to be adapted. Askehave and Nielsen (2005) introduced the ESP approach to web genres by identifying each move or step with a page within the global website. They adapted the genre description model of Swales (communicative purpose>moves>rhetorical structure) to web genres incorporating links as the alternative that breaks up the linear fixed rhetorical structure of printed genres. They indicated that the structure is not fixed but determined by the user, depending on two possible processing modes in this medium: reading mode and a navigation mode. Reading mode occurs when we linearly process the content of any web page, and in this case the rhetorical structure is processed by the succession of moves and steps. For example, this happens when we read the content of the description of a product. In navigation mode readers move away from the rhetorical structure and zoom out to the communicative purposes in the global hypertexts as summarized in the links in view at each moment. In several studies I have adopted the principles of the adaptation of the Swales model by Askehave and Nielsen for hypertexts (Jiménez-Crespo 2009a, 2009c, 2011a, 2012a), combined with the adaptation for technical translation of Gamero (2001) and Göpferich (1995b) to study the conventionalized structure of localized digital genres. These studies started from the description of their source contexts, later comparing and contrasting localized web genres with non-localized ones. Navigation menus and site maps provided the foundation for identifying the different sections in the website. The higher-level sections, identified as moves, are those that are conventionally part of any instance of the genre – such as 'contact us' or 'about us' – while the more specific 'steps' within these sections are integrated as subsections within them. In the case of 'about us', the steps which are possible subsections include 'location', 'history', 'values', 'staff', 'clients', 'quality', etc.

Super, macro and microstructures

Digital texts possess a multiple layered structure that can be analysed at different levels, from the global structure of the hypertext to the concatenation of sentences within a frame or node. From the textual or discourse-analysis perspective, these operative concepts are widely referred to as *super, macro* and *micro superstructures*. These represent the three levels of text representations according to the psychological model of text processing of Van Dijk and Kintsch (Kintsch and Van Dijk 1978; Van Dijk and Kintsch 1983). Micro and macrostructures refer to the meaning or propositional content of the text, the lexico-grammatical content or semantic meaning built up of propositions or sentences. The macrostructure represents the global meaning structure or the gist of the entire text, and it is formed through the text base provided by the microstructures or propositions. Superstructures represent the global structure container or global structure that is characteristic of each genre, or the form in which the macrostructure or textual content is presented. For example, the superstructure of a news report would be the headline, lead, context, and event. In the case of an online contact form, the superstructure would include the presentation of the contact form and invitation to use it, fields to fill out with the contact details, and submission of the contact information (Jiménez-Crespo 2010a).

Superstructures are the primary defining feature in highly conventionalized genres, and they can be used in order to differentiate between different subgenres within a genre (Gamero 2001). In the process of textual analysis, they are considered the starting point for top-down analyses, providing an overall framework for analysing lower-level structures. In the context of technical translations, Göpferich (1995a: 127) defined the notion of superstructure as the conventionalized sequence of elements in a text that develop in a hierarchical, but somewhat flexible, progression that is fixed at the thematic and functional level in order to develop a theme. Contrastive genre-based studies are highly productive, as they can assist in identifying these recurring units of meaning in each structural block within a genre. As an example of a descriptive analysis of the superstructure of digital genres, Table 4.1 shows the prototypical superstructure of 'non-profit websites' in

Table 4.1 Prototypical superstructure of the 'non-profit website' genre in the United States. Adapted from Jiménez-Crespo (2012a: 149–50)

Move	Step-section	% in US original non-profit websites
A. Home		65%
B. Contact us		77.5%
C. About us		77.5%
	C.1. Description-Services	87.5%
	C.2.1. People>Board	52.5%
	C.3. Mission	50%
	C.2.2. People>Staff	37.5%
	C.4. Location	35%
	C.5. Calendar	25%
	C.6. Foundation	22.5%
	C.7. History	22.5%
	C.8. Testimonial	17.5%
	C.9.1. Multimedia>Photos	17.5%
	C.10. Sponsors	17.5%
	C.9.2. Multimedia>Videos	15%
	C.11. Finance	10%

Table 4.1 Continued

Move	Step-section	% in US original non-profit websites
	C.12. FAQ	7.5%
	C.13. Feedback	7.5%
	C.14. Accessibility	7.5%
	C.9.3. Multimedia>Audio	2.5%
	C.15. Brochure	0%
D. Legal		5%
	D.1. Terms of use	25%
	D.2. Privacy Policy	32.5%
	D.3. Disclaimer	5%
	D.4. Equal Opportunity	5%
E. Press		72.5%
	E.1. Newsletter	7.5%
	E.2. Events	22.5%
F. Jobs/Career		45%
G. Donate		60%
	G.1.Volunteer	42.5%
H.1. Interactivity>Site Map		32.5%
H.2. Interactivity>Search		37.5%
H.3. Interactivity>Links		22.5%
I. Resources		35%
	I.1. Publications	22.5%

the United States (Jiménez-Crespo 2012a). The two leftmost columns indicate the identified moves (i.e. home, contact us, about us, etc.) and steps (i.e. history, calendar, location, etc.) in a corpus of 943 websites of US charities in 2011, while the right-hand column indicates the prototypical frequency of use of each. For example, a page for 'contact us' information appears in 77.5% of the websites.

The conventional superstructure of the non-profit website, defined here as appearing in over 50% of instances of the genre (Göpferich 1995a; Gamero 2001), would include seven moves: home, contact us, about us, description of services, board, mission, press and donate. If we compare this genre with other popular homepage genres such as corporate, institutional or personal homepages, one of the main distinguishing features in the superstructure is the existence of two distinctive sections, 'donate-volunteer' (60% frequency) and 'board' (52.5%).

PROPOSED TAXONOMY OF WEB GENRES FOR EMPIRICAL RESEARCH AND TRANSLATION PURPOSES

In this section we will propose a taxonomy of web genres primarily intended for research, training and practical purposes in web localization and related fields. The hybrid, evolutionary and dynamic nature of web genres has meant that, despite substantial efforts, their categorization is still a highly controversial issue. Existing proposals, even within the same discipline, often start from shared frameworks but, nevertheless, differ considerably in some basic premises, such as the unit of analysis (web page, web document, website, etc.), the parameters for classification or even the number of genres identified. Our proposal has been developed following previous efforts in TS (i.e. Agost 1999; Borja 2000; Gamero 2001) for other translation modalities or types, such as legal, medical, technical or audiovisual genres. The criteria for the categorization of these genre systems or genre ecologies within translation types or modes vary widely. In legal translation, proposals take into consideration the function and the tone or level of formality, from hyper-formal (constitution, decrees) to formal (contracts) (Borja 2000: 133). For example, a court sentence would possess a triple function, instructive, expositive and argumentative, while the tone would be very formal. In the case of technical translation, Gamero (2001) indicates that the tone or level of formality used previously in legal genres would not be considered a classifying feature in technical genres. She proposes a categorization in which the function and an element of the communicative situation, the level of specialization, are the main characterizing criteria. For example, genres with an expositive function can be subdivided into those of general communication – technical encyclopedia or science news article – and those of specialized communication – technical report, technical description. These same criteria are also applied to a genre categorization for medical translation by Mayor Serrano (2007: 135). The proposals for audiovisual genres in translation is of great interest for web localization, as they fully incorporate the possibility of multiple functions within one audiovisual genre (Agost 1999: 31). This is the case of the audiovisual genre 'contest' or 'music program', that can incorporate multiple functions for each part of the show.

Following these previous categorization efforts, we will classify web genres in localization according to three main criteria: a supragenre label according the purpose of the genre (advertise, inform, socialize-communicate, entertain or use as a tool), the communicative function (expositive, argumentative, persuasive-exhortative), and the type of communicative process established (mass to individual, community to community, individual to individual, etc.). The first organizing criterion is a set of supragenre labels based on the purpose of the digital genre. All web genres are divided into 'informational genres', 'communicative or interactive genres', 'instrumental genres', 'advertising genres' and 'entertainment genres'. These supragenre labels embody the main purposes for which senders develop a website and present it to WWW audiences: to provide information, to assist in communication or interaction, to use it as a tool or instrument, to advertise products or services, to provide entertainment or a combination thereof.

The next filter is the intended function behind the genre. Hatim and Mason's (1990) proposal is used to divide texts into those that describe or narrate information (expositive), intend to modify the receiver's behaviour (exhortative), or to argue (argumentative). In order to account for multifunctionality in digital genres, they are divided according to the primary and/or secondary functions. For example, corporate websites possess both an expositive and an exhortative primary function, while a discussion forum has a primary expositive function with a secondary argumentative function. In the specific case of web genres, in addition to their main set of functions, there is an additional layer in which all genres possess an exhortative function. This is due to the fact that two guiding principles of web success are that:

1. users should stay as long as possible in a site; and that
2. they should be encouraged to come back as often as possible instead of selecting other sites that provide similar information or services, etc. (Nielsen 2001).

Therefore, in addition to the aforementioned exhortative character of all web genres, most websites also have a secondary exhortative function as the organization, individual or company behind it has the intention of improving or maintaining a positive users' attitude towards them (Bly 2002; Askehave and Nielsen 2005). Finally, the third guiding categorizing feature in the proposed open taxonomy is the communicative situation – more specifically, the main participants in the communicative interaction. Senders and receivers in the communicative situation in these types of genres are divided into: mass, individual, corporations, organizations, institutions, communities and the WWW. The inclusion of the WWW as a participant in the communicative situation is reserved for those genres in which users interact with the content of the web, as in the case of search engines, etc. Despite the fact that search engines embody companies that derive a profit from their activity, users perceive that they are interacting with the content of the WWW as a whole, and not with a company in the strict sense of the word.

Genres represent open categories (Göpferich 1995b), and this categorization should be understood as open-ended, not exhaustive, and in evolution. It should also be conceptualized in prototypical terms (Halverson 1999), without clear boundaries between categories and each categorization principle. The prototypical-cognitive view of genre classifications, in the hybrid world of the WWW, means that boundaries between exemplars represent fuzzy notions rather than clear-cut constructs (Labov 1973). This is precisely what Crowston had in mind when discussing digital genres:

Table 4.2 Proposed categorization of web genres for translation purposes

Supragenre category	Functions	Elements of communicative situation	Web genres	Subgenres
Informational genres	**Primary functions:** Expositive (provide information) Exhortative (modify user's behaviour)	Institution to mass	Institutional websites	– Government – Academic – International organization
		Individual to mass	Personal homepages	– Academic – Leisure – Professional
		Company to mass	Corporate website	– Support website for bricks and mortar company – Online company
		NGOs to mass	Non-profit website	– Intracultural non-profit – International organization non-profit (Red Cross, Amnesty I.)
		Company to company	Intranet	
		Organization to individuals	Documentation source	– Library website – Document databanks
		Association to individuals	Association-community website	
	Primary function: Expositive **Secondary function:** Exhortative	Organization to mass	Academic – research journals Online newspapers Online magazines News aggregators TV station website Radio website	

Table 4.2 Continued

Supragenre category	Functions	Elements of communicative situation	Web genres	Subgenres
	Function: Expositive (narration and description)	Mass to mass	Wikisite	– Wiki encyclopedias – Wiki databanks
		Individual to mass	Hyperfiction Literary websites	
	Multiple functions	Online company to mass	Portals (Yahoo, Google, MSN, etc.)	
Advertising genres	**Primary function:** Exhortative	Company to mass	Promotional website	– Product promotional website – Event promotional website
			Social promotion-rebates	
Instrumental genres	**Primary function:** Expositive (provide information)	WWW to individual	Search engine	– General – Video search – News search – Etc.
		Company to individual	Online store	
		Organization to individual	Documentation source	– Library website – Archives
		WWW to individual	Download site	– Video download – Link collection
Communication-interaction genres	**Primary functions:** Expositive and exhortative	Individual to group	Social networking sites	– General – Professional – Personal interests

Function	Communication	Genre	Subtypes
	Individual to individual	Community connection/social	– Romance/dating – Multi-purpose ads
Primary function: Expositive **Secondary function:** Argumentative	Group to group	Discussion forums	
Primary functions: Expositive and exhortative	Company to mass	Gaming sites	– Individual gaming – Social gaming
Entertainment genres		Bidding sites Adult sites	– Video collection – Personal/mass video connection

> [It] may be helpful to think of genres defined by exemplars and documents as being more or less good examples of a genre rather than attempting to draw firm boundaries
>
> (Crowston 2010: 295)

All the proposed genres should therefore be seen as prototypes that embody core features perceived as central to the exemplar of a genre. For example, a variation of the corporate homepage has recently appeared within social networking sites – the Facebook corporate-promotional homepage. Additionally, we cannot forget about the hybrid nature of digital genres (Tercedor 2005; Santini 2007) and therefore, these genres can combine in different ways.

An additional optional subgenre category is included to account for variations within primary genres. These subgenres emerge from small changes in any of the characterizing features or small differences in their communicative purposes (Bhatia 1993). The criteria for identifying subgenres are more heterogeneous in order to account for different evolutionary trends in primary genres, or even for the purpose of future studies that might employ this taxonomy. For example, some studies might subdivide corporate websites into those of large, medium and small companies. In the case of gaming sites, the above table includes non-interactive gaming and social gaming, the latter being a novel trend with large corporations such as Zynga.

SUMMARY

This chapter started by reviewing genre-based approaches and their significance for localization. The common confusion in TS and Linguistics between the text types and digital genres was discussed. The chapter provided a concise summary of the theoretical approaches to the study of genres in light of the massive amount of research into genres and digital genres from different perspectives. We reviewed how this theoretical and methodological framework could provide an ideal platform for web localization research. The contributions of digital-genre theory to analysing the differences between printed and digital genres were discussed, projecting their findings towards web localization. A model to analyse digital genres based on previous proposals for technical translation was presented. The chapter ended with a taxonomy of digital genres for web localization, based on their purpose, text function and communicative situation.

FURTHER READING

The literature on digital genres, discourse-analysis genre studies and genres within the practice and research of translation is extensive. For an overview of digital-genre research, see the introduction by Santini *et al.* (2011). For the emergence of digital genres see Shepherd and Watters (1998) and Crowston and Williams (1997). The series of proceedings from the Annual Hawaii Conferences on System Sciences represents a comprehensive repository on digital-genre research. Some basic readings for Genre Theory are Swales (1990), Bhatia (1993) and Paltridge (1997). For an adaptation of Swales's approach to hypertexts see Askehave and Nielsen (2005). For the significance of genres in TS see García Izquierdo and Montalt (2002) or García Izquierdo (2005, 2007). See also Montalt *et al.* (2008) on didactic applications of genre approaches to translation education, and Borja *et al.* (2009) for research methodologies using genres. In the series of Jiménez-Crespo's articles readers can find genre analyses of the most commonly localized web genres: corporate websites (2009a, 2010a, 2011a), non-profit websites (2012a, 2012b) and social networking sites (2013). The significance of genre conventions in web localization is reviewed in Jiménez-Crespo (2009a), and in Jiménez-Crespo (2011e) readers can find a compendium of conventions for web writing style. Usability publications also offer key insights into general web genre conventions (i.e. Nielsen and Tahir 2002; Nielsen 2004; Krug 2006). Most alertboxes in Jacob Nielsen's www.useit.com website provide information about specific conventional features of websites.

5

WEB LOCALIZATION AND QUALITY

Translation quality and its evaluation represent one of the most controversial issues in TS and professional web localization. This chapter attempts to provide the groundwork necessary to close the gap between the industry and academic perspectives. It offers a concise overview of the many approaches to assessing translation quality both in the industry and in TS, how they interrelate and, most importantly, what both perspectives can contribute to an integral assessment of web localization. Current practices can be described as experiential and mostly rely on error-based metrics inspired in the LISA QA system with the goal of producing efficient and cost-effective localized websites with 'the look and feel of locally made products' (LISA 2003). Meanwhile, few TS publications have delved into quality evaluation in localization, mostly offering descriptive accounts (Dunne 2009, 2011), case studies (Pierini 2006) or proposals to incorporate functionalist principles and holistic evaluation (Jiménez-Crespo 2009d, 2011a). The main theoretical approaches to translation quality are discussed, while understanding the evaluation of web localization quality as a time- and resource-constrained process. The many elements that can be highlighted in web localization quality are discussed, such as the different components of internal and external quality (Gouadec 2010). The chapter ends with a proposal for a componential scalable model that accounts for the multiple elements of quality that can be highlighted in web localization evaluation.

LOCALIZATION AND TRANSLATION QUALITY

The quest for high levels of quality in all entrepreneurial processes has been reflected in the localization industry, with 'quality receiving more attention than ever' (Bass 2006: 6). Quality is a highly aspirational notion for translation agencies, freelance translators, training institutions, certification exams or translation technology marketing. Yet, despite great efforts from all interested parties (i.e. industry experts, practitioners, scholars, trainers, users, etc.), the fuzzy notions of *quality* and *quality assessment* still seem some of the hardest to pinpoint of all translation-related phenomena. Have you ever wondered why we find translation quality mentioned everywhere but we still debate what it actually entails? As with many other issues, its controversial nature is mostly due to the lack of conceptual common ground among commentators. In fact an attempt by the International Standards Organization to develop a translation quality standard petered out in 2012 due to diverging perspectives among the interested parties. This lack of consensus does not mean that quality evaluation is not implemented: right now, thousands of reviewers are evaluating the quality of localized websites; a Facebook user is voting on which proposed translation would be more appropriate for an interface segment; a linguist is checking the output of a Machine Translation system. These are cases of quality evaluation that are built upon internalized frameworks of quality that guide subjects' decisions, even if they might lack operative theoretical foundations.

As with many other issues, recent research into quality in localization has often followed in the wake of industry developments (Wright 2006; Dunne 2011). Summarizing the main outcomes of this research, it can be observed that:

1. quality should not be understood as a static construct, but rather as a flexible notion that depends on each situation, and/or that
2. it should be planned from the very start of the localization cycle, rather than conceptualizing it as a stage that follows the development and translation stages (Dunne 2009).

Within localization research, most efforts have been devoted to the more standardized and homogeneous process of software localization (Esselink 2001; Wright 2006; Bass 2006; Dunne 2006b, 2009, 2011); very few scholars have tackled the specific issue of quality in web localization from other perspectives, such as TS (Pierini 2006; Jiménez-Crespo 2009d, 2011a; Jiangbo and Ying 2010), web content management (Gibb and Matthaiakis 2007), or cross-cultural psychology applied to web design (Singh *et al.* 2009). Normally, studies into web localization quality indicate the need for further research and analysis, partly because the same set of evaluation criteria cannot be uniformly applied to all translation activity (Martínez and Hurtado 2001: 284). Web localization also represents a relatively new phenomenon and a distinctive translation modality that still has no set of canonized criteria for its evaluation (Wright 2006).

Seen from a TS perspective, one of the most pressing questions is, how much translation and localization theory is necessary to develop and implement quality assessment models? TS scholars have consistently argued that quality evaluation cannot proceed without sound theoretical foundations (House 1997; Colina 2008; Angelelli and Jacobson 2009).

> Evaluating the quality of a translation presupposes a theory of translation. Thus different views of translation lead to different concepts of translational quality, and hence different ways of assessing it.
>
> (House 1997: 7)

This implies that professional views on web localization quality, sometimes referred to as anecdotal or experiential (see below), are necessarily different from those in TS due to the underlying theoretical assumptions. All in all, different approaches to localization quality coexist; for example, recent crowdsourcing approaches to web localization have demonstrated that effective quality assessment can be built without a sound theoretical framework, challenging the House notion of theory-dependent quality (Jiménez-Crespo 2013). Calls for further empirical research to test quality evaluation models, theories and principles are a constant in the discipline but still, the debate on what constitutes quality and how to evaluate it is far from nearing finality. In the industry, quality is marked by the often-forgotten impact of economic, time or situational constraints that dispel the myth of quality as an absolute notion. In fact, accepting these constraints has been crucial to shifting quality from a relatively unachievable abstraction to a practical construct operationalized through a continuum of levels defined by situational criteria.

QUALITY IN THE LOCALIZATION (AND TRANSLATION) INDUSTRY

The notion of quality attracts a great deal of attention within the localization and translation industries (Jiménez-Crespo 2011a; O'Brien 2012; TAUS 2012). It represents a dynamic abstract notion defined according to a wide range of parameters, such as the clients' goals, end-users, perishability of the information, clarity, accuracy, etc. Unlike academic disciplines, current approaches in the industry are governed by the quest not for a fuzzy notion of quality but, rather, for efficiency in a process constrained by timelines and resources. So definitional efforts concentrate on establishing processes to secure the final quality outcome, rather than the notion of quality itself. In broad terms, the industry approach seeks to guarantee quality by following a two-pronged approach:

1. Using quality assurance (QA) procedures intended to guarantee that quality requirements are met; and
2. Establishing quality control (QC) procedures through the entire localization cycle, from source text development all the way to the

delivery of the product. QC procedures check the quality of the products or services offered.

The first prong involves setting up processes to avoid 'failure' and assure a definable level of quality. The second involves checking the end product to identify any failures that have occurred and to prevent them from being handed on to the customer (requester). QC is also considered a subset of the first prong and is normally carried out using a standardized static-quality metric based on error-analysis (i.e. LISA QA). To some extent, these stages help distinguish Gouadec's (2010) notions of internal and external quality: internal quality refers to the intrinsic qualities in the localized text itself, while external qualities have to do with how well it fulfils its intended purpose, how it satisfies the implied client needs, etc. Quality management becomes an essential component in this external approach. For our purposes, it is highly productive to separate both components in professional settings, as theoretical approaches in TS can shed light mostly on intrinsic quality, but not necessarily on extrinsic aspects related to the localization transaction, business aspects, etc. This is also in part why a wide localization industry–academia gap exists, as TS scholars normally highlight internal quality, while industry experts often debate external issues.

If one analyses the industry's literature on this issue, the defining features of internal quality tend to be the equivalence and consistency of a TT in relation to the ST (Dunne 2009). Sometimes similar operative criteria for evaluation in MT environments are also found, such as accuracy, clarity and style (Hutchins and Somers 1992: 163; Fiederer and O'Brien 2009). Nevertheless, external quality is more frequently discussed in industry publications, normally grounded on international standards, whether general – ISO 9000 – or translation-specific, such as the European EN 15038. These standards generally define quality as the capacity to comply with a set of parameters predefined by the customer or client. For example, the ISO 9000 defines quality as: 'the totality of features and characteristics of a product or service that bears on its ability to satisfy stated or implied needs' (ISO 9000). With a very similar perspective, TQM (Total Quality Management) defines quality as 'fully satisfying agreed customer requirements'. Similarly, the definition in the North American ASTM translation quality standard[1] defines it as 'the degree of conformance to an agreed upon set of specifications'. These definitions do not define the notion of quality *per se*, but rather, focus on procedural aspects, as opposed to establishing what could be considered a 'quality' product or translated text. Basically, such definitions govern procedures for achieving quality, rather than providing normative statements about what constitutes quality (Martínez and Hurtado 2001: 274). They are generically process-oriented instead of product-oriented (Wright 2006: 256).

As far as the evaluation itself is concerned, quality assessment in web localization normally involves a triple process: linguistic testing, cosmetic testing and functionality testing (Esselink 2001: 150–4). Linguistic testing intends to guarantee that all translatable textual segments have been rendered adequately, including all text embedded in graphics, presentation, animations, etc. Cosmetic testing focuses on the visual aspects of the inter-active textual segments or interface texts to ensure that everything is displayed correctly in the localized version, while the goal of functional testing is to ensure that the process of localization has not corrupted any of the coding that could result in functionality problems. These different stages are performed consecutively and are usually performed by different evaluators and even mechanical checking, such as automated functionality testing. In the industry there is a tendency to place primary emphasis on functionality testing:

> Because functional aspects of a program can be objectively assessed . . ., people often perceive software development and localization as processes that are akin to manufacturing, while forgetting about the linguistic aspects of the program and the often subjective nature of linguistic quality definitions
>
> (Dunne 2006b: 96)

This primacy of functional and cosmetic testing over linguistic elements is more prominent in the complex process of software localization, a more technologically complex process with limited possibilities of communicative interaction between users and the product itself (Esselink 2001; Dunne 2006b). In web localization, it can be argued that quality is sustained to a greater extent by the 'linguistic' components, given that the technical complexity is lower but the range of textual, discursive and communicative problems much wider. This is due to the large number of textual types and genres poten-tially present in web genres, requiring an evaluation approach closer to other translation types and modalities, such as legal, technical or audiovisual.

In general, procedures for quality evaluation can be subdivided into three distinct types: summative, diagnostic and formative (Martínez and Hurtado 2001). Summative evaluation is carried out to determine the end result or to pass a final judgment; it would be used in certification examinations or professional contexts involving publishable/non-publishable decisions. Formative evaluation appears in translation training and usually requires constructive feedback to be provided by the trainer to the evaluee (Kussmaul 1995). The feedback is normally directed at improving future performance, but in the process evaluators need to identify the etiology or cause of the error or inadequacy. Hence this type of evaluation entails both looking back at performance in the past and forward into the future. The last type, diagnostic evaluation, is directed towards placement, the identification of a relative level of quality achievement, and is mostly used during college admissions or hiring processes. In professional practice, these types are normally mixed and combined. A college exam would be both summative and formative in nature, while the evaluation of web localization, though mostly summative in nature, also entails a distinct process of formative evaluation, as evaluators might need to log the error and provide either a solution or feedback to the person responsible. The same can be said of a hybrid case in which translators log errors made by Machine Translation engines in order to improve future performance.

Industrial approaches also prioritize a wide range of factors in order to evaluate quality, and different models or approaches stress some components more than others, such as:

1. clients and end users
2. commissioners of translation
3. user sentiment
4. usability
5. text type or genre in question
6. perishability/life expectancy of target text
7. time constraints
8. cost
9. end users' or clients' quality expectations, ranging from gisting to full publishing quality
10. professional/volunteer/community/crowdsourced translation
11. evaluation method and/or error typology used.

The interplay and balance between all factors normally determines the actual quality of the final product, and any or all of these factors might be assumed by initiators/clients, translators and end users in order to make a quality judgment. For example, a quick translation with a low cost, such as a crowdsourced translation of tweets from a famous person, might be judged differently from another translation commissioned to a professional over a relatively reasonable timeframe. These factors interact to offer the current dynamic approach to quality, in which constraints exert a powerful role.

Quality analysis as a constrained process

Discussions of quality have effectively moved away from the quest for an illusory absolute to conceptualizations reflecting compromises between interested parties due mainly to cost, time and resource constraints. In the professional world, translation quality can be said to depend on the 'necessary and sufficient rule', that is, guaranteeing adequate quality or 'fitness for purpose' without incurring excessive costs or resources (Wright 2006). Even in TS, scholars working within the functionalist paradigm recognized early on the significance of contextual factors in analysing translation quality (Hönig 1998). This resulted in a move away from a primary emphasis on equivalence relationships, form, errors or style and towards understanding quality in terms of adequacy, compliance to standards, agreed-upon specifications or customizable quality grades that apply to specific projects or types (Dunne 2009; Gouadec 2010). This turn towards the reality of the profession recognizes the inherent limitations of translation and localization as industrial activities and, as a result, sees quality evaluation as a contextually bound and constrained process. According to Gouadec (2010: 272), 'quality assurance almost always comes second to economic considerations' in the professional world. In general, the constraints that operate during the translation and localization process can be separated into the contextual and the procedural:

Table 5.1 Contextual and procedural constraints in web localization quality

Contextual constraints	Procedural Constraints	
	In the evaluation process:	*In the translation process:*
– Budget or monetary constraints – Time for completion – Client quality expectations – Specifications for the project – International standards applied (or lack thereof) – Volume of translation – Subjectivity and lack of agreement on what constitutes quality – Cultural norms as to what is considered quality – Genre/mode/medium – For what purpose: gisting, publishing, training, etc.	– Skills-training-experience of translators and reviewers-editors – QA system (or lack thereof) used – QA procedure used (error-based, holistic, mixed, etc.) – Error typology or holistic categories used (only those categories are implicitly identified)	– Quality of source text and related materials, such as glossary, TMs, etc. – Application of specified terminology, style guides, translation memories during the translation process – Translation-localization technology employed – Translation procedure: human, post-edited machine translation, raw machine translation – Cognitive constraints – Type/genre of text

Quality is thus in practice conceptualized as a balance between the multiple constraints that can operate at both procedural and contextual levels. These constraints can be implicit or explicitly assumed by clients and translators/localizers.

We identify two points of departure or guiding principles for customizing the level of relative quality. In business settings, it is normally compliance with agreed specifications under the umbrella of international quality standards. Dunne (2006b, 2009, 2011) operationalizes this compliance by judging how the projects fulfil the specifications laid out by the client before the actual localization process. This approach requires careful documentation of all specifications and scope of the commissioned web localization project

(Levitina 2011). However, it is not always possible to conceptualize quality in terms of agreed customer specifications, as Dunne points out:

> Clients often cannot provide all the necessary standards, requirements or specifications for the simple reason that they are unfamiliar with the languages, culture, conventions and legal requirements of the target locale(s).
>
> (Dunne 2006b: 100)

In this case, it is up to the evaluators and localizers to provide generic guidelines for quality, or it might even be necessary to educate clients as to realistic quality expectations, depending on the specific constraints (Ørsted 2001; Bass 2006).

From a more theoretical perspective we also find a second point of departure in functionalist principles related to how effectively the website or its subcomponents fulfil the purpose the clients intended (Jiménez-Crespo 2009d). Obviously, the issue with this approach is how to operationalize and quantify whether those purposes were achieved – user-based evaluation can be of great use here (i.e. Nida and Taber 1969; Nobs 2006). This could be operationalized in terms of whether the localized website resulted in more customers purchasing goods or services, whether it attracted more repeat visits, whether a FAQ section resulted in fewer customer service calls, etc. In my opinion, both perspectives are complementary and stem from the same principles, but the functionalist one is more flexible, as it can cope with more of the spectrum of web localization processes that take place in our modern digital world, from small resources to large ones or non-professional to professional types.

The interrelated set of constraints that operate during the whole process results in a series of grades or levels of quality that are agreed upon for each project, domain, situation, etc. Several scholars have proposed different levels or degrees of quality, some of which initially emerged for machine translation post-editing purposes (Allen 2003; Quah 2006; García 2009) or for professional translation in general (Gouadec 2007, 2010). For example, Gouadec embraces a flexible approach to quality and defends establishing quality degrees for different domains or situations upon which quality evaluation and quality judgments can be built, conceptualizing quality in terms of how 'fit for delivery or broadcast' a translation might be. The different customizable degrees of quality would be: 'rough cut', 'fit for delivery (but still requiring minor improvements or still not fit for broadcast medium)' and 'fit for broadcast (accurate, efficient and ergonomic)' (Gouadec 2010: 273).

Research conducted on machine translation quality has also been instrumental in operationalizing quality in terms of a balance between contextual constraints and the needs of end users. Allen (2003), in his study on post-editing machine translation, subdivided the different grades of machine translation post-editing into: no post-editing, minor post-editing intended for gisting

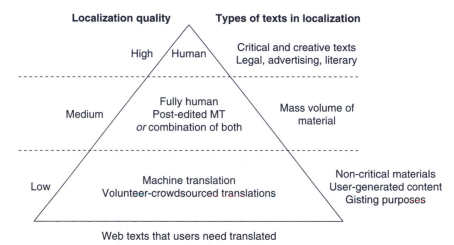

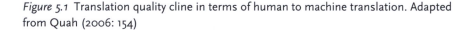

Figure 5.1 Translation quality cline in terms of human to machine translation. Adapted from Quah (2006: 154)

purposes, and full post-editing. Quah (2006: 154) also referred to the cline based on quality from low to high, identifying the need for each level depending on users' needs, and also establishing a cline based on whether machine translation or human translation would be needed (no post-editing is mentioned). The author identified highly creative and critical translation modalities as requiring full quality, and therefore, human-based translation, while translation for gisting purposes – of web articles, for instance – is identified as a low-priority process that can be achieved through machine translation.

In this case, the question in web localization is whether the entire website can be envisaged as a global entity in which the same approach is applied equally to all components (as often happens in the industry), or whether the different text types that make up a website – from ads to complex legal web privacy terms – deserve different treatments. Should different evaluation and models of quality be applied to the diverse types of texts within a site (advertising, audiovisual, legal, technical, literary, etc.), or do the constraints justify the application of a standardized QA system to the entire website? Current approaches are starting to favour differentiating texts within websites according to different quality tiers (O'Brien 2012), sometimes related to levels of risk.

The LISA QA process

The LISA QA model, and others inspired by it, can be considered the most widely used in the localization and translation industries (O'Brien 2012), even though the organization disappeared in 2011. It can be considered to some extent a *de facto* quality metric standard in this sector (Wright 2006). This QA model is an integratable database-driven application that can be used for both translation and localization quality evaluation. It is an error-based system with an open pre-set error typology that covers language, formatting and functionality errors. The seriousness of each type of error is assigned using the following penalties: critical (10 points), major (5 points) or minor (1 point). For each project or translation type, evaluators (one or more) set a threshold for the number of combined minor, major and critical errors that are allowed, and if that threshold is passed the localized text would be deemed 'unpublishable'. This can therefore be described as a summative evaluation process that includes a pass/fail judgment. However, it also incorporates a formative component, in that evaluators might be requested to provide feedback to translators to minimize future errors (Esselink 2001), or they might be requested to propose solutions to all identified inadequacies. The LISA QA model is highly customizable, and all parameters, including error types, thresholds and penalties are assigned normally on a pre-project basis.

This model was developed due to the need to incorporate the interplay between textual and functional components in digital products. It therefore incorporates both linguistic and functionality testing stages that were typical in localization QA (Esselink 2000; Chandler 2005; Dunne 2009). In software, these stages are normally performed by different evaluators or testers, although this might not be true in the less technical process of web localization. The need for interrelating both components is clear: for example, even when the linguistic testing component might measure an outstanding level of quality, functionality errors such as deficient text integration, functionality issues or segments in other languages, would compromise the global quality of a website (Bass 2006: 92). This is an essential aspect that distances all types of localization evaluation from other types of translation evaluation.

However, despite including linguistic, formatting and functionality errors, a higher emphasis on functionality testing can be perceived (Dunne 2006b). In fact, only a third of the evaluation depends on 'language' components. The pre-set language errors are identified as mistranslation, accuracy error, terminology error, language error, style error, country or dialect error, and consistency error. It is easy to perceive the difficulty in assigning any given error to only one of these categories. Some of them overlap, such as language and style errors. One of the main issues with this model is the difficulty in dealing with more serious inadequacies at macrotextual and pragmatic-communicative levels. These types of pragmatic and functional features are more difficult to evaluate than grammar, meaning or spelling (Colina 2008: 125) and therefore tend to be absent in error-based systems such as LISA's. This is partly because the decontextualization of textual segments hinders the evaluation of a global coherent text from a pragmatic perspective. In this model, as with most error-based approaches, evaluators are rather forced into a microtextual level that has difficulties dealing with problems that affect the text as a global unitary entity. Another common problem is that, even when all current models use different severity levels, what counts as a minor, major or critical error is rarely described. This aspect can significantly increase the variability among raters and does not provide a sufficient degree of reliability.

Obviously, the widespread use of the LISA model and others is inspired by many beneficial features, such as the fact that it is componential, or in other words, that it recognizes many aspects of quality. It also implicitly accepts that the search for an absolute standard of quality is impossible. In this case, and from a functionalist perspective, the localized text will be more or less appropriate for the purposes for which it is intended (Nord 1997). Thus, in line with the 'necessary and sufficient rule' (Wright 2006), this approach also presumes that a limited number of errors is unavoidable due to the economic context in which this process is performed (Bass 2006).[2]

Standards in the industry: quality and interoperability

The significance of quality is witnessed by the existence of a number of widely used international standards focused on this issue. In general, standards in professional practices also cover a wide range of objectives – e.g. those related to content creation, translation and localization, terminology, ontologies, locale specification or base standards, such as language standards or character codes (Wright 2006). A complete overview of all interrelated standards and standardizing bodies would be a huge undertaking, and many available publications and websites summarize the main standards that apply in localization (Wright 2006; Schäler 2008b; Lommel *et al.* 2011). However, the analysis of quality cannot disregard the great efforts in the industry to develop and apply these standardized sets of rules, conditions and requirements that define terms, procedures, etc.

In the analysis of web localization processes and products, it is productive to differentiate between two types of standard used in the localization industry:

1. standards that are obligatory, such as base standards for mark-up languages by the W3C and other language standards, and
2. those general and translation-localization-specific standards that can be applied to improving the quality, interoperability, interchangeability and replaceability, such as international quality standards.

Language standards can be either obligatory (such as using HTML) or optional and cover a wide array of issues. According to Wright (2006), they can be grouped under: base standards (mark-up language standards such as HTML, XML, SGML, and metadata resources), content creation, manipulation and maintenance, translation standards, terminology and lexicography standards, taxonomy and ontology standards, corpus management standards and language and locale-related standards. Most obligatory base standards are an integral part of the quality process and are handled by programmers and developers rather than translators/localizers. Some standards by the W3C concerning quality are also optional, for example the W3C accessibility initiative (WAI),[3] which it is nevertheless essential to consider in web localization (Jiménez-Crespo 2009e; Tercedor 2010).

The standards affecting the final quality of a localized website can be divided into functional standards and quality standards. The latter, which normally separate Quality Assurance (QA) from Quality Control (QC), can be subdivided between:

1. general industrial quality standards that can apply to translation and localization as industrial activities, such as the ISO 9000 family,
2. translation quality standards in different geographical areas, such as the European translation quality standard EN 15038
3. translation-quality metrics such as the LISA QA model or the SAE J2450 for the automotive industry.

Wright (2006: 257) also adds a fourth level of translation quality that covers customizable procedures related to the evaluation of source text materials, target text assessment, translator assessment, etc.

The ISO 9000: 2000 family of standards represents a multi-level set of frameworks that provides guidelines and requirements to guarantee quality in industrial and governmental environments. It provides a procedural framework for quality management that defines quality in terms of meeting agreed customer requirements, and it is widely used in order to certify the quality of translation agencies and vendors around the world. The main philosophy behind the ISO 9000 standards can be summarized as:

1. documentation of the quality,
2. a focus on continuing improvement,
3. defining a set of performance metrics,
4. a focus on customer satisfaction,
5. enabling project quality management and corrective actions.

The standard's premise is that errors and issues will arise regardless, but nevertheless, a system should be in place to minimize and correct them (Bass 2006). Some scholars have argued that the ISO standards might be insufficient to guarantee quality in localization, as this process does not produce a new product, but rather, adapts a previously developed one (Dunne 2009). However, it is clear that this procedural approach to quality management can help correct mistakes and lapses in quality from earlier stages and continually improve the overall cycle. A recent standard, the ISO/TS 11669: 2012, covers general guidelines for project management, another effort to ensure quality by controlling how processes are managed.

Inspired to some extent by the ISO 9000, different standardizing bodies around the world have produced translation-specific quality standards, mostly focused on the procedural and transactional nature of the process, such as the North American ASTM 2575-06 or the European translation quality standard EN 15038. Other European translation quality standards, such as the German DIN 2345, the Austrian Önorm D1201, the Italian UNI 10547, disappeared in favour of the European EN 15038. All of them vary in terms of foundations and scope, from more process-oriented EN 15038 to the almost direct adaptation of Nord's (1997) functionalist proposal of quality in terms of function plus loyalty to the client and users in the ASTM 2575-06. Some of the now disappeared standards did not implicitly mention localization, while it appeared in some others such as the Austrian Önorm D1201.[4] Similarly, the notion of quality itself is rarely explicit, except in the German standard in which a quality translation was defined as the one that is complete, is terminologically consistent, uses correct grammar and adheres to the agreed style guide. The EN 15038 standard does not define quality *per se* but established a certain number of procedures to guarantee the quality of the end product, such as the specific university-level translation degree of the parties involved, an obligatory revision by a person different from the translator, etc.

Functional standards normally address the need for interoperability and interchangeability in the industry, and would be related to the quality of the overall technological process and translational transactions, improving the efficiency of localization processes and resulting in cost-savings for all parties involved. Among these standards are the TMX (Translation Memory eXchange) developed by OSCAR group in the now defunct LISA organization. It was designed as a vendor-neutral standard for exchanging translation memories created by different types of computer-assisted tools. One of the problems that initially arose by the implementation of TMX was the different segmentation rules used by existing CAT tools, and therefore, the same group developed a standard to provide ways of stating segmentation rules, the SRX (Segmentation Rules eXchange). Both of these last standards have not been taken over by the Localization Industry Standard group in ETSI.[5] Terminology management is equally important in localization projects, and – although it is implemented to a lesser degree due to its complexity – OSCAR also developed TBX (Term Base eXchange), an XML standard for exchanging terminological data. In the same vein as TMX, a group of localization industry experts, OASIS, developed XLIFF (XML Localization Interchange File Format) a standard intended as a format to store and carry the extracted text from software programs and carry it along in the localization process, allowing multiple providers and localizers working in the same projects to exchange the information. Another standard exclusively for localization was developed by LISA to standardize certain procedures in the localization process, such as counting words in a project (GMX-V), or identifying the potential complexity of a project (GMX-C) or the quality metric used (GMX-Q). Recently, the disappearance of the Localization Industry Standards Association has increased the profile of GALA (Globalization and Localization Association) that is currently involved in the development of standards, such as the Linport, a standard form for sending and receiving translation projects in a standards-based package format – a similar endeavour to the TransWS standard to oversee the overall localization transaction and project flow – and Model Service Elements, aimed at providing concise, cross-industry definitions for all notions and concepts used, such as localization, words or proofreading. All these standards can directly affect the extrinsic quality of the overall localization cycle, and not necessarily the intrinsic quality of the text itself.

QUALITY IN TRANSLATION STUDIES

Quality evaluation is a central but rather controversial issue in TS. Its origins can be traced back to criticism in literary translation, and nowadays most research focuses on two distinct but related perspectives, the professional (i.e. Sager 1989; Dunne 2006b, 2011; Gouadec 2010) and the didactic (i.e. Nord 1991, 1997; Waddington 2001; Delisle 2005; Collombat 2009). Proposals to conceptualize quality evaluation in TS depend to a considerable extent on the underlying theoretical backgrounds and objectives: early approaches tended to base quality judgments on equivalence relationships between ST and TT, while later communicative-oriented scholars such as Nida and Taber (1969) moved towards a more dynamic approach that included assessing the effect on the readers. From the early 1980s, functionalists moved the focus towards whether the translation achieved the purposes for which it was intended (Reiss and Vermeer 1984; Nord 1997), and others proposed elaborating detailed profiles of source and target texts to compare the two using a cultural filter (House 1997). Nevertheless, a common criticism of these theoretical proposals is that they offered generic theoretical principles for assessment in different contexts rather than definitions of what constitutes translation quality *per se*, and also left it up to practitioners to decide how to implement them in professional settings. Some of these proposals are quite complex and time-consuming if fully applied, and, as a result, they have not been fully implemented in professional or didactic contexts. They do, however, bring to the surface specific aspects that are of great interest for conceptualizing quality assessment in web localization.

From a TS perspective, current implemented models can be considered as anecdotal or experiential, as they are based on subjective criteria and lack theoretical foundations (Colina 2009). They are based instead on the accumulated knowledge base of subjects or organizations involved, and their discourse often revolves around notions such as 'faithfulness to the source text', 'equivalence', 'lack of errors', etc. Such models prevail among translation practitioners, philosophers, industry experts, etc., as well as being the main day-to-day approach in professional web localization. This heterogeneous group of approaches cannot be considered as a model of quality, but rather as models based on previous bodies of experience that are partially captured in a diverse range of grading scales, rubrics and error typologies. Scholars argue that the main problem with this widespread approach is precisely the lack of reliance on explicit theoretical foundations, empirical data or solidly defined constructs (Colina 2008; House 2008). Consequently, it is impossible to control the subjective bias of human evaluators, and the two main core principles in evaluation, validity and reliability, cannot be achieved. This subjective bias was already present in the first attempts to study translation evaluation. For example, Nida (1964: 154–7) believed that it is impossible for translators or evaluators to avoid a certain degree of subjectivity in the interpretation of the ST and its reflection in the TT. Ever since, it has been widely accepted that the subjective component of the evaluation process will remain and has to be admitted (Hönig 1998): evaluators assess translations by comparing them to an ideal text that they would have produced themselves, thus projecting their individual standards onto the actual text. As a consequence, it is a basic principle that a single evaluator cannot provide an objective measure of quality in translation (Rothe-Neves 2002).

Theoretical approaches to quality evaluation in TS are the other side of the spectrum. A complete overview of their evolution and current state would obviously be beyond the scope of this section. The objective here will instead be to highlight the main trends and proposals of interest for building a framework to assess quality or to conduct research. For our purposes, it is relevant for web localization quality, first, to review the criticism of widespread error-based approaches – still the main approach used in professional (O'Brien 2012) and didactic (Collombat 2009) settings – as well as alternative holistic approaches, and, second, to analyse what the different theoretical models can add to our understanding of web localization quality. These models can be roughly subdivided into response or reader-based, textual and discursive, and corpus-based approaches.

Error-based approaches

The notion of error continues still today to be central to translation evaluation in professional and didactic settings (Kussmaul 1995; Delisle 2005; Dunne 2009; Collombat 2009). The inevitable presence of error and error typologies in quality assessment, as Gouadec indicated (1998: 135), is always in the minds of translators, trainers, students and researchers. A recent study by O'Brien (2012) reported that all translation companies surveyed (most of which localize web content) use error-based metrics to evaluate quality. Despite their popularity, the error-based methods are perceived as somewhat inadequate, because error identification alone cannot result in comprehensive quality evaluation. Problems often arise from the fuzziness of error categories and their impact levels. Furthermore, this approach narrows the focus of attention to the microtextual level – lexical and grammatical issues – whereas a wide range of errors can occur at higher textual levels, such as communicative, pragmatic or superstructural ones (House 2008). This was rightly indicated by functionalist Nord, who argued that error identification alone was insufficient, as 'it is the text as a whole whose function(s) and effect(s) must be regarded as the crucial criteria for translation criticism' (1991: 166). He suggested a top-to-bottom approach to evaluation to account for this wider textual focus, starting from the overall textual function and its effects and moving on down to lower textual levels, such as lexical inadequacies. For the purposes of a comprehensive understanding of web localization quality, we would need to focus on the following theoretical discussions concerning error-based approaches:

(a) *Defining the notion of error.* The first stumbling block for a common conceptualization of quality is defining the nature of error in itself. Translation errors have been defined from a cognitive and functionalist perspective as inadequately solved translation problems (Nord 1996: 96–100).[6] Hence they can be defined as 'an objective problem which every translator ... has to solve during a particular translation task' (Nord 1991: 151). This process-oriented notion highlights the skills and competence of the translator(s) involved as translation errors arise from deficiencies in training, skills and, consequently, performance. The cognitive reality of the translation task requires a distinction between systemic/recurrent errors and random errors, also known as mistakes (Spilka 1984: 72). A translation mistake is a random error, normally a minor error that translators commit due to the cognitive interference and cognitive complexity of translation tasks. Such errors are normally immediately recognized by translators as random or 'stupid' errors. They are often related to a paradigmatic or direct transfer of ST lexis or structures, as well as to typographic problems caused by technological issues such as typing, etc. Another distinction of interest in defining translation errors is the functionalist dichotomy between absolute translation errors and inadequacies (Nord 1991, 1997).[7] Absolute errors are those that are considered as such no matter the translation type, situation or context. A calque, a distortion or a grammar/syntax error in any target text would be considered as such no matter where it appears. However, functionalist errors or inadequacies are those specific to the translation brief or request, such as using the wrong geographical variety of the language for a localization addressed specifically to one locale, such as using Canadian French for a Belgian website or Castilian

Spanish for one addressed specifically to Argentina. Sometimes, these inadequacies are harder to identify, as they often can be found only by 'comparing the source and target text in the light of the translation brief' (Nord 1997: 76), and native speakers reviewing exclusively the target text might not be able to identify them. This need to review the translation in the light of the translation brief and the source texts is due to the fact these might not just be inadequate in themselves; they become inadequate 'with regard to the communicative function it was supposed to achieve' (*ibid*.: 73). In web localization publications as seen in the LISA QA system, the notion of error encompasses a wide range of issues due both to translators' cognitive processing problems, and to issues related to functionality and layout. These last cannot be directly attributed to incorrect solutions to translation problems, but rather, issues with internationalization, development, interplay of translators and developers, etc.

(b) *Reliance on fuzzy or incomplete error taxonomies.* Error-based approaches are operationalized using concrete and limited-error taxonomies. According to Martínez and Hurtado (2001: 281), the different types of translation errors can be divided according to their etiology or cause into: (a) errors relating to the ST or its understanding, such as false sense, omission, no sense, etc., (b) errors relating to the TT or the re-expression, such as punctuation, grammar, lexical or style errors, (c) pragmatic and functional errors: that is, those related to inadequacies as far as the function or *skopos* of the translation is concerned (Nord 1996), and, in the case of localization, (d) functionality issues related to development or to the interplay between markup and programming development and translation renderings (Jiménez-Crespo 2011a). In general, proposed taxonomies depend on the goal of the categorization, either for didactic purposes (i.e. Gouadec 1998; Delisle 2005; MeLLANGE, 2006), for professional certifications (ATA, CTIC, etc.) or for assessing translations in professional settings (SAE J2450, LISA QA, SICAL, etc.). The error categories among all of them vary considerably, ranging from 675 error types in Gouadec's proposal (1998),[8] via 38 in the open taxonomy of the MeLLANGE project to 23 in the American Translation Association marking scale. These pre-established typologies are often limited or incomplete, and tend to include fuzzy error types, thus making it difficult to provide accurate or complete evaluation outcomes. To solve this problem, it is often indicated that taxonomies should be validated through broad-based empirical studies (Martínez and Hurtado 2001; Angelelli and Jacobson 2009) but, contrary to what might happen in cases such as professional certifications, industrial QA processes are not focused on scientific objective measurements but on providing a satisfactory level of quality for the parties involved. A common issue with error typologies is that they are limited by nature and might not control some components of quality, such as functionalist and pragmatic ones. As pointed out by Jiménez-Crespo (2009d, 2011a), the most widely used QA system, the LISA QA, does not incorporate pragmatic and functionalist errors, and therefore most corporate websites do show a recurrent presence of inadequacies not accounted for in such systems. For example, errors at the macrotextual level, such as using different terms for the same concept in the navigation menu and in the content text – i.e. 'contact us' or 'about us'– appears as one of the main issues in localized websites. Finally, these models rarely control quality components that cannot be directly linked to microtextual errors, such as issues of 'usability', 'readability', or 'content sentiment' (O'Brien 2012).

(c) *Assessing the impact or seriousness of the error.* The impact or seriousness of the error has attracted the attention of scholars and industry experts alike (i.e. Hönig 1987; Larose, 1998; Williams 2004). All marking or grading scales assign a weight or seriousness to errors, from minor all the way to critical. A calquing error might be considered minor while a wrong sense might be considered a major error. Critical errors are normally reserved for those that could make the text unusable, such as an opposite sense in the title of a software test item. Not all weights are necessarily negative. For example, didactic scales often incorporate positive points awarded for exceptional or specially creative translation solutions, although this practice does not appear in profession translation (O'Brien 2012). Different approaches exist in order to assign the weight or seriousness impact for each error: based either on internal linguistic criteria or on extralinguistic ones (i.e. the potential impact on the usability of the text or the impact on the quality appreciation by the end user). The most important linguistic criteria for assessing impact normally differentiate between different textual levels. For Nord (1991) pragmatic or functionalist errors, as opposed to linguistic, cultural or transfer ones are the most serious, while Larose (1998) or Williams (2004) separate errors according to the textual level: microtextual or macrotextual. An example of a macrotextual error would be to directly transfer an argumentative text from Arab into English, or directly translate the structure of a web marketing text from one culture to another when persuasion might be expressed differently. On the other side of the spectrum, more professionally-oriented perspectives in TS maintain that the seriousness of the error depends on the extent to which it infringes the effectiveness or usability of the target text (Hönig 1987; Gouadec 1998, 2010). This latter view can be considered the prevailing one in the industry, and lately it has also been adopted in certification exams, such as the American Translation Association marking scale. In this approach the impact is assessed on a scale from whether an error would be undetectable or slightly bothersome to the receiver, all the way to making the text unusable.[9] One key issue in web localization is that the superimposed network of textual structures in websites implies that the error's impact should also be determined by the level at which it occurs: navigation menus and interface texts that mediate the interaction are considered part of the macrostructure or textual skeleton of the hypertexts; therefore an error in these structures would be more serious than, for example, an omission or false sense within a 'Our History' page. Errors at these superstructural levels can also render the text unusable, as users might be frustrated and abandon the site, thus vitiating the purpose of the localized site.

(d) *Quality thresholds.* These are set up on a project or company basis, and localizations or translation are deemed 'publishable' or 'unpublishable' in relation to them. Adjustable error thresholds appear in all evaluation metrics according to the quality requested. Quality is therefore seen as a relative notion rather than an absolute. These thresholds are framed in terms of a combined number of minor or major errors, and often no critical errors are allowed.

Holistic evaluation approaches

Holistic approaches to quality evaluation emerged as an alternative to error-based approaches and stem mostly from functionalist principles. They assess the global target text in a componential manner through different layers of what might constitute quality using different series of customizable components such as 'specialized content and terminology', 'target language', 'functional and textual adequacy', 'meaning', or 'usefulness/transfer', etc. (Waddington 2001; Colina 2008, 2009). These models provide an instrument for evaluating the often-neglected communicative/pragmatic adequacy of localized texts, 'rather than being limited to grammatical and or stylistic errors at the sentence level, and changes in meaning' (Colina 2008: 107). The evaluation is carried out on the translated text as a whole, providing a more reliable assessment of certain components of quality than would be possible by evaluating single segments separately. According to a study by Waddington (2001), error-based and holistic approaches were equally effective at establishing internal quality rankings of translation quality. This type of evaluation is carried out through judgments on different categories based on descriptive statements that follow a continuum, thus allowing for evaluation decisions that can be more complex than absolute error/non-error ones. For example, Colina's holistic proposal for evaluating medical brochures in the US incorporates the following statements in the category 'non-specialized/meaning':

a. The translation reflects or contains important unwarranted deviations from the original. It contains inaccurate renditions and/or important omissions and additions that cannot be justified by the instructions indicative of very defective comprehension of the original text (on the part of the translator) . . .

c. Minor alterations in meaning, additions or omissions

d. The translation accurately reflects the content contained in the original, insofar as it is required by the instructions without unwarranted alterations, omissions or additions. Slight nuances and shades of meaning have been rendered adequately.

(Colina 2008: 129)

The evaluator makes a judgment by selecting one of these descriptors for each category. The evaluation also allows for the possibility of indicating examples or comments about the errors or inadequacies that justify the decision, but does not include a complete listing of all identified errors. This makes this model most useful in summative evaluations: that is, when the object of the process is to evaluate the entire translated text to identify a sufficient degree of quality. This type of summative evaluation appears in web localization during the so-called 'in-country' reviews, for example, when the localized website is analysed directly in the targeted country. In general web localization assessment the documentation and elimination of all identified errors is required, and therefore the exclusive application of this model would not be fully applicable. However, in Jiménez-Crespo (2009d) I argued for a mixed evaluation system that would incorporate current error-based approaches with an additional holistic final evaluation. The holistic section could, through an efficient and not necessarily time-consuming process, provide a reliable basis for evaluating certain pragmatic and functionalist aspects that revolve around global texts, rather than segments. Currently, an extremely small number of companies incorporate a holistic component in their QA (O'Brien 2012), even when the componential models include procedural aspects of quality linked to quality standards rather than linguistic ones.

Textual and pragmatic approaches in TS

Textual and pragmatic approaches appeared in the 1970s and helped to shift the focus away from exclusively identifying and counting errors towards incorporating textual, functional and communicative aspects. These approaches began by taking complete texts and their functions as the main criteria for evaluation, proceeding later to error identification within the global framework of the text. Among these theoretical proposals are the text type model of Reiss (1971), the functionalist proposals of Reiss and Vermeer (1984) and Nord (1997), the argumentative macrotextual approach of Williams (2004) or the pragmatic/functionalist model of House (1997). The last two models, despite different theoretical foundations,[10] suggest compiling profiles of the source and target text that take into account cultural and pragmatic differences and using a contrastive analysis of the profiles to assess the translation. Functionalist models, on the other hand, only provide a series of programmatic guidelines based on their theoretical model which takes the essential element to be that the text meets the requirements of the translation commission. All these models have been criticized as too complex and time-consuming to apply in professional settings, and, besides, some of them do not explain how to proceed with the actual evaluation.

Despite the fact that these proposals can be said not to have impacted professional practices,[11] many principles in functionalist models can be of interest when defining and evaluating quality in web localization. Functionalist approaches in the 1970s and 1980s were instrumental in moving the focus of the evaluation process away from highlighting some sort of equivalence with the source text (Reiss 1971) and towards the purpose or *skopos* or function of each translation assignment (Nord 1997). This entailed a shift in the definition of a quality translation, from one that was somewhat 'equivalent' to a source text to one where the entire text had the ability to fulfil the communicative purpose for which it was intended. It also introduced into mainstream Translation Studies the notion we have already noted of 'adequacy' in the evaluation process. In this shift, the receivers and commissioners, together with their sociocultural context, play an essential role. The industry's objective of producing websites that look like 'locally-made products' (LISA 2004), perfectly fits into the function-driven conceptualization of the translation process that focuses on the function of the text and the expectations of receivers. In the industry, quality is measured *de facto* in a compromise between loyalty to the clients' commission and how well the text accomplishes the purposes for what it is intended (Nord 1997). A localized website can therefore be regarded as having accomplished its purpose if it is received as a locally made one (i.e. it is clear and fluent, it matches the linguistic, genre and cultural conventions that users expect), its web usability is not compromised (it matches all the interactivity, visual and functionality conventions) and it is functional (i.e. there are no functionality errors or screen formatting issues). It was also functionalists who more strongly stressed the role of conventions in the global evaluation process, as it is key to guaranteeing that target texts contain whichever conventions users expect in whichever genre is translated or localized (see Chapter 4).

Corpus-based approaches to localization quality

The last theoretical approach of interest for web localization is the *corpus-assisted approach to quality evaluation* (Bowker 2001). For over two decades, the use of corpora during translation and evaluation has been widely promoted, mostly from within TS, for both didactic (i.e. Bowker 2001; Zanettin *et al.* 2003; Beeby *et al.* 2009) and professional practices (i.e. Bowker and Barlow 2008). Lynn Bowker pioneered the use of corpora during translation evaluation because this process 'entails making judgments about appropriate language use, [and] it should not rely on intuition, anecdotal evidence or small samples' (2001: 346). In translation, Bowker (1998: 631) also indicated, 'corpus-assisted translations are of a higher quality with respect to subject field understanding, correct term choice, and idiomatic expressions.' Additionally, Bowker indicates that the quantitative approach provided by evaluation corpora can be better than using conventional resources such as dictionaries, because these 'are not always highly conducive to providing the conceptual and linguistic knowledge necessary to objectively evaluate a translation' (2001: 346). A carefully constructed evaluation corpus constitutes a source of conceptual and linguistic information that can objectively support evaluation decisions and judgments. Corpusbased evaluation does not represent a stand-alone evaluation process but, rather, an effective assistance tool that can be used both during the actual evaluation process, or in a preliminary stage by quantitatively identifying recurring patterns of general errors, as well as genre- or languagecombination-specific ones.

In general, the basic premise behind the use of large computerized textual corpora in translation, and by extension in evaluation, is that it can help produce more natural-sounding translations (Zanettin 1998). It can also minimize the extent to which elements from the ST may 'shine through' in the TT (Teich 2003), or in other words, that lexical, syntactic or pragmatic features of the ST might end up represented in translations. Thus, even when one or a group of evaluators eliminate any language or cultural errors in the localization, and the sites seem to appear lexically and syntactically correct, the combination of lexical or syntactic items might not appear totally natural to end users. To a certain extent, this is due to the fact that the localized text does not show the combination of lexical and syntactic items that users are primed to expect in specific communicative situations (Hoey 2005). In a sense, corpora provide a tool for translators to identify these attested 'units of meaning', that is, conventional ways of expressing specific meanings and performing specific functions in the relevant text-type variety within the target language (Tognini-Bonelli 2001: 131). This is due to the premise that the large body of texts that belong to the same text type and genre and have been naturally produced by speakers of any specific discourse community represents, to some extent, the subconscious set of expected features in any genre. This shared knowledge of how specific genres and text types is accumulated by repeatedly exposing members of any discourse community to any genre.

Very few studies have focused on the use of corpora in localization (Shreve 2006b; Jiménez-Crespo 2009c, 2011a) and the only existing proposal for an evaluation corpus in Translation Studies is the above-mentioned proposal of Lynn Bowker (2001). This evaluation corpus proposal is intended for a didactic setting, and it was presented as assistance to evaluators when making evaluation judgments. It comprises four different components, a comparable corpus, a quality corpus, a quantity corpus and an inappropriate corpus.[12] The combination of the large amount of data in these corpora would 'make it possible to spot patterns more easily, to make generalizations, and to provide concrete evidence to support decisions' (*ibid.*: 353). This use of corpora during evaluation has been criticized mostly on the grounds that the proposal for evaluation does not include a fully-fledged evaluation method, but rather, a way to support the evaluator's intuition (Colina 2009). Another criticism is that the use of corpora is also reduced to the microcontext, that is, it is mostly geared towards finding the most common lexical or syntactic combinations, 'collocations' and 'colligations'.[13] Both these features are related to the appreciation of naturalness in texts, as they point to the more frequent combinations in users' minds.

Using corpora for evaluation on a regular basis might be time-consuming in certain environments, but these corpus-based contrastive analyses can highlight and bring to the evaluators' attention patterns of errors that are difficult to identify using error-based metrics, or errors of frequency – that is, accumulations of individual adequate items that, nevertheless, could be considered as a frequency error if any pattern is repeated often. Another application of the corpus-assisted approach in localization is, by comparing large numbers of original and localized websites, to identify recurring error patterns that can assist in elaborating and customizing error typologies for specific situations or genres. Table 5.2 shows the error typology developed from a contrastive 40-million-word corpus of original and localized corporate Spanish websites (Jiménez-Crespo 2011a). The empirically grounded typology that resulted from this study is structured in four categories: (1) transfer errors, (2) errors related to the target language, (3) pragmatic and functional errors and (4) localization errors – a category that only appears in this translation modality. The classification of errors related to the target language is further subdivided into three additional categories that match the levels of textual analysis – lexical, syntax and stylistic – with a separate typographical level.

In a subsequent case study included in the same publication, this error typology was applied to a localized Spanish version of a popular technology company website. The most recurrent errors were:

1. lexical calques
2. lexical coherence at the microstructural level
3. lexical coherence at the superstructural level
4. inconsistent capitalization in headings and titles
5. syntactic calquing
6. not using diacritical marks and signs
7. obscure wording or phrasing
8. cacographies
9. gender or number agreement in nouns and adjectives
10. the use of inadequate prepositions.

Table 5.2 A corpus-based error typology for web localization. Adapted from Jiménez-Crespo (2011a)

Transfer	Expression in target language				Pragmatic	Localization
	Lexical	Syntactic	Stylistic	Typographic		
a. Wrong sense	a. Loanwords	a. Syntactic calque	a. Phrasing/wording	a. Cacography	a. Appellative function	a. Untranslated segments
b. Nonsense	b. Barbarisms	b. Treatment (formal/informal)	b. Short sentence	b. Diacritical marks*	b. Sociocultural norms	b. Segments in other languages
d. Addition	c. Calques	c. Gender, number, case, verbal agreement	c. Appellative function	c. Inconsistent capitalization	c. Explicitation	c. Encoding
e. Omission	d. False friends	d. Dialectal syntax	d. Register	c.1. Capitalization: borrowings	d. Genre conventions	d. Incorrect syntax
	e.1. Lexical coherence: superstructural	e. Prepositions	e. Ambiguity	c.2. Capitalized sentences	e. Cloned structure	e. Incongruent text/image
	e.2. Lexical coherence: microtextual	f. Pluralization of acronyms	f. Omission/incomplete	c.3. Capitalization: months, languages, etc.	f. Other pragmatic	f. Visual metaphor
	f. Wrong lexical item	g. Ambiguity		c.4. Decades		g. Formatting/layout
	g. Acronyms			c.5. @ sign		h. Functionality
	g.1. Punctuation or spaces in acronyms			c.6. Punctuation in numbers		
	g.2. Capitalization in acronyms			c.7. Format currencies		
	g3. Anglicisms in acronyms			c.8. Quotation marks		
				c.9. Capitalization: abbreviations		
				c.10. Ampersand &		

DIFFERENT APPROACHES, DIFFERENT OUTCOMES: WHERE DO WE GO FROM HERE? TOWARDS A REAL-WORLD MODEL OF WEB QUALITY

From what we have seen, approaches to measuring quality in translation in general, and to web localization in particular, seem to be varied and rather polarized: scholars and researchers on one side advocating the introduction of theoretical and empirical approaches, while industry specialists continue developing QA methods with efficiency and cost-effectiveness in mind. To some extent, both groups claim that the other does not fully understand their position, and obviously this is due to the different natures of intellectual-academic endeavours and practical professional approaches. Industry practices continue to search for scalable grades of quality grounded in error-based measurements that do not incur excessive or prohibitive costs, seeking to balance existing constraints with constant improvements in QA processes. Nevertheless, theoretical and empirical research into translation quality can certainly help in developing more comprehensive and efficient quality evaluation methods. It can bring into the picture different levels and dimensions, such as pragmatic and functionalist issues or cultural aspects (Singh *et al.* 2009), to help tailor evaluation models to the needs and constraints of specific projects or digital genres. One example of the impact of translation theory on evaluating localization is the introduction of functionalist approaches that closely match the industry discourse for the goals of the process. As seen above, a common approach to localization quality is to ensure that, before the localization process starts, the commissioners provide a detailed list of specifications – the commission or brief – upon which to base evaluation of whether the quality objectives have been achieved.

Figure 5.2 represents how linguistic and textual approaches typical of the evaluation of other translation types relate to the functionality and usability components of web localization quality combined with industry approaches based on satisfying customer commissions. The user-based approach of web usability rests on the remaining components: the adaptation of functionality, textual/linguistic, and cultural adaptation issues. According to usability principles based on user-based experimentation, higher usability is achieved if the other three aspects match the expected set of features that repeated exposure to innumerable instances of any digital genre have accustomed users to (Nielsen and Tahir 2002).

Another issue of interest in which both perspectives can be merged relates to how to assess the seriousness or impact of an error. For example, user-based approaches have been proposed both in TS and in the industry, to assess the impact on users' appreciation of quality and/or how well the text achieves its intended purpose. This evaluation of error impact is normally operationalized in different levels, from 'undetectable to average user', via 'would annoy the user' all the way to 'would make text unusable'. This impact evaluation model is currently applied to the intratextual linguistic quality of

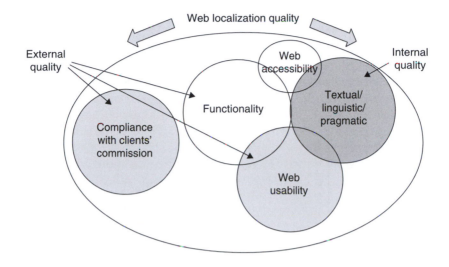

Figure 5.2 The different components of web localization quality

the text (such as the new American Translators Association marking scale), and it can be used in all the interrelated components of web quality, such as usability, web functionality, etc. Another issue related to the effect on the user is the potential damaging consequences of errors or unintentional infringements of cultural values or norms – such as the initiation of lawsuits against a company, institution or organization, or negative effects on its brand name.

Figure 5.3. shows how to potentially combine both existing perspectives on assessing error impact levels, based on both impact on user quality appreciation, and the level at which the error occurs.[14] As seen in Chapter 4, these textual levels go from microtextual or segmental to superstructural. Superstructural errors occur in interface texts such as navigation menus, gateways, homepages, sitemaps or interactive emergent messages, and are considered more critical as these texts provide the necessary coherence to the website (Williams 2004; Larose 1998). They are also repeated throughout the website, which magnifies the seriousness of these errors.

A PROPOSED FRAMEWORK FOR EVALUATING WEB LOCALIZATION

To bridge the gap between industrial and TS perspectives, the proposed framework adopts a flexible approach that combines and adapts existing trends to the specifics of web localization. It incorporates intratextual and extratextual components and introduces the real-world practical approach that assumes the existence of inevitable constraints, therefore facilitating the application of the 'necessary and sufficient' rule (Wright 2006). At the same

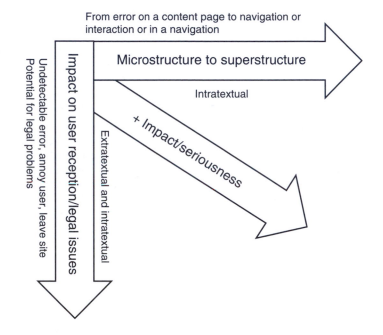

Figure 5.3 Assessing the impact of errors in web localization

time, it incorporates different aspects of translation evaluation theory that can be easily incorporated, such as the combination of error-based and holistic methods or the functionalist principle of adequacy, in order to assess the degree to which the adaptations are appropriate in light of the translation commission and intended purposes. The proposed framework does not entail a complete evaluation method *per se*, but rather a flexible template, in order to enable customized evaluation frameworks to be developed. It incorporates a global network of criteria that holistically make up web localization quality, and, in light of existing constraints, it is designed to prioritize whichever components the responsible parties (i.e. clients, initiators, agencies, developers, translators-localizers) deem appropriate for each specific situation. The five main criteria for evaluation are divided into three dimensions: intratextual, extratextual, and relationship to source text. The intratextual elements are divided among the linguistic aspects in the rendition of the source text, such as lexical, syntactic, pragmatic and typographic elements, as well as discourse-based criteria (i.e. genre and text type conventions, adherence to web style principles, etc.). The extratextual elements of web localization quality are divided among functional criteria (i.e., functionality, text insertion, formatting, programming, internationalization, etc.) (Esselink 2001; Dunne 2009), while the framework specifically

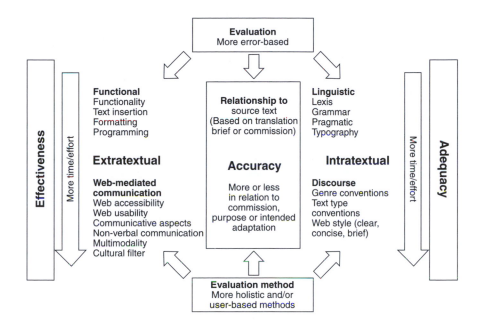

Figure 5.4 A proposal for a customizable framework to assess web localization

addresses other aspects related to web-mediated communication, such as web usability, communicative issues, and non-verbal elements (i.e., images or presentations, multimodality, web accessibility, cultural filters or dimensions). The dimension relationship to the source text depends on the translation brief or commission, including the localization grade requested. It varies according to the level of adaptation needed to make the website look like a local production.

Related to these three dimensions are the three properties that can be considered to be part of a quality localized website, adequacy, accuracy and effectiveness. These properties are somehow related to the criteria advocated for machine translation post-editing quality, although they differ in that this model is not based on any sort of equivalence relationship to the source text. Extratextual elements, such as functionality issues, or criteria related to web mediated communication, such as usability, can be evaluated according to how effective the target website is. Some criteria are culture- and language-independent (i.e. web usability principles or web accessibility), while other can be more culture- or language-pair-specific, such as the cultural filter. Effectiveness is also related to the three overall generic purposes of all websites in order to measure their success: their usability – how easily users interact with the site and achieve whatever goal they had in mind when opening the website (find information, make a purchase, entertainment, etc.), the site's ability to attract repeated visits, and its stickiness (the ability to keep users on it for as long as possible).[15] At the same time, the intralinguistic dimension depends more on an adequacy relationship to the norms at different levels of the target language and culture. Accuracy applies to the relationship between the source and target text, identifying issues such as omissions, wrong sense, etc. And this relationship can also be judged in terms of adequacy when the commission requires adaptations of all types to achieve the intended purpose.

The customizable aspect of this framework resides in the fact that from top to bottom, items are more or less critical to produce a quality website. This does not mean that some criteria are irrelevant, but rather, that some basic issues are more important than others when prioritizing the elements to consider in the context of a constrained process. Basic issues of language hygiene, such as appropriate lexical and syntactic uses, as well as functionality issues of the websites are critical regardless of the resources and time available, while adaptations to web usability or developing specific graphics or images represent a more complex and resource-consuming effort. Thus, this flexible framework to evaluate quality can be easily tailored for all types of websites from semi-professional environments in non-profit associations to websites of large corporations. The progression is indicated by the arrows showing the time/effort involved.

At the same time, the framework incorporates the two possible evaluation methodologies, error-based and holistic approaches, and it separates the different criteria according to which method is more appropriate for evaluating which issues. For example, functionality or formatting issues and accuracy in relation to the ST or TL expression issues can be more easily evaluated and corrected using error-based methods, while compliance with target genre conventions, adherence to web style guides, usability principles, adequacy of adaptations according to the commission or cultural issues are more conducive to evaluation using a combination of error-based and holistic methods. In the context of web localization, in which any error or inadequacy should be corrected, the more to less time required to perform the assessment and correct discrepant items also applies to the evaluation method intended. Processes in which resources allocated for quality evaluation are scarce should ideally employ error-based methods, while larger projects could benefit more from a combination of both methods.

This model can also be useful for researching the quality of websites worldwide from a descriptive perspective. By focusing on the actual evaluation method used, and overlaying it on the proposed framework, a hypothesis can be formulated as to how current methods of quality evaluation deal with the different components where the global quality of any localized website resides. The interplay of agents in the entire localization process can also be researched in light of sociological approaches to translation in order to observe chains of decisions and strategies, and how they affect the overall quality.

QUALITY MADE TO ORDER

This chapter has traced the current state and debate of translation and localization quality evaluation and highlighted the need to put aside the quest for a perfect, one-size-fits-all approach to its conceptualization. Multiple approaches have been explored, and quality evaluation has been seen from a real-world perspective as a compromise between the goals of the process (or commission), the needs of the end users and the constraints that operate both at the contextual and procedural level. In this regard, it has been argued that web localization quality involves answering a number of inter-related questions:

Quality evaluation

1.   For what purpose?
2.   For whom or which users?
3.   For which texts or digital genre?
4.   Under which constraints?
5.   When? Before, during or after?
6.   Of what? A product, a process-cycle, translation transaction or all of these?
7.   For what set or subset of translations, activities, mental processes, etc.?
8.   For a holistic global website, or for separate textual, visual or non-verbal aspects?
9.   How can it be achieved (technological help, use of TM tools, co-operative process, etc.)?

These answers can help all stakeholders interested in improving quality in web localization, even if they initially espouse different approaches, to reach a consensus on the object of their discussions. As far as the research perspective is concerned, as has happened with other attempts at generalizing in translation theory (Chesterman 2004), it may be time to step back and understand quality both as a prototype and as a theoretical construct to be studied under specific sets and subsets (professional/non-professional, highly time-constrained/regular time constraints, specialized web content/general content, advertising content/user interface content, large monetary investment/low budget, etc.). This approach would lead to a conceptualization of quality in general, and in localization in particular, in terms of 'under X conditions quality Y (should) happen(s)'. Such a strategy cannot only lead to practical gains in professional settings but also to testable hypotheses for future studies. Thus, this area opens up an attractive field for interdisciplinary research that can benefit TS and the profession, as well as providing a good departure point for starting to close the gap between industry and academia.

SUMMARY

This chapter started with a review of current literature on quality and quality evaluation both in the industry and in Translation Studies. We have argued that current practices in the industry are subject to a number of contextual and procedural constraints that require conceptualizing localization quality in relative terms, depending on the translation commission or job order, the constraints and the type of content localized. This chapter outlined the main contributions of theoretical approaches to quality in TS towards building a model of web localization quality that is both practical and realistic. Error-based approaches were discussed, as well as user-based, textual pragmatic, and corpus-based approaches. I have advocated closer collaboration between industrial practices and TS research in order to improve current models. The chapter ended with a proposed flexible framework for evaluating web localization quality in which adequacy, efficiency and effectiveness appear as the main components of quality in localized websites. This flexible evaluation method allows primary importance to be assigned to whichever components of quality the creators of the translation commission require in light of existing constraints. The different components can thus be separated according to whether error-based or holistic methods, or a combination of both, would be most effective. The chapter ended with a brief discussion of the notion of 'fit for purpose' or 'quality made to order', which is the prevailing present and future approach to quality in web localization.

FURTHER READING

For an overall perspective, in-depth summaries of research on quality within TS are offered in several volumes (Depraetere 2011; Angelelli and Jacobson 2009; Williams 2004) and in articles/chapters (Martínez and Hurtado 2001; House 2008; Gouadec 2007: 74–9, 2010). Some practical books offer descriptive accounts of quality assurance in software and web localization (Esselink 2001: 145–225). Dunne has published a series of papers on localization quality in which industrial approaches are combined with functionalist principles (2006b, 2009, 2011). For a commentary on error-based approaches in web localization and a proposed error typology, see Jiménez-Crespo (2011a), or see Jiménez-Crespo (2009d) on how to incorporate pragmatic and functionalist errors in web localization evaluation. The study by O'Brien (2012) offers an interesting summary of current quality evaluation practices in the industry, while Wright (2006) and Lommel et al. (2011) offer an in-depth summary of all international standards.

6

WEB LOCALIZATION AND EMPIRICAL RESEARCH

New textual forms and discursive and communicative practices require the constant adaptation of research methodologies and theoretical models to support research efforts. To serve as a basic introduction to web localization research, this chapter reviews the main paradigms, models and methods used in TS, as well as the basics of planning research projects (Williams and Chesterman 2002; Orozco 2004). It aims to provide a foundation for planning research efforts in this area, helping to locate potential projects within the wider framework of TS as an interdiscipline. It reviews how methodologies have been adapted to the specifics of web localization, as well as the main challenges that researchers exploring this phenomenon will face. Current trends and studies are included throughout the chapter as examples, and new directions are offered in this almost unexplored field.

RESEARCHING WEB LOCALIZATION

Since the emergence of web localization, scholars from different perspectives and disciplines – such as international business and marketing, Internet linguistics, discourse analysis, communication studies, computer science, computational linguistics or cultural anthropology – have focused on this phenomenon as an object of enquiry. However, its impact on TS is still surprisingly marginal despite growing interest in the current 'technological turn' (O'Hagan 2012b) and the fact that we are moving from print to digital distribution models. Web localization, thus, represents a largely untouched area for theoretical and empirical research into the complex interplay of translation, technology, medium, societies, power and cultures related to both the translation task and the context surrounding it. Research into web localization phenomena appeared in the late 1990s with the explosion of the WWW, and initially most projects approached it as an extension to software localization (i.e. Esselink 2001). This comes as no surprise, as most practices were initially modelled on established procedures in this area (Esselink 2006). Web localization did not appear as an independent object of inquiry until the 2000s, when the number of web users increased fivefold.

The first attempts could be described as applied research into industry processes, best practices and the improvement of workflow models. The authors of these publications were practitioners and industry experts, and as with translation in general, their works were prescriptive and practical in nature (Chesterman and Wagner 2002; Gile 2010).[1] The scholars who looked into this phenomenon adopted the prevailing applied approach, combining localization procedural descriptions with best practices. This led to outstanding joint industry–academic collaborations helping to close the gap between the localization industry and the scientific community, as the volumes edited by Dunne (2006a; Dunne and Dunne 2011) or Reineke (2005) show. All the same, web localization was generally lumped together with software localization. Some journals that focused on localization also emerged, such as the *Localization Focus* and *Journal of Internationalization and Localization*. From the TS camp, research in the 2000s mostly revolved around theoretical studies (i.e. Sandrini 2005; Neuert 2007; Pym 2010), which we will define here as centred on 'intellectual processing of ideas', while some empirical research started to appear. Empirical research revolves 'around the collection and processing of data' (Gile 1998: 70) and starts from experimentation and observation. It can be considered as the main objective of TS according to its founding fathers, Holmes (1988/2000: 172) and Toury (1995), and it requires sound theoretical and methodological foundations, careful planning, rigour, systematic character and thoroughness. It also requires highly specialized researchers trained in research methods and the nature of empirical research, as well as a thorough critical understanding of the models, paradigms, and theories that underlie any project, as well as researchers' biases (Gile 2010).[2]

WEB LOCALIZATION AND INTERDISCIPLINARY RESEARCH

In planning research, it is necessary to remember that TS is an interdiscipline (Snell-Hornby 1988; Hatim and Munday 2004), nurtured by a multitude of imported and home-brewed paradigms, theories and models since the 1970s; theoretical models and methods are consistently borrowed and merged with existing ones. Interdisciplinarity obviously occupies a central role in web localization, whose practice reflects a unique convergence of fields: foreign languages, linguistics, computational linguistics, translation, computer science, desktop publishing, graphic design and layout, documentation science, information management, usability or international business

(Folaron 2006: 206). Web localization has thus brought new perspectives into TS that further validate Tymoczko's (2005: 1094) prediction that TS will become more interdisciplinary in the coming decades. Any new research needs to account for this interdisciplinary nature and attempt, when possible, to create links with related disciplines. This represents an exciting challenge for scholars embarking on web localization research. The relationship between interfacing disciplines here should not be fixed; rather, it represents a constant dynamic flux of ideas and exchanges (Munday 2012). Figure 6.1 represents the wide range of interactions and interdisciplinary synergies between TS as the parent discipline, Localization Studies, and the variety of disciplines they interface with. In the centre we find disciplines such as Linguistics or Sociology that interface with both TS and Localization, while at either end of the spectrum we find the disciplines that relate more to one than the other. For example, literary studies represent one of the most prolific points of departure for TS interdisciplinary research, while web accessibility only concerns web localization.

But we should be cautious about incorporating related disciplines, as interdisciplinarity can also constitute a threat – the more so if the partner discipline has greater financial means, status, or power (Gile 2004: 29). The

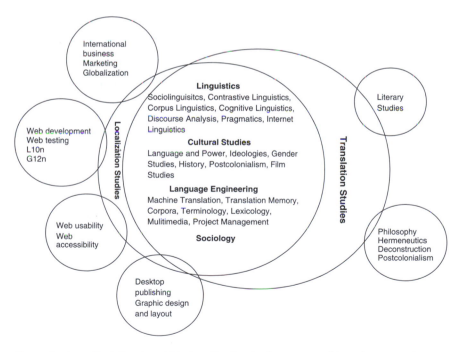

Figure 6.1 Interdisciplinarity within localization in the context of Translation Studies. Interdisciplinary map of TS adapted from Hatim and Munday (2004: 8)

problem can occur in this field, especially when some theoretical models used as points of departure dismiss translation as a less complex stage, reducing it to an equivalence-replacement operation.[3] The opposite is also true, as TS scholars have also partially integrated models and methods from other disciplines. Additionally, as is often pointed out, methods, models and procedures are frequently borrowed from associated disciplines without a full understanding of the partner discipline (Chesterman 2002). Collaboration is essential to producing interdisciplinary research. We should, however, embrace interdisciplinarity as 'it challenges the current conventional way of thinking by promoting and responding to new links between different types of knowledge and technologies' (Munday 2008: 14). The current multiplicity of approaches to web localization research testifies to this.

PLACING LOCALIZATION RESEARCH WITHIN TRANSLATION STUDIES

It is essential to place web localization research within its parent discipline as a sub-branch of TS. First and foremost, this can be done by placing potential projects within the general framework of the discipline laid out by the so-called founding father Holmes, and, secondly, by identifying the main research paradigms, models and methodologies within the discipline.

The seminal proposal of Holmes (1988/2000) is generally accepted as the foundation for modern TS (Gentzler 2001), despite multiple revisions, criticisms and additions (i.e. Sun and Shreve 2012). It is generally understood as a framework for dividing the labour among all researchers in this field (Toury 1995: 9), and as such, it makes a good starting point for mapping new research of existing trends. In general terms, Holmes subdivided the discipline into Pure and Applied TS (see Figure 6.2 for an adaptation of the map of Localization Studies). The general goals of the Pure branch are the description of translation phenomena and the establishment of general principles that can explain and predict them. This branch was further subdivided into Theoretical and Descriptive TS. Two sub-branches were proposed for the former: general and partial theories. General theories intend to cover, or account for, every type of translation and to make generalizations about translation as a whole.[4] Partial theories, on the other hand, are restricted according to different criteria: medium, area, rank, text type, time- and problem-restricted. Initially, it looked as if localization research would be part of the medium-restricted branch initially envisioned.[5] However, a closer look reveals that most theoretical research into web localization can generally be located in several categories in the proposed framework, which often leads to Holmes's map of TS being adapted to accommodate for new technological realities (Quah 2006; Vandepitte 2008). And Holmes himself insisted that more than one restriction can apply simultaneously, so partial theories pertaining to web localization can be medium-restricted and problem-restricted. Web localization as a whole can be of interest for most of the restricted areas, except for the time-restricted one, due to its relatively recent origin. As pointed out in Jiménez-Crespo (2011b), web localization studies can also help test general theories that claim to pertain to all translation phenomena.[6] So far, very few theoretical studies have focused on web localization *per se*, and most work has been carried out by Pym (i.e. 2004a, 2010, 2011a), while others have attempted to conceptualize this modality in light of existing functionalist theories (Sandrini 2005; Neuert 2007).

Empirical research falls mainly within Descriptive Translation Studies (DTS), whose objectives are the examination of the product, the function and the process of translation. These three foci lead to the subdivision of the discipline into Product-oriented, Function-Oriented and Process-Oriented DTS:

1. Product-oriented DTS focuses on existing translation, comparing and analysing single ST and TT pairs, multiple translations from a ST into one or more languages, etc. These types of studies cover the booming corpus-based translation studies often applied to web localization research.
2. Process-oriented DTS is concerned with the psychological component of translation, trying to find out what happens in the black box (Shreve and Diamond 1997) of the translator. This area has been increasingly explored empirically during the last decade, mostly using imported methodologies from experimental and cognitive psychology (i.e. Tirkkonen-Condit and Jääskeläinen 2010; Shreve and Angelone 2010; Alvstad *et al.* 2011).
3. Function-oriented DTS relates to the study of a translation's function in the sociocultural context of reception, focusing on the contexts of translations rather than the texts themselves. This area, which Munday (2008: 11) nowadays refers to as 'cultural-studies-oriented TS', has gained great popularity since what is known as the cultural (Bassnett and Lefevere 1990) and sociological (Wolf 2010) turns in TS. These new models focus on the larger context in which translation occurs, and both social and cultural issues are of interest, as they have been consistently highlighted in web localization research.

The theoretical and descriptive branches are not independent; rather, the findings of research in the latter feeds into the theoretical branch to develop or test a general or a partial theory of translation. Similarly, theoretical research can lead to testable hypotheses within the descriptive branch.

The last branch is the Applied TS (ATS), which focuses on performance rather than knowledge, and Holmes considered it as a branch 'of use'. Its objectives are related more to prescription than description, even though recently it has been recognized that descriptive studies are also needed within this branch (Ulrych and Anselmi 2008: 166). Holmes originally envisioned three main components in ATS: translation training, translation criticism, and translation aids. Holmes also mentioned translation policy, where translation scholars can advise on issues related to the role of translation in society, while recent publications suggest adding translation and localization management (Dunne and Dunne 2011). Holmes described this branch in less detail, as he was mostly concerned with providing the more scientific foundation for the discipline that the theoretical and descriptive branch provides. He predicted that TS is a field of pure research pursued for its own sake, quite apart from any direct practical application outside its own terrain. Its relationship with the pure branch is dialectical: applied research is always founded on theoretical knowledge and dependent on empirical descriptive data. In its turn, the applied branch provides materials for the other two branches. Nevertheless, Holmes assumed that there is no direct transfer between the descriptive TS and the applied branch, while Toury assumed that theoretical and descriptive studies would provide information to the applied branch in terms of prescriptive statements. The transfer of knowledge between these two branches has recently been the objective of further elaboration and reflection in publications (Rabadán 2010; Ulrych and Anselmi 2008; Scarpa *et al.* 2009). Another main difference between the ATS and DTS is the audience or users they address; professionals and practitioners are the core objective of ATS,[7] while scholars and researchers are targeted by theoretical and descriptive ones. The role of professionals and experts in the realm of ATS is always a matter of debate, mostly due to the pressure from this collective to convert research findings into applicable knowledge (Gile 2004). However, it should be mentioned that for our purposes, research carried out by an applied professional can be used as a prescriptive hypothesis for testing within the discipline, such as the study of whether breaking a cultural norm in a localized website will produce the expected undesired effect, or if a specific model used to produce a localized website, such as professional vs. volunteer-crowdsourced, is in fact more effective (Jiménez-Crespo 2013).

The nature of TS has changed due to the impact of technological developments, as seen throughout this book, and this has considerably changed its nature since Holmes first envisioned the map. Scholars have proposed changes to this framework, such as expansions (Hermans 1999; Munday 2012), to accommodate the impact of translation in technology (Quah 2006: 42) or to add localization management (Dunne and Dunne 2011: 6–8). For our purposes, it is of interest to review the adaptation proposed by Quah (2006) that incorporates technological developments, mostly in the translation aids section. Originally, translation aids were conceived as CAT translation tools, dictionaries and grammars. The proposed enlargement advocates a distinction between automatic translation tools (MT) and computer-aided translation tools, such as translation tools (TM, Terminology management tools), linguistic tools (dictionaries, glossaries, concordances, etc.), and localization tools (document management, project management). Quah indicates that nowadays most tools are multifunctional and combined, and obviously this trend will continue to evolve as current systems routinely incorporate MT within TM systems (see Chapter 8), and some are set up to allow for online collaboration by volunteers. It can be easily seen that within ATS, the translation aids section would be the one that would evolve and change the most, therefore needing constant research and updates.

One of the most interesting aspects of ATS is its full interdisciplinary nature. According to Rabadán (2010), this branch draws from other disciplines and partly relies on their procedures, borrowing models, theories and methodologies, and combining them with TS ones. For example, translation training relies heavily on general theories of teaching, and research on translation aids relies upon computational linguistics and other related areas. Applied research on web localization necessarily borrows from a wide array of technology-related areas, and will continue to do so. This is true of most research carried out at the crossroads between Computational Linguistics and TS at the Centre for Next Generation Localization or in the Localization Research Centre at the University of Limerick.

Mapping Localization Studies research into TS

The emergence of so-called 'Localization Studies' (Munday 2012) can easily be conceptualized as a sub-branch of general TS interfacing with and feeding off all the three branches of research but also incorporating connections with a number of new disciplines not previously connected to TS, such as information management or international business strategies. The framework to be proposed here can, as Toury (1995) points out, help 'separate the division of labour' among all researchers interested in this phenomenon. It can also assist in mapping existing research in the discipline from the last decade. In this proposal, Localization Studies could be divided into Pure and Applied LS. Pure LS would include a theoretical and a descriptive branch. The former would cover general theories of localization like those put forward by Pym (2004a, 2010), as well as partial theories restricted to a localization type (software, web localization, videogame localization, small device and app localization), rank, problem, text type or genre, etc. Descriptive LS could be divided between product-based, function-based and process-oriented.

Current research in web localization has largely focused on product-oriented studies using mostly corpus-based methodologies. One objective has been to examine proposed general tendencies of translations, such as conventionalization (Jiménez-Crespo 2009a) or explicitation (Jiménez-Crespo 2011b), strategies seen in websites when dealing with calquing, borrowing, or terminology (Diéguez 2008), or the adaptation claim by the localization industry (Jiménez-Crespo 2010a, 2012a). From a discourse-analysis perspective descriptive product-based studies have also contrastively examined the localization of a number of digital genres, such as institutional websites (Fernández Costales 2012), computer service websites

(Bolaños 2004; Bolaños *et al.* 2005), embassy websites (Pedrola 2009), corporate websites (Jiménez-Crespo 2008a) and/or non-profit websites (Jiménez-Crespo 2012a, 2012b).

Function-oriented studies focus on the sociological and cultural context of localization and are also steadily growing. Examples include Austermühl and Mirwald's (2010) study of sociological issues concerning the image of translators in localization industry publications, the study of the profile of localizers in the industry by Reineke and Sánchez (2005), and McDonough's culture-oriented approach to researching national identity in localized websites (McDonough 2006a, 2006b, 2010). Other examples of function-oriented studies relate to the new developments in crowdsourcing and volunteer translation and localization on the web (see Chapter 8). Finally, due to the relatively novel nature of process studies, no empirical process/cognitive studies have so far been carried out exclusively on web localization, although some have focused on the impact of technology such as TM on the process (O'Brien 2006; Torres-Hostench *et al.* 2010).

The proposed Applied LS covers a great deal of existing applied research on localization, even when many of the studies do not develop from, or necessarily share, TS models, methodologies or theories. The categories envisioned for ATS fit squarely into the pattern of current and future research needed on localization: localization training, localization evaluation (including quality) and translation and localization aids. We could also add localization management, given the current impact in the field (Dunne and Dunne 2011). As we have seen in previous chapters, research into these areas is steadily growing, and some of the findings of descriptive studies are being applied to localization training (Jiménez-Crespo and Tercedor 2012; Jiménez-Crespo 2008c), localization evaluation and quality (Jiangbo and Ying 2010; Jiménez-Crespo 2011a, 2009d; Pierini 2006), and localization tools and standards (i.e. Wright 2006; Filip 2012a).

Within the emerging field of Localization Studies the possibilities for research are still endless. Following the basic areas of research indicated by Williams and Chesterman for general TS (2002), LS could look to different phenomena such as:

- Text analysis and web localization
- Web localization Quality Assessment
- Localization of digital genres and other genres often embedded into websites
- Multimedia localization that includes the audiovisual component
- Localization and Translation technologies
- History and development of localization
- Ethics of localization
- Terminology and terminology management in localization

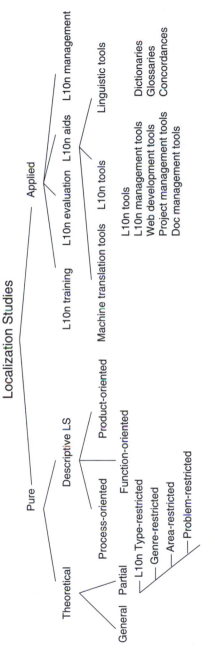

Figure 6.2 Proposed map of Localization Studies. Adapted from the map of TS from Holmes (1988) and Toury (1995: 10)

- Localization process and the cognitive translation process within localization
- Localization training
- The characteristics of the localization profession and its relationship to other translation job profiles.

And we could also add to the list, in combination with the proposed directions indicated by Folaron (2006: 206–11), the following:

- Localization management
- Globalization and Internationalization in web localization
- Information management and the life cycle of documents
- Localization and translation standards, how they impact the task, to what extent they are followed, etc.
- The non-professional, volunteer and crowdsourcing practices that are booming thanks to the Internet
- Web accessibility and localization (Jiménez-Crespo 2009e; Tercedor 2010)
- Usability research and the impact of localization.

However, the development of this discipline can only progress with sound research based on solid theoretical and research models that provide the necessary scientific rigour. Careful evaluation of the researcher's biases and preconceptions, as well as the paradigms and models, is essential when starting research on localization. It is therefore essential to review some basic notions in the discipline such as research models, designs and methodologies.

APPLYING RESEARCH MODELS AND PARADIGMS IN TRANSLATION STUDIES TO WEB LOCALIZATION RESEARCH

During the last four decades, Translation Studies has amassed a vast amount of knowledge, developed through theoretical, applied and, to a lesser extent, empirical research. The progression can be broadly described as leading from experiential/anecdotal prescription to conceptual/theoretical research and the introduction of the empirical paradigm in the 1980s. These should be considered as cumulative stages, as the scientific method relies on theories being empirically tested, while the findings provide feedback to existing theories or originate new ones. Additionally, applied research is eventually conducted to provide prescriptive recommendations based on empirical research and theoretical models. As with any new research, projects in web localization need to start from the existing context of the discipline(s) where it is located (Halverson 2010); also necessary is critical examination of the theoretical assumptions (or lack of them) that underlie that starting point, as they condition the project itself and the potential validity and reliability of the outcomes.

It is beyond the scope of this chapter to provide a comprehensive review. A number of TS publications offer detailed insights into the different theories (i.e. Baker and Saldanha 2008; Pym 2010; Gambier and van Doorslaer 2010; Malmkjaer and Windle 2011; Munday 2012), overviews of research in the discipline (Gile 2004), and the main research methodologies and models (Williams and Chesterman 2002; Orozco 2004; Neunzig 2011). The objective here is to provide a brief and concise overview of TS paradigms, models and directions to locate potential web localization research projects within this antecedent TS framework.

Translation paradigms

Generally speaking, there are two notions in TS literature that are useful in orienting research projects: translation models and translation paradigms. The general notion of the former was introduced by Thomas Kuhn (1962) to analyse major change processes in scientific disciplines. Within TS, paradigms have been defined as 'sets of principles that underline different theories . . . when we find ideas, relations and principles from which there is internal coherence and shared points of departure' (Pym 2010: 3). Examples of these ideas are the use in theories of terms such as 'source', 'target', 'equivalence' or 'translation function'. For example, some theories are based on natural or directional equivalence between source and target texts, while others, such as cognitive translatology, might completely disregard any type of equivalence relationships (Muñoz Martín 2009).[8] The first basic dichotomy of interest in TS is the distinction between the liberal arts and the empirical science paradigms (Gile 2004). The first is focused mostly on philosophical or hermeneutic research methods – the science of interpretation – while the latter is based on the natural science scientific paradigm. The beginnings of TS were clearly marked by the liberal arts paradigms that afforded researchers greater freedom to propose and argue theories, while the more empirical approach to translation research emerged in the 1980s. Nowadays it can be said that both paradigms co-exist within the discipline. These two paradigms should not be confused with the distinction between conceptual and empirical research. According to Williams and Chesterman (2002: 58), conceptual research aims to define and clarify concepts, to interpret or reinterpret ideas, to relate concepts to larger systems, to introduce new concepts or metaphors that allow a better understanding of the object of research. Empirical research, on the other hand, is geared towards generalization, prediction or explanation. It sets out to provide new data on which hypotheses can be tested or reformulated, to refine existing ones, to propose a new hypothesis and ways to test it, or even to suggest connections between hypotheses that can lead to new theories (Chesterman 2001). Both approaches are necessary in research, as nothing can be observed without any preliminary theory or concept of what is being observed. As an example, the definitions of concepts that have been previously analysed in this book – such as localization, text, genre or quality – are necessary to conduct rigorous research. Otherwise, how can a study focus on quality evaluation of localized texts, for example, if we do not have an operative definition of what a 'text' is? Furthermore, whether the definition or text model includes images, graphics and animations must be taken into account. A lack of concretization can result in the findings being impossible to replicate or challenge – a basic premise of the scientific method.

In his overview of translation theory, Pym presents the basic paradigms throughout the history of TS, such as theories based on natural and directional equivalence, purposes, descriptions, uncertainty, localization and cultural translation. He rightly mentions that the succession of paradigms within TS is not exclusive nor progressive, as, for example, we have witnessed in localization industry discourse a return to the 1960s natural equivalence paradigm (Pym 2010). All other paradigms can offer a foundation for specific research projects in web localization, with the exception of the natural equivalence paradigm whose theories might be said to be obsolete in TS. In fact, theories and models based on the paradigms of purpose, description and cultural translation underlie most web localization research. Identifying oneself with one paradigm does not mean that one has to fully subscribe to a single one, but rather:

> [W]e should feel free to move between the paradigms, selecting ideas that can help us solve problems. That is the way that I think translation theories should develop . . . there is no need to start [research] in any one paradigm.
>
> (Pym 2010: 165)

In any case, the most important issue would be to have the widest possible understanding of paradigms, approaches and models in order to research any specific research question that we might pursue.

Translation models

Discussions about translation or web localization also entail theorizations about different concepts and ideas employed, what they represent, why some problems should be solved in a specific way, etc. As we have seen, a common difference between views of localization is whether it is a part of translation or *vice versa*. All these underlying ideas can be considered as localization (or translation) models,[9] or, in other words, the interrelated networks of concepts that we use to discuss translation or localization (Pym 2010). Such models can conceal very powerful guiding ideas that condition our understanding of these phenomena. Different models can emphasize different guiding principles during the localization process: the source text, the client's instructions, equivalence, the effect on the user, adaptations, etc.

The basic difference between models and paradigms is that the latter represent the grouping of ideas underlying theories that only emerge once theories have been proposed or have been consolidated. Translation models are basically different from theories and paradigms in that they are less abstract (Chesterman 2000: 15), and they are understood as intermediary constructs between theories and actual data. Models provide the preliminary framework to orient the project and to provide conceptual tools.

One of the most renowned proposals in TS is the threefold classification of Chesterman (2000), according to which there are three main research models in the discipline:

1. The comparative model. In this model translations are aligned either with their source texts or with untranslated texts, and the analysis focuses on the relationship between them. Corpus studies and contrastive studies are examples of this model.
2. The process model. It focuses on different phases of the translation process. This model is represented by communicative approaches, and also by some cognitive approaches.
3. The casual model. In this model translations are regarded as caused by antecedent conditions and as causing effects on readers and cultures. This model is centred on the question of 'why' the translation or localization is the way it looks and what effect it might have on its audience, receiving society, culture, etc.; comparative and process models look into the questions of 'what', 'how' or 'when'. Causation is a very complex phenomenon, and Williams and Chesterman (2002) differentiate between three possible levels of causation: translation cognition, the translation task or the external conditions of the translation, and the sociocultural level, related to factors such as norms, traditions, history, ideology, power, economic goals, languages involved, etc.

Another complementary and useful distinction between translation research models is the didactic distinction offered by Josep Marco (2009) that, while including the previous models by Chesterman, acknowledges the different approaches or schools of thought in TS. These models are offered in order to make a 'closer connection between research method . . . and underlying theoretical approaches and conceptual tools' (2009: 15). In this proposal, Marco distinguishes between the following:

1. The textual descriptivist model, which combines notions from textually oriented theoretical approaches and Descriptive Translation Studies. Despite the differences between both approaches, Marco argues that the descriptive focus and text linguistic or discourse-analysis tools often converge in research. For example, textual analysis of translation always resorts to grammatical or lexical criteria. This is due to the fact

that DTS scholars often resort to linguistic categories in their research. It focuses on concepts such as translation techniques or shifts (the technique used by the translator to solve a specific problem, such as using calquing, modulation, addition or omission), constraints and norms. It is mostly influenced by Discourse Analysis, although it also has influences from other disciplines. Corpus-based translation studies are included in this model, as they are very closely connected both in theoretical assumptions and ultimate goals, differing only in the analytical tools used. It mainly focuses on the products of translations.

2. The cognitive-oriented model, which studies the translation process from a cognitive science or psycholinguistic perspective. It attempts to discover the processing happening in the black box (Shreve and Diamond 1997; Shreve and Angelone 2010). It focuses on the process of translation rather than the product, and uses methods usually borrowed from psycholinguistics, such as think aloud protocols, computer records, interviews and questionnaires. The methods are normally experimental.

3. The culturalist model, whose goal, according to Marco, is the study of the complex social, political, cultural and ideological forces which shape translation practices. It is related to the 'cultural turn' (Snell-Hornby 2006), and it attempts to uncover the socio-economical and political motivations hidden behind norms, rather than describe them as in the case of DTS. It uses a wide range of methods, interfacing with a number of antecedent disciplines, such as cultural studies, postcolonialism, gender studies, feminism, queer studies, etc.

4. The sociological model. It is often argued that this model is almost established in the discipline (Wolf 2007, 2010). It draws from sociology of professions to describe sectors of the translation profession based mostly on concepts proposed by major scholars such as Bourdieu (1972). It analyses the profession using notions such as 'habitus' or the totality of professional dispositions and attitudes of agents, such as translators or localizers, within a given field of practice. This habitus is acquired by professionals by 'inculcation in a set of social practices' (Inghilleri 2005: 75). The object of study of this model is not the translations *per se*, but rather, the translators and agents involved in the process and their relations to the wider field, understood here as a historically constituted activity with its own institutions and laws of functioning. According to Wolf (2010: 29), the sociocultural model:

> comprises the cluster of questions dealing not only with the networks of agents and agencies and the interplay of their power relations, but also the social discursive practices which mold the translation process and which decisively affect the strategies of a text to be translated.
>
> (Wolf 2010: 29)

Marco indicates that all three models previously proposed by Chesterman – comparative, process and casual – can be found in each of his proposed models based on schools of thought in TS.

PLANNING RESEARCH IN WEB LOCALIZATION: RESEARCH METHODOLOGIES AND RESEARCH DESIGN

In planning research, in addition to the epistemological or conceptual and theoretical foundations previously discussed, the basic issues may be summarized as:

1. coming up with tentative research questions,
2. selecting the most appropriate research methodologies, and
3. developing the design of the research project.

The global process normally involves different stages: the conceptual stage in which the study is planned, the methodological stage and the analytical stage. This is a circular process in that the final stage goes back to the conceptual during interpretation of the analysis of the data. At this stage, hypotheses or research questions can be supported, rejected or redefined, or new ones might emerge. Figure 6.3. shows the research stages for empirical research design in TS by Orozco (2004).

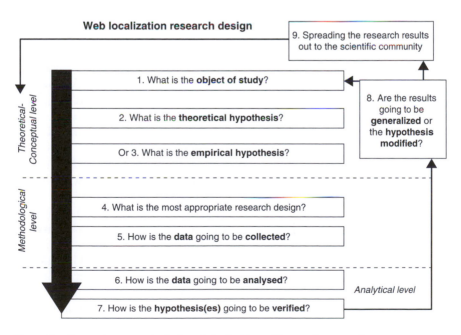

Figure 6.3 Stages in research design. Adapted from Orozco (2004: 99)

The first step consists in narrowing down a specific issue that is going to be researched: in other words, the specific articulation of the question that is going to be studied (Halverson 2009). It can be articulated as a claim or hypothesis that will be tested, or as a question that is going to be tentatively answered. For example, a study of internationalization strategies in web localization, such as Jiménez-Crespo (2010b), can start with the research question (What are the strategies of companies regarding the use of international Spanish versions?) or from a hypothesis (Large corporations will favour an international Spanish version of their websites for all Spanish-speaking countries instead of local ones). Research questions emerge through two distinctive methods, induction or deduction. With inductive methods, questions emerge after analysis or observation of the data or phenomenon (i.e. recurrent errors or some types of localized errors), whereas with deduction the point of departure is a theory or hypothesis that will be somehow tested (i.e. the application of XYZ evaluation models will reduce errors in localization). This process can lead to theoretical or empirical hypotheses. Research questions determine and guide a great number of steps in the process, such as the literature review, the design of the study, the data to be collected (if any), the analysis, etc. Online TS bibliographies such as BITRA[10] or the Benjamins Bibliography of Translation Studies can assist in the literature review process. Questions should be clear, concise, linked to established theories and studies in the field, not too broad or narrow, and have potential to make a contribution to the existing body of knowledge (Bryman 2004). According to the often-used summary by Chesterman (2001), the types of hypotheses that can constitute a research question can be:

(a) Conceptual. They include interpretative hypotheses, in which X can be interpreted as Y, or others more related to theoretical research
(b) Empirical. They can be divided into:
    1. Descriptive hypotheses that intend to generalize: e.g. all X have feature Y/ belong to class Y.
    2. Explanatory hypotheses: e.g. X is caused/made possible by Y.
    3. Predictive hypotheses: e.g. in conditions ABCD, X will (likely) occur.

This will lead to research questions that may in principle be explanatory in nature (why?) or descriptive (what is going on?).

Once the research question is formulated, the next step would be to select the most appropriate research methodology(ies). This notion can be defined in terms of the 'process of research', i.e. the planning and carrying out of each stage of a scientific study (Orozco 2004: 99). The methodology is clearly determined by the type of question, and whether qualitative or quantitative methods will be used, or a combination of both. TS has imported and adapted a range of research methods from the social sciences (Bryman 2004), and the following could be applicable to web localization research:

1. Documentary research methods: analysis of existing documents that contain information about the phenomenon we wish to study. Payne and Payne (2004) describe the documentary method as the techniques used to categorize, investigate, interpret and identify the limitations of physical sources – most commonly written documents, whether in the private or public domain. The localization industry has produced plenty of primers, documentation, best practices, etc., such as those by the LISA and GALA organizations. Research into the documentation produced by the localization industry has been used in analysis of the image of translators (Austermühl and Mirwald 2010).

2. Observationalist research methods. These involve the direct observation of subjects – either translators during their tasks or end users in their use of localized websites – in a manner similar to Usability studies (i.e. all of Jacob Nielsen's studies). Reception studies in web localization could have a great impact on issues related to localization quality and the usability of localized websites.

3. Interactionist research methods. Here the investigator interacts with informants by means such as questionnaires or interviews, and can focus on all the potential participants in the whole web localization cycle, from commissioners, initiators and localizers all the way to users and receivers of translations and localization (e.g. O'Brien 2012; Reineke and Sánchez 2005)

4. Ethnographic research methods. These methods require the immersion of the investigator in the translator's community, either as an overt monitoring agent or a 'covert' observer. Studies of web localization can focus on translators' and localizers' work conditions or the actual inter-actions between agents in the global localization process.

5. Quantitative research methods. Empirical quantitative methods are mostly related to corpus studies in TS. A number of studies have compiled extensive corpora of websites, both original and localized, that have looked into a number of research questions (see above).

6. Experimental research methods. These rely on controlled experimental conditions that involve subjects, either translators themselves compared to novices, bilinguals or general population. Most experimental studies in translation have been devoted to uncovering the hidden processes in the 'black box' during translation processing, and lately some studies have also focused on the impact of technology, both TM and MT, in translation tasks. These studies normally use spy software that capture all typing and/or online search behaviours as well as a potential triangu-lation with eye movement (O'Brien 2006). As previously mentioned, no

studies on web localization *per se* have adopted an experimental approach but, nevertheless, the findings from all experimental studies on translation are of great interest in the study of cognitive issues related to localization processes, such as the review of professional vs. novice performance described in Chapter 7.

It should be borne in mind that all models are complementary, and in all methods different translation models can be applied. No social research method excludes other research methods. For example, current quantitative corpus-based research that seeks to draw inferences from the process itself resorts to triangulation, that is, using corpus studies from an inductive approach and later testing potential claims of hypothesis through subject experimentation with eye-tracking and keystroke-logging. This type of triangulation is normally needed in cognitive approaches (Alvstad *et al.* 2011).

Once the research question and the methodology used have been established, the next step in the research cycle would be the research design itself. In empirical research, we can find the different categories set out by Bryman (2004): experimental, quasi-experimental, cross-sectional (corpora), longitudinal, case study and comparative. The difference between experimental and quasi-experimental is that in the former the subject groups are randomly assigned, while in quasi-experimental ones groups are divided according to naturally occurring categories, such as professional localizers vs. localization students. Cross-sectional design entails collecting data from more than one case at one point in time, to collect a body of data that is quantifiable and qualitative in connection to more than one variable, enabling patterns of association to be observed (Bryman 2004). Corpus studies are considered a case of cross-sectional studies. Longitudinal cases entail collecting data over time. An example is Jiménez-Crespo's (2010b) study to review the evolution of localization strategies in different dialectal varieties of Spanish by 100 of the largest US companies. A case study entails the detailed and intense analysis of a single case, such as examining the use of certain translation strategies in specific localized websites. Case studies are of special interest for web localization research, and this design has often been used in the area, including for the first studies of web localization, in which the dialectal variation of terminology used in the Mercedes website was analysed (Bouffard and Caignon 2006). Some other studies, such as the Pierini's (2006) study of website quality in localized tourist sites, can also be considered case studies. They often include as much information as possible about the case under investigation and tend to describe the context and setting in which the case occurred. The main issue with case studies is that the results often tend to imply some sort of generalization, and this is one of the main problems associated with this type of design. According to Bryman (2004: 52), another potential issue is the tendency to draw conclusions from extremely limited samples. Instead, the issues to consider in case studies are related to the quality of the theoretical reasoning behind them rather than quantification or potential generalizations. Finally, comparative design involves the comparison of two cases, and often this design is combined with the other types above.

PLANNING RESEARCH INTO WEB LOCALIZATION: A SUMMARY AND CHECKLIST

Having briefly reviewed the issues related to research questions, methodologies and design, we can summarize the questions that need be addressed during the planning of any empirical research project, as indicated by Chesterman (2001: 22):

- Research question/aim: Clearly stated? Why is this a good question/an important or interesting aim?
- Other relevant research: How well can you relate what you are doing to what others have done?
- Hypothesis: Are you starting or concluding with a specific hypothesis? What kind of hypothesis is it? Why is it interesting/important? Is it well justified?
- Theoretical model: Why did you choose a particular theoretical model or approach/a particular variant of that model? What about other possibilities? Why did you reject them? Have you adapted the model at all? Why?
- Central concepts and categories: Adequately defined? Justified against alternative concepts, categories and definitions? What kind of categories? What kind of classification?
- Material: What is your empirical material? Why did you choose it? How did you collect it? Is it representative?
- Relationship between variables: What kind of relationship are you looking for/do you think you have found? Between what variables, exactly?
- Counter-evidence: Considered? Borderline cases dealt with adequately? Counter-arguments? Alternative explanations?
- Reliability: Is the analysis reliable? Explicit enough to be replicable? Calculations accurate? Classifications consistent? Statistics appropriate?
- Validity: Are the conclusions valid? Hypotheses supported or not? Adequate evidence? Logical argument?
- Follow-up: Now what?
- Implications: So what?

For anyone embarking on research, it is of great interest to analyse several previous studies to discern and find answers to all the questions previously stated. This is a good exercise that helps to develop the ability to plan rigorous studies and make a contribution to the body of knowledge on web localization phenomena.

MAIN CHALLENGES IN WEB LOCALIZATION RESEARCH

Research into web localization entails challenges and difficulties that concern both the conceptual-theoretical and the methodological level, mostly related to:

1. the theoretical models employed
2. methodologies, and
3. technologies used for data collection and analysis.

This section focuses on challenges that are specific to web localization research and are not necessarily equally shared with other types of research. Consequently, they require the adaptation of existing methodologies and/or the development of novel approaches. This should not discourage anyone from research in this area as, given the scope of web localization and the relative lack of research, any type of rigorous and solidly conducted research will be most welcome to the scientific community.

The challenges in theoretical research, including applied research that analyses, improves or describes best practices and workflow models in the industry, concern issues such as:

1. the models used
2. the definition of concepts, and
3. the interdisciplinary context in which localization occurs.

The adoption of a model or a set of related models in interdisciplinary efforts represents a cornerstone of research, as it guides the type of analysis and the interpretation of the findings in the study. Interdisciplinary approaches in this area often fail to adopt a well-defined theoretical model of translation, and consequently we tend to find an oversimplification of translation phenomena. The opposite can also be true, if TS scholars do not possess a full understanding of the models from partner disciplines. Wider partnerships for conducting research, involving both scholars in related areas and industry-academic collaboration could help produce research that fulfils the theoretical and conceptual demands and does not stem from obsolete theoretical models such as natural equivalence. Similarly, and depending on the goals of research projects, the epistemological or conceptual foundations should be clearly stated. For example, what is understood by 'adaptation', 'term', 'segment' or 'text'? Why was this definition chosen and not others? What is the unit of analysis and why? Are we best served by using these definitions and this model?

The methodological challenges are equally significant when embarking on empirical research on web localization. Most of them lie in:

1. technological issues
2. access to data and copyright
3. the compilation of whichever type of data the research question and method require
4. its analysis.

Some methods can be easily applied without any adaptations, such as interventionist methods in which the main data collected are interviews and questionnaires. Often, studies have used questionnaires emailed to different agents in the localization world. As already mentioned, experimental studies on web localization have not taken off yet, and the main issues in this area are access to the intended subjects and the costly technology used to capture data, such as spy software (Translog or Proxy), eye tracking, etc.

Most empirical studies on web localization have so far focused on the product, the translated or localized texts themselves, and two methodological approaches can be identified:

1. retrieving data from live websites online without downloading a corpus
2. compiling web corpora of different kinds according to explicit criteria to account for the representativeness requirement (Biber 1988; Kenny 2001).[11]

The first type of analysis accounts mostly for case studies and focuses on finding data that illustrate a specific point. The issue with this methodology is that the dynamic nature of web information adds a temporal dimension to the study. The specific date and time of the data-collection process should be clearly indicated, as the issue of replicability might be compromised once the data are modified or disappear. One potential solution to this issue is the introduction of novel Internet time machines or archives that allow one to travel back to snapshots of different websites, such as Waybacktime machine (http://archive.org/web/web.php).[12] For example, it is possible to review whether the quality problems in localized versions of the main Colgate site were modified throughout time or how a localized version evolved over the years.

A web corpus can be defined as a body of 'texts put together in a principled way and prepared for computer processing' (Johansson 1998: 3). In general, linguists and translation researchers have been increasingly interested in the web as a source of linguistic data (Baroni and Ueyama 2006), and it is necessary to clearly separate three types of corpora. 'Web corpus' generally refers to the following related concepts (Fletcher 2007, 2011):

1. a static corpus with a Web interface,
2. one compiled from websites or pages, and
3. the body of freely available online texts accessed directly as a corpus.

In the first type, texts are not specifically written for the web but simply stored in a format that can be retrieved through a web interface. This should be the case with most current large corpora, such as the BCN, the CREA corpus of Spanish or the Corpus of North American English. The second and third types are of interest to empirical web localization studies, since they help distinguish between current practices and, in the case of the second type, using the 'Web for Corpus' (WfC), as a source of machine-readable texts for corpus compilation, and with the third type using the 'Web as Corpus' (WaC), that is, consulted directly for localization practice or research purposes. This should be the case when Google is used to check any term or phrase directly, as well as the use of engines that use the web as a corpus (Webcorp, Webconc). The types of WfC that might be compiled can be either monolingual, parallel or comparable (Baker 1995; Kruger and Munday 2011).

Parallel corpora consist of source texts aligned with their translations into one or several languages, while web-comparable corpora consist of localized websites alongside non-translated similar websites. Parallel corpora require alignment, either manual or automatic of source texts with their target texts, a process hampered by the fact that many websites are not normally fully localized, or that pages might show structural differences (Jiménez-Crespo 2012a). For example, localized versions of websites might only incorporate 70% of the source website translated, depending on the localization level. The only possible solution is to pair those pages or sections of the websites that are localized with the source ones, documenting and quantifying the existing degree of localization. Parallel corpora also align textual segments, and the current developments in multimodal corpora would be highly beneficial to account for non-textual elements in websites. Comparable corpora, on the other hand, do not require alignment, as they represent two distinct textual populations, original and localized websites. For both types of corpora, the compilation process entails technical difficulties related to:

- The dynamic nature of websites: The dynamicity of websites is probably the most complex issue, as many websites require active connections to servers in order to display properly, and novel server-based architectures mean that a single website *per se* might not exist but, rather, that different ones are assembled out of content according to the user or browser preferences. Nevertheless, despite differences in content, the basic architecture or hypertextual structure of the digital genre in question is usually similar – navigation menus or sitemaps, for example. Studies can still focus on the common aspects of the genre structure.

The dynamic nature of websites represents a challenge to translation theory in general, as the notion of static text that underlies translation and corpus-based TS does not exist in this case (see Chapter 3). One common solution is to compile corpora out of textual segments of websites, such as legal texts, navigation menus or news posted on them. However, using this methodology might pose problems for generalizations, given that localizers normally work on all types of critical vs. low-frequency or less critical segments while processing websites. A common approach is to download 'content text' from websites (i.e. Jiménez-Crespo 2013), without navigation menus or highly interactive segments. This is often the approach taken when the object of study is not localization as such, but web corpus compilation and use in translation.

- The download process, the extent to which the websites are downloaded and whether all types of multimedia content are included or not constitute another issue. Stripping textual website components from their presentation and other interactive, visual and multimedia elements is a common approach, but it does entail compromising the multimodal nature of texts. It also does not allow for a complete analysis of the text as users will receive it. Some studies have included the multimodal aspect of websites in their analysis, like Pedrola (2009), but in this study a corpus was not downloaded but consulted online. Also, given that websites represent repositories of information or open structures, some elements are often left out, such as .pdf documents, as they represent printed e-texts that the party responsible for the website wants to make available online. The download process should occur after careful selection of the websites to obtain a representative sample of the population under study. It can normally be accomplished using download engines such as Httrack,[13] ideally on a synchronic basis.
- Encoding difficulties. These often relate to the fact that different websites use different encoding, resulting in problems once texts with different encodings are mixed and then analysed with lexical analysis tools. Normally, most websites might use Unicode, but some might use older versions. This problem is especially relevant for languages with diacritical signs or character sets that do not appear in English.
- Copyright issues. This is a recurring issue in most corpus compilations (Olohan 2004: 48). Normally websites incorporate legal terms that specifically address the written consent needed to use and download the materials in the website (Jiménez-Crespo 2011c). Nevertheless, it is often impossible to get in touch with the party responsible for providing copyright clearance.

In Jiménez-Crespo and Tercedor (2010) we addressed some of the other challenges in the compilation and analysis of web corpora for empirical translation, some of which have also been covered here in previous chapters, such as the difference between printed texts posted online and digital texts created directly for web distribution, the adoption of digital genre models to define the population under study, genre embedding issues that hamper the compilation due to multiple potential genres within a site, such as flash advertising, movie clips, etc. Some other issues that have been reviewed relate to the analytical stage, like the hypertextual nature of websites resulting in lexical repetition, due to the inclusion of hypertextual or navigational maps in each page of the website to enhance internal coherence. Thus, lexical analyses of web corpora often show that lexical items related to the super-structure of a website are the most frequent items. A possible solution to this is to include an additional analysis in which all the terminology in navigation menus is added to a stop list, a list of words that corpus analysis tools ignore.

SUMMARY

This chapter started from the premise that the lack of theoretical research on basic issues in web localization has somewhat hindered the development of empirical research in the field. After examining the significance of inter-disciplinarity in TS and web localization, we reviewed Holmes's map of TS as a way to provide continuity within the discipline for future projects. This chapter also proposed a tentative map of the emerging Localization Studies built upon one from the parent discipline. As a guide for anyone embarking on web localization research, the basics for planning any project were presented, such as the main translation paradigms, models, research designs and methodologies. Existing studies and trends in web localization were offered as illustrations throughout the chapter. The chapter ends with a discussion of the main challenges in web localization research with an emphasis on corpus-based studies.

FURTHER READING

Required reading for anyone attempting to venture into web localization research are basic translation theory monographs, such as Munday (2012) and Pym (2010). Another key item is the basic introduction to research in Translation Studies by Williams and Chesterman (2002). Numerous other publications by Chesterman provide a basic framework for planning and implementing research projects (2000, 2001, 2002), as does the last chapter of Munday's introduction (2012: 295–310). For general methodology and research design, see Orozco (2004) and Neunzig (2011). For useful commen-taries on Holmes's and Toury's maps, see Munday (2012: 15–23) and Quah (2006). For a full development of all potential research opportunities within the discipline, see Vandepitte's (2008) ontology for Translation Studies. Given the prominence of applied research in this field from professional perspectives, see Rabadán (2010) or Scarpa *et al.* (2009) on how findings from ATS can travel to the Theoretical Pure and Descriptive branches of the discipline. For basic understanding of corpus-based research, see Baker (1995), Laviosa (2002), Olohan (2004), Mahadi *et al.* (2010) or Kruger and Munday (2011). Jiménez-Crespo and Tercedor (2010) review the main theoretical and methodological issues in web corpus research on web localization. See Fletcher (2011) for an overview of web corpora, and the *International Handbook of Internet Research* (Hunsinger *et al.* 2010) for an outline of models and methods in the area. Borja *et al.* (2009) offer an account of research methodologies using specialized genres. Folaron (2006) offers interesting directions for research in TS, as also does the introduction to Jiménez-Crespo (2011c).

Part III

LOCALIZATION AND THE FUTURE

7

WEB LOCALIZATION AND TRAINING

This new translation modality requires the development of training models that can help prepare the next generation of localization experts. This chapter begins with an overview of intensive research into translation training (i.e. Kiraly 2000; González Davis 2004; Kelly 2005), expertise in translation (i.e. Shreve 2006a; Jääskeläinen 2010) and translation competence (Bell 1991; PACTE 2001, 2005, 2009, 2011), moving on to the basis for planning and implementing translation education programmes globally. After reviewing the ambiguous status of professional localizers *vis-à-vis* translators, it continues with a proposed model of 'localization competence' that builds upon translation competence research. Localization competence is understood as a specialized subset of general translation competence with larger technological, management, textual and genre components. It will be argued that the shift toward web-based information means that handling web-based texts will be a core competence for all future translators. Given the reality of the localization profession, this chapter discusses how to accommodate the proposal for two pathways for developing localization expertise: progressing from general translation trainee to localizer (including the treatment of textual translation as a component), and from localization engineer or expert (who only deals with engineering and management issues) to web localizer. It ends with a discussion of how to build localization training programmes based on the proposed notion of competence.

WEB LOCALIZATION AND TRAINING

As the significance and volume of web content continues to increase, processing texts created for web distribution can no longer be considered a peripheral task for most translators but, rather, as a core component of their work. Web localization has effectively started to extend beyond the highly specialized niche of web localizers, as processing all sorts of text for web distribution is now considered a highly desirable skill for future translators (Jiménez-Crespo 2011e). Training needs will therefore continue to increase; not only will the highly specialized model in which localizers work with complex websites with automated CMS systems continue, but most translators will need to tackle all sorts of web texts and genres, such as smaller texts posted online or incorporated to databases for web distribution. Training efforts in this area have suffered from the lack of conceptual consensus we have seen before, and so the first step towards web localization training is to define the very nature of localization, how it relates to other translation modalities and specializations, and what the role is of the professional 'localizer', as opposed to a 'localization engineer', 'technical translator', 'localization manager' or 'technical translator'. Without a clear consensus on what localization expertise entails, what makes a 'localizer' different from a 'translator', and/or what skills different agents in the localization process possess, comprehensive efforts to build training models can hardly succeed. We have already discussed some of these issues previously. The present chapter reviews current trends and research in translation and localization didactics and proposes a scalable flexible model for web localization training based on current research into translation competence (PACTE 2001, 2005, 2011; Göpferich 2009), translation expertise (Shreve 2006a) and translation competence acquisition (Kiraly 2000).

At first glance, localization training seems as polarized as many other issues: industry approaches often highlight the technological component as the main distinguishing feature when compared to 'regular' translation. As a result, training normally focuses on knowledge of tools, technological processes and workflow management, giving procedural technological knowledge preference over other considerations – something often seen in the language-neutral setting in which these courses take place. This knowledge is supposed to be the core competence of a professional localizer in light of the industry discourse that separates regular translation from the fancier and more desirable localization, understood as a translation + technology model (Quirion 2003; Pym 2006; Austermühl and Mirwald 2010). Several training bodies and institutions have emerged offering courses, seminars and certifications, such as TILP, The Localization Institute or the SDL Trados certification, that provide state-of-the-art training in the use of the latest technology tools.

On the other hand, TS academics often argue that their objective should be not to 'train' students through compartmentalized workshops on small technological components but rather, to 'fully educate' future localizers (Folaron 2006; Pym and Windle 2011b). This argument resonates with the recurrent debate between professionals and academics on the significance of translation theory and the relative inability of academic institutions to train students for the real-world market (Pym and Windle 2011b; Gouadec 2007). We would like to argue that this distinction between 'training' and 'education' often found in TS (Pym 2011b; Angelelli 2005; Bernardini 2004) represents one of the main starting points for conceptualizing the discussion on the didactics of localization. The goal of translator education, according to Bernardini (2004: 19–20), is to promote the growth of the individual, to develop cognitive capacities, and 'those attitudes and predispositions that will put [the individual] in a position to cope with the most varying (professional) situations'. Translation training aims to 'prepare learners to solve problems that can be identified in advance through the application of pre-set, or "acquired" procedures'. The former is generative, as it aims at developing 'the ability to employ available knowledge to solve new problems, and to gain new knowledge as the need arises', while the latter is cumulative. Folaron (2006: 204–5) specifically reviews the benefits of education instead of training for localization, highlighting the development of cognitive skills related to logic, reasoning, complex problem solving or conceptualization. Translator education is also related to the ability to learn and the ability to adapt to how learning processes occur (Wright 2004), a necessary skill in the ever-changing world of technological innovation. These different approaches do not necessarily contradict each other; rather, they represent complementary perspectives on the education of competent future localizers.

The interest in closing the existing gap currently falls mainly on the institutional side, with more and more translation scholars and researchers advocating a closer connection between research and the real job market. In the introduction to a special issue on professionalism in translation, Jääskeläinen *et al.* indicated this pressing need to move general translation education closer to the real world.

> The links between research and the reality of the translation market may need critical scrutiny in terms of how we define our concepts, how we design and implement research, how we use research findings to bring about changes as well as how we educate future translators.
>
> (Jääskeläinen *et al.* 2011: 145)

However, in the case of localization, it seems that the industry discourse exerts a more powerful influence on institutional education than *vice versa* (Pym and Windle 2011b). Web localization training is often incorporated in undergraduate courses covering the loose umbrella of translation technology, often including translation memories, audiovisual translation, localization tools, etc. In her review of translation technology teaching, Alcina indicates that 'the translation of websites. . . requires translators to have a wide, thorough knowledge of computer science of the kind that was previously possessed only by specialists' (2008: 80). At first glance, this approach is not much different from professional training approaches.[1] Nevertheless, in the course of their studies translation students seeking a university degree acquire a wide range of competences that complements the technological skills acquired in web localization courses (Quirion 2003; Austermühl 2006), creating a continuum on the path towards advanced localization expertise.

LOCALIZATION AND THE TRANSLATION PROFESSION

The world of professional localization emerged in the 1980s mostly through in-house training of existing translators or multilingual developers in reaction to the constant challenges posed by technological innovation. These localizers were normally trained on the job (Esselink 2006), with companies that had large stakes in localization dedicating resources to localization training. Ever since then, the localizer has had a real and distinct professional role (Gouadec 2007; Schäler 2010). A quick look at technology job portals such as Dice.com shows this. It was often pointed out that many translators acquired advanced technological skills in order to move up to the more desirable and better-paid area of localization and, once they achieved it, they firmly defended their separate professional status against regular translators. In the same fashion, as many translators shifted towards management or QA positions, translators and localizers filled the positions opening up in localization management and QA specialities, including the new area of localization engineering. A debate then ensued on the specialized nature of localizers, mostly regarding the extent to which technological, management, engineering, or QA tasks are part of the localization profession, as opposed to that of regular translators. Gouadec (2007) indicates that the drive to separate localizers from translators is driven mostly by marketing and self-appraisal motives – localization represents, after all, a translation modality that requires specialized technological skills. Nevertheless, localization engineering and localizers embody distinct job profiles within the global localization cycle (Esselink 2002).[2]

Another interesting debate involving the status of localizers in the translation profession is whether the recurring practice of extracting textual elements from localization and then sending them to freelance translators justifies the separation between regular translation and localization itself (Quirion 2003; Austermühl 2006). Nowadays, web localization is normally performed by localizers using translation technology and management tools with different degrees of separation between tasks depending on the project, setting, company, level of professionalization, etc. For example, Gouadec (2007: 43–5) identifies four different professional profiles in the course of a web localization project: localizer, project manager, developer and quality assurance operator. In his review of the web localization cycle 29 different steps are identified in the standard overall project, ten of them being similar to other translation tasks, while the other 19 can be either performed by the localizer, managers, developers or QA operators. Gouadec rightly indicates that the localizer him/herself can perform any and all the tasks required for a web localization project. In the case of the more complex process of software localization (Esselink 2006), the collaboration between localizers and other technical agents is required. It can then be argued that it is precisely here that the frequent confusion arises in identifying the localizer's skills, the potential merging of management, QA and engineering tasks in web localization projects. Websites range from those of highly complex multinational corporations to smaller more static websites of small companies, such as restaurants or small hotels. One of the obvious ways to clarify this confusion is to identify the role of the localizer as a translator who possesses an expandable degree of technological and management competence, ranging from the combination of advanced translation competence – handling technical, legal, advertising, literary, scientific texts, etc. – with basic localization technology tools up to advanced knowledge of localization and terminology management tools and processes, QA tools and procedures, etc. Thus, depending on the situation or hosting organization, localizers' profiles may vary.

In any case, it is clear that the two main components of any professional localizer are an advanced translation competence and a degree of technological and management skills, some of which – such as advanced use of translation memory tools or dealing with tagged texts – might be shared with other translation modalities. Professional localization can then be conceived as an extension or addition to general translation competence, and therefore research into translation competence is key to studying the definition of expert localizers' skills.

TRANSLATION COMPETENCE, COMPETENCE-ACQUISITION AND EXPERTISE IN TRANSLATION (AND LOCALIZATION) TRAINING

Research into the didactics of translation and interpreting has been based upon the notions of translation and interpreting competence, as well as the interrelated notion of competence acquisition. This competence is assumed to be different from natural translation (Harris 1977; Harris and Sherwood 1978), it is mostly operative knowledge – knowledge about how to do something – rather than declarative knowledge – knowledge about something (Hurtado 2001; PACTE 2011, 2005). It is also considered expert knowledge (Shreve 2006a), a notion that in the field of cognitive psychology is defined as a 'consistently superior performance in a domain' (Ericsson 2006: 3). This expert knowledge has to be consciously developed through systematic training and 'deliberate practice' (Shreve 2006a). Translation competence relates to translation expertise in that the former refers to an overall body of knowledge needed to 'professionally' translate, while expertise focuses on the actualization or realization of this competence: that is, the actual performance. Over the last two decades the notion of translation competence has been extensively researched from theoretical and empirical perspectives, but to date there is no consensus on the different components that make up this abstract notion. One of the largest empirical efforts examining the components and development of translation competence is the PACTE research group, whose model can be considered as one of the most complete so far. Its framework will be used later in this chapter to propose a holistic model for localization competence (see below).

In parallel with the emergence of translation competence research, the tentative notion of 'localization competence' also appeared (Wright 2004; Pym 2006; Folaron 2006; Jiménez-Crespo and Tercedor 2012). In tune with research on general translation competence, research on the different components and skills that professional localizers possess (as opposed to bilingual regular translators or translator trainees) could lead to an empirically grounded model beyond experiential or anecdotal approaches based on knowledge of technology tools. This emphasis on technology leads to atheoretical localization competence models in which technological skills are added to bilingual skills (and not localization engineering or project management *per se*). Nevertheless, if this technological knowledge is not accumulated on top of specialized translation competence in its wider sense, including cross-cultural, cross-linguistic, communicative or textual skills, the resulting profile is simply a localization engineer, localization manager or a bilingual natural translator without specialized translation competence. In the often changing world of localization, a prototypical global model of what professional localizers can do or perform constitutes a prerequisite to organizing training programmes. For example, this effort is carried out in the description of competencies within Masters that include localization in the common European Union educational space. This prototypical model can initially be deducted, as indicated by Wright (2004), from interviews with leading companies in the field as carried out by LISA in 2000, or optimally by a combination of industry and academic approaches that combine real-world experience, theoretical and future empirical studies using professionals, translators not specialized in localization and translation trainees (Jiménez-Crespo and Tercedor 2012). Additionally, the cognitive approach to expertise can be highly beneficial in this case. In this approach, research can focus on the prototypical problems encountered by experts in the field and what type of strategies are applied or can be applied (Shreve 2006a).[3] This interrelates a great number of skills and rests on complex cognitive processing, making it harder to justify training that incorporates exclusive technological training: experts know a lot more than just how to use some tools; they know, for example, how to solve complex problems (including identifying the right person in the team) by applying problem-solving strategies to a wide array of potential translation, technological, procedural, problems, etc.

A review of experimental research findings into what professional translators can do, as opposed to bilinguals or trainees (see Göpferich and Jääskeläinen (2009) or Pym and Windle (2011b)), can shed some light as to what makes an expert in the field. Obviously, many of the features are also essential to defining professionalism in localization. Professional translators can:

1. Use top-down processing (macro-strategies), moving constantly between the micro and the macro level and referring more to the translation purpose, an essential skill in localization due to the potential segmentation and lack of context due to CMS and translation memory;
2. Use more periphrasis and fewer literal calquing strategies;
3. Process larger translation units;
4. Spend longer reviewing their work at the post-drafting phase but making fewer changes when reviewing;
5. Rely more on encyclopaedic knowledge;
6. Express more principles and personal theories, essential for justifying certain decisions and strategies to a localization team;
7. Incorporate the client in the risk-management processes;
8. Automate some complex tasks but also shift between automated routine tasks and conscious ones;
9. Display more realism, confidence and critical attitudes in decision-making;
10. Read the text differently from monolingual readers, based on the task that they are going to perform later.

Let's review in greater depth the notion of translation competence in order to propose a tentative model of localization competence.

Translation competence

Translation competence and its acquisition occupy a central role in the development of TS and its didactic applied branch, with innumerable theoretical and empirical studies (i.e. Bell 1991; Wilss 1992; Nord 1991; Hönig 1995; Kiraly 1995; Risku 1998; Pym 1992, 2003a; PACTE 2001, 2005, 2009, 2011; Göpferich *et al.* 2011). The relevance of this research is paramount for translation training, as these empirical studies and models help trace the progression from bilinguals to novices and then professional translators, thus providing a framework for translation training programmes. Three different research areas have focused on defining what entails being a professional translator. The first area of research, involving the PACTE (2011) or the Transcom (Göpferich 2009; Göpferich *et al.* 2011) research groups, has resulted in detailed translation competence models that have been empirically tested using translation trainees, professional translators and language teachers. In a second area of research, 'translation expertise', the performance of bilinguals or trainees is compared to that of professional translators (Ericsson 2000; Englund Dimitrova 2005; Jakobsen 2005; Shreve 2006a). In the third area, related to evaluation and assessment, mostly in certification exams, the focus is on the elaboration of evaluation instruments that can validly and reliably assess a predetermined level of performance (i.e. Angelelli and Jacobson 2009).

As already mentioned, translation competence research rests upon the notion of 'natural translation' (Harris 1977; Harris and Sherwood 1978), the innate ability of any bilingual to translate naturally. Translation competence is operationalized through componential models that represent the network of specialized knowledge that professionals or experts (Shreve 2006a) possess, as opposed to bilinguals or trainees. Translation competence is normally defined as the underlying knowledge system needed to translate (PACTE 2005) or 'the knowledge and skills the translator must possess in order to carry out a translation' (Bell 1991: 43). Others, from a market perspective and a minimalist approach, define translation competence as the 'whole range of skills required by the labour market' (Pym 2003a).[4] There is consensus that translation competence is composed of several interrelated subcompetences, even if the nature of these and how to define them is still a matter of debate. Nevertheless, and for our purposes, a review of all models shows that at least three basic subcompetences play an essential role: communicative and cultural competence in a source and target language, strategic-transfer or macrostrategic competence in order to plan and carry out the task, and tools and research competence. Additionally, there is a wide consensus that there are more subcompetences involved, and that the sum of all subcompetences makes up a whole greater than the sum of its parts. This means that, despite outstanding knowledge of two languages and cultures and the use of technology tools, it is the ability to interrelate and mobilize them to solve specific problems that really matters. Different competence models incorporate different sets of subcompetences, but for the purposes of web localization training two models offer key insights: Hönig's (1995) and Pym's (1992, 2003a) dual model of associative and 'macrostrategic' competences and PACTE's comprehensive model upon which our proposal is based.

The minimalist proposal of Pym is partly based on Hönig's (1995) competence proposal that separates:

1. an associative competence, and
2. an ability to deploy a macrostrategy and apply it consistently throughout the translation.

According to Pym, the training of translators should be focused on:

> The ability to generate a series of more than one viable target text (TT1, TT2 . . . TTn) for a pertinent source text (ST) [This corresponds to what Hönig calls associative competence]; The ability to select only one viable TT from this series quickly and with justified confidence. [This corresponds to Hönig's macro-strategy and the ability to employ it consistently.]
>
> (Pym 2003a: 489)

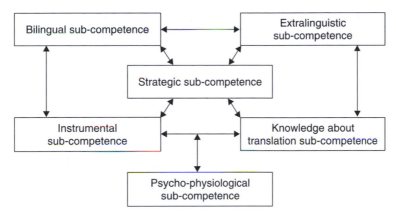

Figure 7.1 PACTE group translation competence model (PACTE 2005: 610; 2011: 331)

The author then refers to the fact that translators need to know a fair amount about grammar, terminology, market forces, teamwork, etc., but it is still these two minimal subcompetences that relate exclusively to translation itself. This translation subcompetence model can be quite useful in localization, as in part the atomization and segmentation of source texts requires advanced skills from the translator to cognitively switch from the micro or segmental level to the macro level in order to contextualize each potential chunk within the wider framework of the overall website. This ability of expert translators to maintain a cognitive balance between the macro and the micro levels has been related in localization to higher levels of quality (Bass 2006: 82) and has been empirically shown to be one of the main processing differences between professionals and non-professionals (Séguinot 1989; Tirkkonen-Condit 1989, 1992; Göpferich 2009).

One of the most comprehensive translation competence models is the one that since 1997 the PACTE research group has been empirically researching and testing with professional translators, translation students and language teachers. This consists of five interrelated subcompetences plus physio-psychological components such as memory, logic, attention, etc. All these subcompetences represent 'a system of competencies that interact, are hierarchical, and subject to variation' (PACTE 2000: 43).

Figure 7.1 represents this model. Its main component is the strategic subcompetence that, to some extent, is similar to the macrostrategic subcompetence of Hönig's and Pym's models. This subcompetence is the most important of them all for:

> [S]olving problems and guaranteeing the efficiency of the process. It intervenes by planning the process in relation to the translation project, evaluating the process

> and partial results obtained, activating the different sub-competencies and compen-
> sating for deficiencies, identifying translation problems and applying procedures to
> solve them.
>
> (PACTE 2005: 610)

This subcompetence represents mostly operative knowledge, and it inter-relates and mobilizes all other subcompetences in order to solve specific translation or localization problems.

The bilingual subcompetence includes 'pragmatic, socio-linguistic, textual and lexical-grammatical knowledge in each language' (PACTE 2005: 610). It includes knowledge about the communicative situation, such as participants and sociocultural norms, illocutionary competence (knowledge about the functions of language) and advanced textual competence. It also includes the ability to control the interference between the language pair or 'interference control'. The PACTE group indicates that this component is shared with other bilinguals – and in fact many components of translation competence are shared with other professionals (Kiraly 1995: 108; Kelly 2005). However, it should be mentioned that professional localizers posses advanced knowledge in general and specialized areas, including the advanced knowledge of main digital genres, specialized skills in copywriting, such as legal, technical or advertising writing, etc. Obviously, not all college-educated bilinguals possess the ability to draft legal or technical texts that are acceptable to specialists as appropriate and efficient in form and style. This requires the acquisition of advanced writing skills and socialization in specialized groups. The same can be said of web writing style and the multiple specialized components in websites (Price and Price 2002; Jenney 2007): advanced knowledge of textual production of a wide range of specialized web genres and types is required. Some scholars differentiate between language and textual competence (Neubert 2000; Kelly 2005), although both are included under the same category in the PACTE model. Separating these two components might be productive in order to highlight the often forgotten acquisition of advanced knowledge on web style and digital genres and types. In fact, an approximation based on digital genre theory can be seen as an effective tool in order to acquire the textual competence required for specialized translation (Montalt *et al.* 2008).

The extralinguistic subcompetence includes 'encyclopedic, thematic and bicultural knowledge' (PACTE 2005: 610) and it is mostly declarative knowledge. It includes both accumulated knowledge about the world and specific advanced domain knowledge related to whichever field a translator specializes in. According to PACTE, the bilingual and extralinguistic compe-tences can be shared with other bilinguals, and therefore only the other three represent the actual subcompetences found exclusively in translators – and, I would add, in localizers.

The knowledge about translation subcompetence is mostly declarative knowledge, both implicit and explicit, about what translation is and aspects of the profession.

> It includes:
> (1) knowledge about how translation functions: types of translation units, processes required, methods and procedures used (strategies and techniques), and types of problems;
> (2) knowledge related to professional translation practice: knowledge of the work market (different types of briefs, clients and audiences, etc.).
>
> (PACTE 2003: 92)

Finally, the instrumental subcompetence was not present in earlier competence studies, but cannot be ignored with the advent of technology in translation. This subcompetence is also known as 'tools and research' competence (Göpferich 2009) and refers to two distinctive types of knowledge:

1. the translation technology tools and other technology applied to the entire cycle, and
2. research and documentation sources and strategies, including paper or online dictionaries of all kinds, encyclopedias, grammars, style books, corpora, translation memories, etc. (PACTE 2005).

This subdivision seems necessary in order to conceptualize training efforts in technology-tools-intensive modalities such as localization.

Finally, the PACTE model includes a separate component that is not considered a subcompetence as such; it is not specific to translation competence but, rather, 'an integral part of all expert knowledge' (PACTE 2003: 91). The psycho-physiological components include:

> 1. cognitive components such as memory, perception, attention and emotion;
> 2. attitudinal aspects such as intellectual curiosity, perseverance, rigour, critical spirit, knowledge of and confidence in one's own abilities, the ability to measure one's own abilities, motivation, etc.;
> 3. abilities such as creativity, logical reasoning, analysis and synthesis, etc.
>
> (PACTE 2003: 93)

The development of all, or most of, these components, despite not being part of translation competence *per se*, can be easily related to the goals of the 'translation education' model previously discussed (Bernardini 2004; Pym and Windle 2011b). It also relates in part to the benefits of the development of cognitive skills that higher education provides for future localizers following the proposed model of Folaron (2006).

Translation competence acquisition

Closely related to the notion of translation competence is that of '*translation competence acquisition*', the pathway or progression by which bilinguals acquire the components of professional translation competence (PACTE 2001; Toury 1995: 241–58; Shreve and Diamond 1997; Göpferich 2009). This process is understood as a dynamic and cyclical process in which the development of the strategic competence or operative translation knowledge plays an essential role. The heterogeneous and complex nature of translation and localization also means that the acquisition of translation competence is a non-finite process (Neubert 2000), requiring translators to continually add knowledge and merge it with existing knowledge. Consequently, they need the capacity to be creative and adapt themselves to novel as well as existing situations.

As previously mentioned, the starting point for acquiring this competence is normally natural translation (Harris 1977; Harris and Sherwood 1978) or, in the case of the PACTE group, 'pre-translational' competence. During the acquisition process, learning strategies help to develop and integrate translation subcompetences, resulting in the development of different degrees of translation competence. All subcompetences are not necessarily acquired at the same time or in parallel fashion; rather, they develop unequally and they interrelate and compensate. Similarly, depending on the language direction and translation type (legal, technical, medical, etc.) some subcompetences might be more relevant than others, and the process might develop at different speeds. Obviously, the acquisition method also influences the process, and the competence of individuals will vary widely depending on their pre-translation competence, the methods, or the specific subcompetences targeted in the learning process. As an example, a programme focused primarily on technology acquisition will not guarantee that the end result, the actual performance of the individuals who take part in it, will generate quality legal translated texts (such as terms of use) if the many interrelated subcompetences are not specifically targeted.

TOWARDS A MODEL OF LOCALIZATION COMPETENCE

The foregoing review of studies of translation competence and its acquisition reveals that the acquisition goals of localization training, the skills possessed by professional localizers, easily fits within models such as those by the PACTE group or the Transcom group. The emphasis the industry places on technological, workflow, management or engineering skills is part of the instrumental knowledge about translation subcompetences, or, we might say, translation-localization. The main component, the strategic subcompetence, merely rests upon a larger knowledge base of these two subcompetences in order to solve prototypical problems found in this modality as well as the ability to solve new ones. Localization competence also requires developing advanced bilingual and extralinguistic subcompetences, which in this case incorporate advanced knowledge of the main digital genres, types, central contrastive problems, pragmatic issues, knowledge and impact of internationalization and globalization strategies, etc.

If we track down the first mention of the notion of 'localization competence', it was Wright (2004) who first proposed a model of localization competence based on a survey of members of the LISA association about the skills deemed necessary for future localizers. The proposed model therefore emphasized knowledge of tools and technological processes as the most desirable components of localization competence, including translation and cross-cultural knowledge as part of the model. During the 2000s, other researchers and industry experts offered more or less detailed models of localization competence (DiFranco 2003; Quirion 2003; Archibald 2004; Austermühl 2006; Folaron 2006; Pym 2006). These normally incorporated both software and web localization, and only one proposed model focused exclusively on the latter (Jiménez-Crespo and Tercedor 2012). Within the context of TS and mostly emphasizing terminology knowledge, Quirion (2003) also offered a model for university programmes in which localization competence was subdivided into four main components:

1. translation and adaptation skills,
2. technological skills,
3. knowledge of the main process and methodologies in the life of a localization project, and
4. knowledge of project management.

This first effort addressed the confusion then existing in university translation programmes about how best to incorporate localization into the overall curriculum of graduate and undergraduate translation education.

Aimed at building bridges between academic and industry training efforts, Folaron's (2006: 212–17) model of localization competence can be considered as the most detailed so far. It is not grounded in current research on translation competence and its acquisition, and the detailed list of components is subdivided into management, technology and language-culture sections. This model offers a defence of the development of specialized cognitive skills in university education, as opposed to the training setting in which industry efforts take place. Anthony Pym (2006) also introduced the notion of 'localization competence', even if a complete model was not offered. Nevertheless, he offered a useful insight into the differences between general translation and localization competences: that the latter entails a collaborative effort in which the final product can be the result of multiple interactions and a team approach. This leads the author to advocate a more collaborative approach to localization training in tune with Kiraly's (2000) socio-constructivist approach or Gouadec's (2007) approach to translation based on projects.

In Jiménez-Crespo and Tercedor (2012) the adoption of the PACTE translation model was introduced as a potential foundation for localization competence. This specialized skill is seen as a specialized subtype of translation competence, like subtitling competence, with enhanced knowledge about translation-localization and instrumental subcompetences. It broadly shares competences with many other specialized translation areas, such as technical translation, legal translation, audiovisual translation, etc. Figure 7.2 shows how localization competence models could be built upon the PACTE model. The localization competence model puts greater emphasis on acquired instrumental competences when compared to regular translation competence, as well as focusing more on processes, management, teamwork and workflows within the knowledge about translation competence. This later subcompetence is renamed as knowledge about translation-localization competence, as many of the principles – such as dealing with different clients, adjusting a task depending on the commission of the project, billing, basic editing, etc. – are shared. Similarly, this flexible model can also accommodate other more specialized roles within the localization world, such as localization management or QA operators, through tailoring the necessary skills. In the case of localization management, the bilingual subcompetence would be less critical than that of translators or localizers, while the instrumental subcompetence would be similar to that of a localizer. Additionally, the main distinguishing feature of localization management competence would be a greater focus on knowledge about localization subcompetence, with a larger share of the strategic component devoted to carrying out tasks and solving problems that to a lesser degree require bilingual or extralinguistic subcompetences.

At this point, it should be mentioned that the PACTE group indicates that the bilingual and extralinguistic competences are shared with other bilinguals and different specialists, and therefore translation competence involves only the other three subcompetences. Nevertheless, if we apply the same to localization, a large base of knowledge about localization and instrumental subcompetences, without any advanced bilingual, strategic or multilingual subcompetences, would result in a localization technical or development profile. It's easy to argue that localization managers should ideally be competent at least in one language pair to be able to plan and solve a wide array of problems due to cross-cultural and cross-linguistic issues, while a linguistic (not technical or functional) QA operator should obviously possess expert bilingual, multilingual and transfer skills in the languages and cultures involved. It should also be borne in mind that strategic competence, that is, operative knowledge, is the main foundation of localization competence. Thus, a componential training model should focus on problem-solving that requires mobilizing all other subcompetences and not just a single one. For example, this means that the objective of a technology course should not necessarily be learning to use a tool but, rather, how the advanced use of this

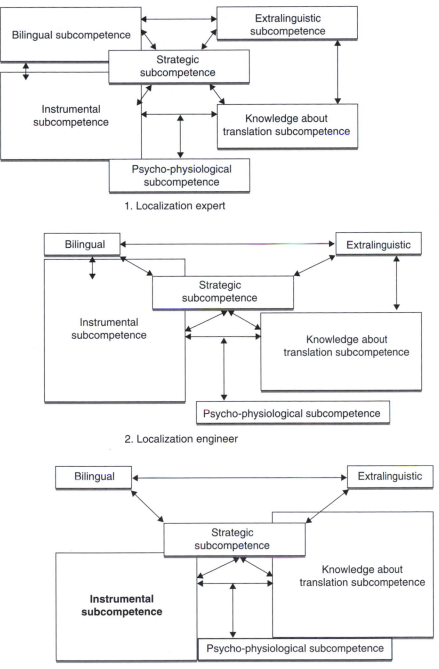

1. Localization expert

2. Localization engineer

3. Localization manager

Figure 7.2 Different localization competence models, depending on job profile

tool interrelates with problems emanating from cross-linguistic problems (i.e. how to solve issues related to space constraints), extralinguistic ones (i.e. how to best solve an issue of cultural references without resorting to explicitation, such as neutralizing it), using technology to expedite the process in cases of tight deadlines without losing quality, etc.

One of the positive aspects of using this model is that it allows one to itemize the prototypical components of each subcompetence in order of importance, and it can provide a flexible tool to establish localization training curricula (Kelly 2010, 2005). Prototypical components can be introduced in the learning process through different didactic methodologies, such as socio-constructivist (Kiraly 2000) or functionalist approaches (Nord 1997, 2005), allowing one to set the goals of the learning process that will be assessed or evaluated (Kelly 2005). Below is an open list of core competences that can be arranged or expanded as necessary. It focuses mostly on localization-specific components although each starts with general translation components shared with other modalities and types.

Instrumental-technological subcompetences

Instrumental-technological subcompetences, also referred to as 'tools and research competence' (Göpferich 2009), are an essential element in all modern translation competence models, and constantly reshape translation training around the world (Pym 2012). For the purposes of localization competence, they could be subdivided into technological subcompetences and research-documentation ones. The main prototypical technological competences for web localization are:

1. Technological subcompetences
   - Basic computing skills (word processing, handling of files, different file types, Internet communications, etc.)
   - Understanding of technology tools applied to translation
   - Knowledge of translation memory tools, including processing hypertext with tag editing tools.
   - Knowledge of localization tools
   - Knowledge of main web development tools
   - Knowledge of CMS
   - Knowledge of terminology mining tools
   - Knowledge of terminology management tools
   - Knowledge of quality management processes and tools
   - Basic knowledge of mark-up languages, HTML, XML, Cascading Style sheets, etc.
   - Basic knowledge of scripting languages
   - Basic knowledge of exchange standards such as XLIFF, TMX, etc. (see Chapter 5)

- Thorough knowledge of file formats encountered in localization projects
- Knowledge of character sets, Unicode, and Unicode locale repository
- Knowledge of corpus analysis tools
- Visual tools for editing embedded graphics
- Knowledge of database organization and how data is applied to multilingual processes
- Technologies used to create content and the technologies that separate translatable elements from non-localizable elements
- Process of post-editing machine translation output.

2. Research-documentation skills
   - Ability to identify appropriate Internet resources to solve specific problems
     - Monolingual dictionaries
     - Bilingual dictionaries
     - Terminology databases, IATE, Microsoft language portal, etc.
     - Monolingual reference corpora
     - Parallel corpora or online translation memories (Linguee, Glosbe, TAUS, Europarl, etc.)
     - Specialized parallel texts
     - Etc.
   - Ability to identify paper resources necessary to support translation decisions
   - Knowledge of the process in order to identify the specific participant in the localization process who might help solve a problem.

Knowledge about translation-localization competences

Knowledge about *translation-localization competences* involves:

1. Metalanguage of translation and localization
2. Knowledge of the GILT process and specific constraints and types
3. Knowledge about basics of localization cycle, stages, and involved agents
4. Knowledge about the basics of project management
5. Management of multilingual content
6. How to assess and implement the level of web localization commissioned
7. How to communicate, negotiate and defend decisions or proposed solutions to problems
8. Knowledge of standards that apply to web localization
9. Knowledge about preparing a project, assessing budget-costs, arranging human resources and project for all locales, etc.
10. Ethical issues regarding localization, globalization, role of translators-localizers in society, etc.

11. Basic legal aspects of localization
12. Basic knowledge of machine translation systems.

Specialized bilingual and extralinguistic subcompetences

These two subcompetences are shared to some extent with general bilinguals, advanced bilinguals or general translators. These two subcompetences nevertheless include specialized components that need to be specifically developed for web localization, as this modality includes a wide range of different genres, text types and specializations, such as legal, technical, literary, journalistic, advertising, and audiovisual translations.

1. Bilingual subcompetence
   - Graduate-level language competence in two or more languages
   - General expert contrastive knowledge of both languages
   - General contrastive knowledge of main transfer strategies between both languages
   - Advanced technical writing skills in the target languages
   - Advanced textual production skills in different domains: legal, technical, journalistic, literary, advertising, audiovisual, etc.
   - Advanced translation skills of the main types found in web localization: legal, technical, journalistic, literary, advertising, audiovisual, etc.
   - Knowledge of terminological, phraseological, discursive and pragmatic conventions in the main digital genres
   - Advanced knowledge of recognition and expression of speech acts in digital interactive texts (stating, asking, commanding, promising, etc.) and illocutionary acts, etc. (when a pop-up window indicates 'date format is wrong', the illocutionary act indicates that we should refill the field with the requested format)
   - Ability to write for screen (brief, concise, clear)
   - In-depth knowledge of cultures involved
   - Contrastive knowledge of pragmatic issues
   - Producing texts that comply with web style guides
2. Extralinguistic competence
   - Development cycle of a website
   - Knowledge of hypertext theory, hypertextual structures, linking, etc.
   - Knowledge of Web 2.0
   - Technological paradigms in our contemporary world
   - Impact of globalization on our modern world.

Strategic subcompetence

Strategic subcompetence is the most important of all, and it entails mostly operative knowledge. It therefore requires not only the ability to solve the most recurrent problems in all web localization tasks, but also the ability to cope with new and unpredictable ones by applying specific strategies and solutions based on situation, context, client, commission, etc. In this sense, localization, just like translation, is understood as a problem-solving activity (Lörcher 1991; Wilss 1992) and an expert skill (Shreve 2006a). This subcompetence would include a larger or smaller general translation strategic competence depending on the professional profile, developed differently in the case of QA operators.

1. Solving general transfer problems due to source text comprehension or target text reformulation
2. Identifying tasks and problems that might appear and how to propose different viable solutions based on the commission and problem at hand
3. Solving problems effectively and efficiently within short deadlines
4. Applying internal (mental) and external support (dictionaries, online resources, reference materials, etc.) to solve source text comprehension problems and target text reformulation
5. Conceptualizing problems at the microtextual or segmental level within the wider framework of the macrotextual website overall. Switching effortlessly between both levels in cognitive tasks.
6. Applying advanced knowledge of digital genres and their communicative situations in order to solve instances of lack of context in the comprehension of segments (either in a list format, extracted by a CMS system, etc.)
7. Applying world, sociocultural and specialized knowledge, sociocultural and translation-localization norms, acquired skills and common sense to specific problems
8. Ability to continue learning specific methods for resolving classes of problems and organizing the application of those methods in optimal ways, including problem representation or 'chunking' at higher levels of abstraction or according to different principles than novices (Shreve 2006a)
9. Ability to adjust the overall translation and localization task to different localization levels, including arranging the process and prioritizing items to process and adapt

DIFFERENT GATEWAYS INTO LOCALIZATION TRAINING

The multiplicity and collaborative nature of localization, together with the fuzzy boundaries of job descriptions in the field, means that the acquisition of localization competence often begins from different scenarios or pre-skills sets. Universities offer localization courses after students have completed extensive coursework on principles of translation, documentation skills, terminology, specialized translation, etc., while industry workshops target a wide range of professionals with heterogeneous backgrounds and skill sets. Translation competence models refer to the notion of 'pre-translational competence' (Presas 1996) or the body of knowledge that subjects possess before they acquire translation competence. Applying this notion, the starting point for designing or establishing localization-training curricula should ideally be 'pre-localization competence'. This represents the accumulated body of declarative and operative knowledge that trainees would have before localization training. The problem here is that this starting point is often quite variable, and different starting points might require different approaches. Quirion (2003: 240) already anticipated the possibility of creating distinctive training scenarios depending on the background of the students, whether it is university students trained in translation during or after completion of their degrees, or individuals with a computational or technical background. The one aspect not in question at this point is that, at least for training purposes, acquiring localization competence does not normally follow on directly from pre-translational competence or even natural translation (Harris 1977). Localization training is normally conceptualized as a specialization within a larger framework of translation training, and so can be seen as an advanced and specialized stage in acquiring translation competence on the one hand, and in computational engineering on the other. This would clearly separate the role of the localization engineer, whose normal tasks do not involve cross-cultural and linguistic-textual transfer and who performs engineering and management tasks exclusively, from the localizer, who carries out over 50% of cross-cultural and linguistic-textual transfer but does do some routine technical and management tasks.

Figure 7.3 shows a proposed framework upon which to develop localization competence acquisition models. As we have seen, this notion is generally understood as a specialized subset of translation competence that, nevertheless, includes a set of skills related to both instrumental subcompetences (localization tools, technological processes, etc.), and other subcompetences related to knowledge of pragmatic, socio-linguistic, textual and lexical-grammatical knowledge associated with digital genres, text types, conventions, etc. This localization framework acquisition can be applied to all localization types. Following Esselink (2006), it is understood that the continuum in the acquisition of localization competence progresses from less technically complex types towards more textual-based but less technologically complex ones. Software localization usually requires more advanced instrumental competences, but the potential variation in digital genres and text types can be quite limited, thus allowing trainers to concentrate mostly on technological aspects without losing sight of other translation aspects related to the software product as a unitary digital genre. At the other end of the spectrum, web localization requires less advanced instrumental subcompetences, but the potential variety of textual and digital genres, and hence textual and linguistic difficulties, is much wider. This is because, even when most digital genres, such as corporate pages, networking sites, etc., are highly conventionalized (Kennedy and Shepherd 2005;

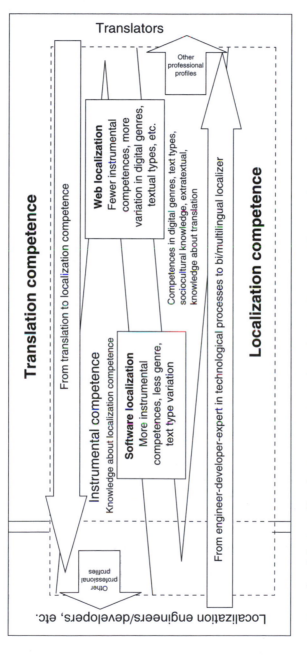

Figure 7.3 Towards a definition of localization competence. From Jiménez-Crespo and Tercedor (2012: 1001)

Jiménez-Crespo 2009a), hypertexts are by nature open structures that can incorporate any type of genre in them (see Chapter 4).

Following the PACTE (2005) translation competence model, Figure 7.3 separates the bilingual, extratextual and translation knowledge competences from instrumental competence. The graphic clearly reflects the two current pathways into localization: from translator or translation novice to multilingual localizer or from localization/internationalization engineer or developer to localizer. In the latter, trainees might be extremely proficient in their instrumental competences, but they might still need to acquire the remaining subcompetences related to general translation competence, such as contrastive knowledge of the language pair, knowledge of general principles of translation as a process and as a profession, etc. In the opposite direction, translation trainees who have already acquired the basics of translation competence need to concentrate not only on advanced instrumental competences, but also on specific issues related to digital genres, their macrostructural and microstructural levels, formats, the degree to which a product is to be localized, etc. The graphic also separates the subcomponent 'knowledge about localization' from the subcompetence 'knowledge about translation' in the PACTE model. This localization-specific subcomponent accounts for specialized knowledge of internationalization and localization processes, management, translation QA procedures, standards, workflows, etc.

This framework also accounts for the fuzzy area between a localization expert with a translation background and the multilingual developer or engineer who can produce natural translations but nevertheless intends to become a localizer. This is represented by the gap between translation competence and the localization engineer profession that, however, overlaps in some areas with localization competence. Hence anyone in either of the two potential profiles, translators and developer-engineers, can always concentrate on expanding and enhancing their acquisition of the specific competences they lack: the instrumental or bilingual subcompetences respectively. As in any other professional field, any expert who overlaps job profiles can, with specific advanced training in his/her weaker competences, potentially become an expert in both areas. This is indicated in the graphic by the arrows that read 'other professional profiles'.

LOCALIZATION COMPETENCE AS A MODEL FOR TRAINING

Translation competence has been used as the foundation for the development of translation curricula around the world (Kelly 2005, 2010; PACTE 2005). It provides a guide for establishing curricular design, specific didactic units and modules, sequencing, evaluation and assessment criteria, quality evaluation of coursework, tracing the acquisition process, etc. To date, only a few proposals for web localization training have been proposed, such as the ones found in the Ecolore,[5] Ecolomedia[6] or Ecolotrain projects, or

Bolaños (2004) and Díaz Fouçes' (2004) proposals. The last can be seen as a professional approach based on project learning similar to Gouadec's (2007), in which all the stages of the project are documented, and students are introduced to all steps in the process of web localization, from assessing the project and creating estimates, all the way to QA and delivery of the localized website. This approach combines mostly components of instrumental subcompetences together with management skills under 'knowledge about translation-localization'. To some extent, this mirrors the experiential approach prevailing in the industry, in which training is organized around the acquisition of a series of skills, mostly technological, that are supposed to lead to professional localization performance.

Localization training would greatly benefit if the previously proposed model of localization competence were applied to planning and assessing learning in this field. The application requires a flexible approach starting from constraints such as available time, resources, students' prior knowledge or stage (if any) of translation competence acquisition, trainer's background, objectives of training, etc. This approach, based on localization competence, can be implemented identifying the components in each subcompetence to be acquired – from the prototypical central ones to more specialized ones, depending on the goals – taking into account that the strategic competence represents the main and most complex one. As previously mentioned, translation competence is normally understood to be 20% declarative knowledge and around 80% operative or procedural knowledge. It is the bilingual, instrumental and strategic subcompetences that mainly represent operative-procedural knowledge, and so, arguably, they represent the bulk of the skills possessed by expert localizers. If the aim of the programme is to acquire a more technical management profile, following the framework offered in Figure 7.2, a stronger emphasis on processes and procedures related to localization and translation would be targeted. The diversification and specialization of job profiles within the industry means that training also needs to take into consideration the generic or highly specialized nature of some agents in the localization industry, and prioritize whichever components are prototypical in the relevant area. This is precisely what Ferreira-Alves indicated in his review of the evolution of the translation profession in light of localization and new technologies.

In the face of this new configuration of the translator's profile and function, it seems important that the kind of training provided should be as polyvalent and versatile as possible, as well as sufficiently multifaceted, integrated and multimodal. It should be geared towards the so-called new satellite professions or extensions of the task of the translator (i.e. localization industry) and conveniently open and available so as to solve the problem posed by the specialist/generalist dichotomy.

(Ferreira-Alves 2010: 15)

This openness and the necessity to prepare students for a continued learning curve is the reason why I maintain that the emphasis should be placed on the development of the strategic component and the ability to cope with recurrent and new problems that require mobilizing several subcompetences. This would be parallel to the acquisition of prototypical targeted components in each subcompetence. The combination of complex problem-solving together with the development of specific components, such as learning to use localization or QA tools, allows for the development of cognitive resources necessary to constantly adapt to new trends and professionally excel within the fuzzy and shifting job descriptions in the localization industry.

PLANNING LOCALIZATION PROGRAMMES

Planning localization programmes based on localization competence models also needs to be placed within the context of current trends in general education planning. Dorothy Kelly (2005), in her handbook for translation trainers, adapted general education planning to the specifics of translation education, and she arranged the stages as follows:

1. setting the objectives and outcomes,
2. adjusting the training to the participants, both trainees and trainers,
3. organizing the curricular content,
4. establishing the necessary resources,
5. choosing the right methodology to apply,
6. arranging the learning sequence, and
7. assessing the targeted components.

The researcher places great emphasis on taking into consideration the social and market needs in the first stage: planning the objectives and outcomes. The same can be said of localization, where technological evolution constantly challenges localizers to adapt to new developments. The proposed localization competence model is open in nature to add or modify any instrumental or knowledge subcompetences to the evolution of technology and processes (Alcina *et al.* 2008), constantly incorporating the most up-to-date set of skills possessed by professionals working in the field. The need to adapt educational endeavours to current social and market needs is a constant in translation training publications, and to some extent, this mirrors how industry associations justify the need to conduct their own educational programmes (Pym 2006). The objectives of the learning process are also established according to whether the programme is a stand-alone localization course or is part of a larger general translation training programme, as many other skills, such as advanced technical translation, can be acquired in other courses (Austermühl 2006: 71).

The issues related to participants concern both the trainees and the trainers as their skills and prior knowledge base and their pre-localization competence determine the objective, methodology, progression and evaluation. The issue of translation education and localization trainers is also of paramount importance (i.e. Kelly 2008). Normally, two main types of trainers dominate localization training, academics with a wide knowledge base on translation theory, training methods, assessment issues, etc. – but possibly lacking a closer connection to state-of-the-art professional practices – and industry experts who transition to training either part- or full-time, normally with a technical profile and a higher emphasis on technological procedures (Altanero 2006). A shared localization competence model informed by theoretical and empirical research in TS and related disciplines and informed by industry experts can represent a common base for localization training acquisition resulting in better outcomes.

Two main didactic methodologies can provide the foundation for localization training: Nord's functionalist approach (1991, 1997, 2005) and Kiraly's socio-constructivist (2000) proposal for translation education. Nord's student-centred approach based on functionalist theories provides a sound theoretical foundation for targeting the recurring cultural adaptations in industry publications. The approach is based on translation and function-oriented text analysis in which students should always be exposed to realistic translation assignments based on a commission or translation brief. These detailed translation instructions should include indications of who is to transmit to whom, for what, by what medium, where, when, why, with what function, and what subject matter he/she is to speak about, in which order, using which non-verbal elements, in which words, in what kind of sentences, in which tone, to what effect, etc. (Nord 1991: 144). Nord's represents one of the first student-centred approaches that emphasizes learning over teaching, moving from transmissionist paradigms in which the teacher is supposed to pass on knowledge to students while they passively incorporate it to a student-centred environment. Nord's approach also represents a more realistic approach to the training of what she calls 'functional translators' (Nord 2005) that can adjust to the demands of the professional market.

Kiraly's approach is based on the adoption of a social constructivism, or the sociological theory which maintains that groups construct knowledge for one another, collaboratively creating a small culture of shared artefacts with shared meanings. This entails a collaborative approach to translation training, in which students' self-concept and their socialization within the professional community are the most important elements. This approach is implemented through authentic translation projects in which students identify and collectively solve problems encountered. This approach fits into Gouadec's (2007) situational project-based model and in Díaz Fouces' (2004) approach to web localization training, although these two are merely project-based and not founded upon a socio-constructivist collaborative approach. In our opinion, a combination of Nord's functionalist approach based on real localization commissions with the possibility of elaborating different target websites based on different commissions or instructions, together with a project-based, collaborative approach based on Kiraly's model can provide the optimal framework for localization competence acquisition. Units or sessions can be arranged around the acquisition of specific subcomponents according to planning and sequencing, and the task-based collaborative approach can help build the strategic subcompetence vital to expert performance in translation and localization. New cloud translation technologies, such as Wordfast Anywhere, that allow for collaborative translation can provide the perfect environment in which to conduct many of these projects. Finally, it should be mentioned that the most recurrent methodology for localization training is similar to the task-based paradigm proposed by Hurtado (1999) and largely by González Davies (2004, 2005), in which concrete and brief exercises help practice specific points, all in a continuum that leads towards mastering a global task. This is understood as a chain of activities that make up a planned holistic task, such as terminology-mining exercises, project planning, cultural adaptation of multimodal components, etc.

SUMMARY

This chapter argued that the point of departure for web localization training programmes is the notion of localization competence, a compendium of the expert knowledge possessed by web localization experts, which is not possessed by bilinguals or general translators. It functions as a flexible guide to building training programmes based on a set of skills that trainees should acquire, serving also as a benchmark by which to evaluate students' progress. This chapter identified the main problem concerning a definition of localization competence as the unclear status of the localization profession within the general translation industry, the differences between componential training and translation education, the different points of departure for students or the progressive differentiation – but not always separation – of the different roles within the industry: localizers, localization engineers or localization managers. It was argued that web localization competence seamlessly fits within current translation competence models such as PACTE (2005) or Transcom (Göpferich 2009; Göpferich et al. 2011) and consequently, it was conceptualized as a specialized subset with advanced additional technological, management and textual competences. A full description of the different skills that make up the componential proposed model was presented. Web localization competence is here necessarily seen as a complex advanced subset, as it encompasses an extremely wide range of translation specialization – technical, legal, advertising, audiovisual, creative, etc. – as well as advanced knowledge about localization-translation and instrumental subcompetences (that include management, QA, basic engineering tasks, etc.). The chapter ended with a discussion on translation-training programme development and teaching methodologies, using the proposed model of localization competence as a flexible foundation to accommodate different settings.

FURTHER READING

There are many useful overviews of translation training approaches such as Pym and Windle (2011b) or (Kelly 2010). Some basic and useful readings on translation training for anyone interested in localization training are Kiraly's (2000) volume on socio-constructivist approaches, Nord's (1997) didactic review of functionalism and González Davies's (2004) task-based approach, as this can offer a guide on how to build a componential training progression of use for localization. Kelly's *Handbook for Translation Trainers* (2005) provides a good overview on how to organize a comprehensive programme. Alcina (2008) is of particular use in placing web localization within general translation training programmes. All of PACTE's publications (i.e. 2011, 2009, 2005, 2003) as well as those from the Transcom research group (Göpferich 2009; Göpferich *et al.* 2011) are of interest to fully conceptualize localization competence as an extension of translation competence. For early attempts at disaggregating the components of localization competence, see Folaron (2006), Gouadec (2003; 2007: 45–7) or Wright (2004), although the last is harder to find. Jiménez-Crespo and Tercedor (2012) offer a first attempt at conceptualizing web localization competence from an empirical standpoint. For those with knowledge of Spanish, some research on web localization training has been done in this language, such as Díaz Fouçes (2004) and Bolaños (2004).

8

FUTURE PERSPECTIVES IN LOCALIZATION

In a fast-moving and unpredictable field such as localization, this last chapter looks ahead with a discussion of potential issues that may help shape new developments in localization that will continue challenging Translation Studies scholars and practitioners alike. This chapter starts with a discussion on current trends that affect how web localization will continue to evolve, and then moves on to look at the issues of professionalization, the boom of crowdsourcing and volunteer practices facilitated by the Internet, as well as the effect of Machine Translation post-editing practices. The chapter finishes with a discussion on how the impact of unpredictable technological developments on societies and communicative practices will continue to shape the theorizations, practice and training in the field.

LOOKING AHEAD IN WEB LOCALIZATION

It was over four decades ago that Nida, arguably the first renowned theorist in TS, proposed using target readers to assess the quality of translation (Nida and Taber 1969): several translations of a segment would be offered and the readers would vote on which one was preferred. Nida understood that translation quality would be achieved if the target text produced in users the same effect that the source text produced in its original audience. Letting a group of users decide, rather than the translators, would help get to the most effective translation. Over the years, this approach was criticized for being unpractical, time-consuming and for using non-expert translators in the process (i.e. Rothe-Neves 2002; Colina 2008).[1] Who would have thought, even a few years ago, that Facebook would precisely implement this crowdsourced user-based approach, possible thanks to the Web 2.0, massive online collaboration and the stunning success of social

media (Jiménez-Crespo 2011d). The same goes for Michael Cronin's prediction of an era in which 'translational cyborgs . . . can no longer be conceived
of independently of the technologies with which they interact' (2003: 112).
Nowadays, the life of any translator cannot be conceived without a computer
and the Internet as a tool, for communication and networking purposes
and for the massive online repository of term bases, parallel texts or translation memories (i.e. TDA TAUS, Linguee, Webitext, Mymemory).[2] In web
localization, this dependency is fundamental, being a modality bound by the
technology that gave raise to it and that, at the same time, facilitates it. It is
part of human nature to look ahead, but can we predict the future of web
localization or even translation in general, given the uncertain impact of
technological progress? Will, for example, the move towards digital distribution of content mean that general translation and web localization are
bound to merge? Here we will review some trends that have the potential to
revolutionize how web localization will evolve, as well as reflect on how
future technologies might affect the practice, training and theorizations of
web localization.

If we look into current trends that will shape the future, two main areas
are of special interest: the impact of technology on the web localization
process and the effect of web localization on Translation Studies in general.
The latter issue relates to the role that technological phenomena will play in
the discipline and whether trends that started in web localization will, in
fact, revolutionize the general practice and theorizations of translation. One
such trend is the expansion of online collaborative translation for all types
of translation, with online crowdsourcing services such as MyGengo, or
exchange marketplaces providing free volunteer translations such as
Cucumis.org. Crowdsourced translations, produced free by a collective of
motivated users and facilitated by the interactive nature of the Web 2.0,
have expanded to embrace translations for small payments at rates considerably lower than professional ones (via Getlocalize, Tolingo or Minna no
Hon'Yaku, for example), opening a new niche between volunteer and
professional services. Will more translation be moved online and produced
by collectives of professionals or non-professionals, rather than through the
classic individual process? Will the traditional prepare–translate–edit–
deliver model be replaced in the fast WWW world? Renowned translation
theorist Munday rightly predicted that 'the emergence and proliferation of
new technologies have transformed translation practice and are now
exerting an impact on research and, as a consequence, on the theorization
of translation' (2012: 268). Web localization fits precisely into this niche,
and research into technology trends and their impact on TS represents an
exciting opportunity for anyone embarking on web localization research.
Whether TS will embrace the 'technological turn' is another issue of interest,
as Translation Studies' general lack of engagement with technology, such as
the development of CAT tools or Machine Translation (MT), has resulted in

contemporary translation theories becoming limited in their scope in the eyes of translation technologists (O'Hagan 2012b). In fact, the booming area of MT has followed a completely separate track from TS, and the latter does not normally inform the former (Austermühl 2011). Additionally, it will be of interest to see whether TS will be expanded to incorporate the wider field of localization, including management and other technological components and synergies within the process, or, as indicated for audio-visual translation by Remael (2010), it will be detached from the main discipline as part of an independent Localization Studies.

As for the impact of technology on web localization, we should first consider the constant evolution of the WWW and how this will shape local-ization. Since its origins in the 1990s (Berners-Lee 2000), the WWW has evolved from the static model of the Web 1.0, in which users were mostly passive consumers of static information, into the interactive Web 2.0: a two-way information highway on which users are at the same time consumers and producers of content.[3] The term Web 2.0 was coined by Tim O'Reilly in 2005 to describe a number of services that enable today's Internet users to interact and share information efficiently. This unstoppable evolution continues with the Web 3.0 that hinges around the complete integration of web, social media, apps, widgets, etc., and the accumulation of knowledge and personalization of each user's experience. We are currently experiencing this transition, with all major websites creating compatible smart phone apps whose localization processes are integrated with the existing efforts of web localization. If the Web 2.0 has led to a boom in user-generated content in all languages, its intersection with Machine Translation (MT) has led to instant translation of this type of content, such as using MT for updates and user comments on Facebook, the crowdsourced post-editing of MT tweets, blogs or postings in Wordpress. The move to cloud computing and the change from local storage on a hard drive to hosting software and content on the web directly will also affect web localization as we know it. This is leading to a blurring of boundaries between web and software localization, in which the platform or medium blends in with the application, creating a new hybrid, web-enabled user interface. A similar interweaving process is happening with smart phone apps that merge social websites with smart phone applications, reusing the localized content from the web to the apps.

Two more issues influencing web localization are quality and interopera-bility. Quality will continue to be at the core of future theorizations of web localization, mostly due to expansion in the use of MT and non-professionals in many web localization tasks, both for the overall common content of websites and user-generated content. These issues will undoubtedly raise questions affecting overall theorizations of translational phenomena in the coming years. As seen in Chapter 5, the industry's current stance favours the customization of quality depending on the type of content and the user's needs: the 'fit-for-purpose' model. The volume of content on the web is escalating, and different web texts will continue to be classified in various tiers according to whether the content is more or less critical. Different translation models will be applied to cope with this content surge, such as full professional translation, a mix involving crowdsourcing, or a combination with raw MT or MT post-edited either by experts or members of the community. The interoperability and the development and evolution of standards in the industry will also impact the development of web localization. Recently, efforts have been geared towards developing new standards and the improving and/or adapting of existing ones, such as TMX or XLIFF (Filip 2012a; Filip *et al.* 2012).

Finally, and, given that translation and (even more so) localization is 'bound up with the technical environment which makes it possible' (Cronin 2003: 25), the unpredictable future of technical developments will continue to influence procedural changes in the translation task and in the daily lives of those working on web localization (Cronin 2013). No other modality is so dependent on technology as all localization types, and technology's fast evolutionary pace only means that localization processes and those involved with them will perforce continue adapting rapidly to whatever challenges may be thrown at them. In fact, if compared to the slow pace at which other types such as legal translation have evolved, web localization seems to be moving at quantum speed. This only means that more and more practitioners and researchers will be needed to cope with these new challenges, creating a continuous need for new professional training and research.

Within all these changes, the two main trends that can be identified with certainty as having the potential to radically change this process as we know it are: the emergence and consolidation of non-professional crowdsourcing and volunteer translation, and the progressive shift towards a post-editing MT environment, sometimes combined with crowdsourcing and professional translation, in a trend that is already replacing the consolidated TEP model (Translate–Edit–Publish) for less critical content. Let us, now, review them in more detail.

PROFESSIONALIZATION

Since the early days of localization the industry has insisted on the different character of the localization profession and its highly specialized nature. Many efforts have been devoted to informing the wider public about the complex nature of translation-localization and consolidating its status as a highly skilled profession in society. Nevertheless, it is precisely web localization that has widely popularized non-professional collaborative practices that, even though they have existed since antiquity (Pym 2010), are now regarded as something of a threat to the profession (Stejskal 2009; O'Hagan 2011).[4] The perceived threat to the professionalization of web localization seems to come from two fronts: the increase of volunteer and crowdsourced translation through online massive collaboration, and the relentless improvements in MT as a process that has found its niche in the localization of web-based content. Some scholars have indicated that the potential threat jointly posed by these two trends will be in terms of changes in processes, required skills, and the wider impact on societal perception and views (García 2010). Nevertheless, as industry discourse and job postings show, web localization will continue to become a mainstream specialization for translation practitioners even if the boundaries of job profiles will probably continue to be fuzzy. The current trend favours the existence of localization engineers/managers working in-house, with over 80% of translation content being outsourced to freelancers (Dunne and Dunne 2011). Whether the role of web localization specialist will become a completely independent one within TS and the industry is one of the unforeseeable issues that the future will help clarify.

Without any doubt, all translators will need to specialize in translating text created for online distribution, mostly due to the convergence of web-mediated communications and increased online delivery of technical, legal, promotional or audiovisual content. It is foreseeable that, as web localization represents a more textual and less technological modality compared to software localization (Esselink 2006), it will become a basic component of general translation competence, such as the ability to adapt translations to both printed and web-style writing (Jiménez-Crespo 2011e). Additionally, whether the prototypical profile of the web localizer will include ever-increasing technological and management skills, or whether the roles will be more compartmentalized is still up in the air. It is likely that the new interoperability standards such as XLIFF and more web-based localization tools will require less technical expertise than a decade ago. What is certain is that these new non-professional practices have led to the emergence of new specializations. One of these is the community translation manager (Désilets and van der Meer 2011; Austermühl 2011) or the crowdsourcing quality manager (Kelly *et al.* 2011). In fact, even though Facebook and LinkedIn were what caused the initial commotion in the professional translation community, these websites still hire professional translators to oversee the entire process, verify the quality and provide the necessary superstructural coherence and quality that segment-based community translation tools cannot provide (Jiménez-Crespo 2011d).

Professional translators working in web localization will also experience dramatic changes in the ways translation tasks are performed. It seems to be true that more and more web localization processes will be carried out through MT post-editing within TM environments. As García indicated, 'soon . . . professional translators in the localization industry will no longer translate texts (like their literary counterparts) or segments (as in the TM heyday), but just post-edit machine output' (2009: 208). Working with tag-protecting TM tools will still be with us in the near future, mostly in smaller websites for non-profit organizations, small companies or personal sites. Nevertheless, is it likely that the work of professional localizers will revolve around MT post-editing, terminology management and other technological management tasks. Still, it should be borne in mind that the Web 2.0, with its democratization and boom in user-generated content, means that web localization has to be understood not as a tightly structured process but as a prototypical notion that varies from highly structured websites of multinationals to social networking sites or smaller tourist sites localized in a variety of ways.

CROWDSOURCING

The participatory and interactive nature of the Web 2.0 has fostered the development of new modes of collaborative translation and localization that are revolutionizing the traditional production cycles. Massive Online Collaboration (MOC), an umbrella term that refers to the joint implementation of tasks by a large collective through social networking technologies, started to flourish in the middle of the first decade of the twenty-first century. In the realm of translation it has resulted in two distinct but related phenomena:

1. Crowdsourcing – a term coined by Howe (2006, 2008) that in our case is defined as volunteer translation produced in some form of collaboration by a group of Internet users forming an online community, often using specific platforms (O'Hagan 2012b). It is a phenomenon tied to the Web 2.0 that originally emerged through web localization and later expanded to include other types of translation types and modes.
2. Open translation tools and resources (Austermühl 2011: 15), such as CAT tools, TMs, terminology databanks, online corpora, global content-management systems, crowdsourcing web platforms, collaborative online CAT tools, open-source translation software, etc.

Crowdsourcing, in translation, refers to a phenomenon in which the Internet provides a platform for completing tasks relying on the knowledge of a self-selected community of volunteers on the web. Other terms referring to this type of collaborative translation process include 'user-generated' (O'Hagan 2009; Perrino 2009), 'open' (Cronin 2010), 'community' (Ray and Kelly 2011), 'volunteer' (Pym 2011b), 'hive' (García 2009) and/or 'collaborative translation' (Kelly 2009; Ray and Kelly 2011). Nevertheless, the term currently most favoured by the industry and scholars alike is 'crowdsourced translation-localization', mostly referring to so-called solicited translations (O'Hagan 2009), in which a company or institution purposefully puts out a call to the community to complete a specific localization task. This is the case of the growing number of popular websites such as Facebook, Twitter, LinkedIn, Hi5, Foursquare, Hootsuite, Yeeyam, etc. Other types of solicited translation are those with a non-profit purpose, mostly from NGOs, such as the cases of Kiva (Munro 2010), Translation Without Borders (Petras 2011) or Kotoba no Volunteer [Volunteers of words] (Kageura *et al.* 2011). Another case of collaborative translation on the web is 'non-solicited translations', in which self-selected collectives of users undertake without any specific request self-organized translation tasks that are later distributed through the WWW, as in the cases of subtitling (Wu 2010; Díaz Cintas and Muñoz Sánchez 2006), roamhacking of videogames (Muñoz Sánchez 2009), fansubs, scanlations (O'Hagan 2009) or non-profit websites.

The different types of crowdsourced translation and localization can also be subdivided according to the purpose or goal of the process, such as cause-driven, product-driven or outsourced efforts (Kelly *et al.* 2011). Cause-driven processes are those in which a collective is motivated to produce collaborative translation for a specific common goal, such as having a localized version of Facebook in Basque or Swahili or to help with translation in disasters, as happened in the 2010 Haiti earthquake (Munro 2010). Volunteers work without monetary compensation and translate at their own convenience. Product-driven efforts may occur when a company would not normally localize a product, due to the small market potential of any specific minority language, but with the help of crowdsourcing this might become a reality. This is mostly the case with software such as OpenOffice, Mozilla and Flock Lion browsers or other products partially crowdsourced[5] such as Adobe products, Symantec antivirus, Sun, etc. Finally, outsourced crowdsourcing is represented by web portals in which crowdsourced translations are offered, sometimes in combination with professional translation and/or MT. The number of portals offering these services is steadily growing, with services such as Gengo, Getlocalization, Smartling, Lingotek, Tolingo, Transifex, or MNH. Most of these services are centred on web localization or web content localization, even when nowadays many have expanded to offer all types of translation. Participants are sometimes anonymous users or translators approved by the service, such as Gengo, and some of them offer different levels of translation service based on the expertise of the participants involved. Thus, the term 'community' cannot be loosely understood as an anonymous collective of users, but rather, depending on the model, the community can be controlled and limited in terms of access, skills, degree of involvement, etc. For example, any volunteer participating in Facebook should have an account and the motivation to execute the translation application, get acquainted with it, etc. Similarly, new outsourced for-profit ventures on the web offer different controlled types of collectives, from bilingual students to professional translators, etc.

The use of non-professionals has also attracted the attention of scholars (McDonough 2011; Drugan 2011) and institutions (European Commission

2012) from an ethical point of view. Some of the main ethical questions that the crowdsourcing model raises involve the implications of relying on unpaid volunteers when a consolidated localization industry exists, and whether large corporations exploit the crowd for their own benefit in the solicited model. Other issues concern the visibility of volunteer translators and the benefits for minor languages that can enjoy localized websites and software otherwise unavailable in for-profit scenarios. Without any doubt, the fact that volunteers are not remunerated is one of the main points of contention, even when users' motives are other than monetary, such as prestige, enjoyment, participation or even to unleash their 'cognitive surplus' (Shirky 2010). Offering payment of small amounts might even have a detrimental effect on their motivation, as it could lead to feelings of exploitation (McDonough 2011). In regard to ethical codes, a study by Drugan (2011) identified that professional and non-professional translation codes are quite different, and one of the main differences between them is that the latter indicates specific penalties if ethical principals are violated. Ethical aspects of crowdsourcing also involve other issues such as human rights (Anastasiou and Schäler 2009) and copyright, the latter being involved mostly in cases where volunteers take over protected content, and issues related to the rightful ownership of the labour of the crowd.

Despite the popularity of the crowdsourcing movement in translation and the perceived threat that it represents for the professional community, this process still focuses on very specific purposes and is employed 'in very narrowly defined contexts' (Kelly et al. 2011: 92). Therefore, it is not expected to make a big dent in the web localization market anytime soon. For large corporations it is often perceived as a mechanism for cutting costs, even when the largest crowdsourcing efforts, such as Facebook, incur the same costs as professional localization (DePalma and Kelly 2011). Normally, the reasons for crowdsourcing in this context are speed, quality and global reach. Solicited crowdsourcing has typically been restricted to segment translation, with less success in cases where the translation entails longer paragraphs or even entire texts. However, this has in part been addressed by new crowdsourcing platforms where users post-edit MT, as the case of GTS in Wordpress for localizing blog entries or the platform Tradubi (Forcada 2011). In these cases users progress from segments to paragraphs to entire texts, depending on their motivation or time availability. The wider adoption of crowdsourcing practices has led experts to start developing best practices in the field, as not all efforts can count on an enthusiastic motivated community such as Facebook's. DePalma and Kelly (2011: 401–6) identified as the key strategies for fostering success: careful planning for crowdsourced translations, building and supporting the community, and making sure an efficient platform or tool that allows for seamless collaboration is built.

The debate about the lack of professionalization also reflects issues of quality, one of the main arguments of the professional side. It is often argued that quality might be lower than if using professionals, even though in some cases the 'crowd effect' might lead to higher quality (Zaidan and Callison-Burch 2011; Désilets and van der Meer 2011). Nevertheless, it has been shown that in some cases crowdsourced websites might show equal quality to those of professionally localized ones. The approach taken by the industry is to let the crowd control the quality through the natural peer-review process (i.e. Wikipedia); to review all translations by professionals, as in the cases of Kiva.org, Translators without borders or Facebook; or else to implement voting systems like the one on Facebook, in which users both propose translations and vote for the best ones. In Jiménez-Crespo (2011d) it was argued that this system is similar to the user-based quality-evaluation methods proposed by Nida (Nida and Taber 1969), and represents a probe into the evolving subconscious set of conventions that the community of users expect for the specific social networking site, as advocated by both functionalist (Nord 1997) and corpus-assisted approaches to quality evaluation (Bowker 2002).

From the point of view of Translation Studies, the massive collaboration of volunteers facilitated by technological developments represents a new phenomenon that is attracting the attention of an increasing number of scholars (i.e. Cronin 2003; O'Hagan 2011; McDonough 2011, 2012). Its opens up novel research perspectives and also allows us to revisit existing translation theorizations and leads to new perspectives (Jiménez-Crespo 2011d, 2013). As already mentioned, the online collaborative translation platforms originally created for web localization are currently widely used by the industry to crowdsource all types of content, from subtitles to literary works. As an example, subtitling is another modality in which non-professional translation has thrived with the advent of the Internet, with websites such as Dotsub or TED Open Translation Project. It is also currently impacting translation training, as scholars are reflecting on the potential use of crowdsourcing sites as a gateway into the professional world for trainees (O'Hagan 2008; Desjardins 2011). Special issues on non-professional translation and localization by the journals *Linguistica Antverpiensia* and *The Translator* show that non-professional and collaborative translation practices, mostly fuelled by the novel avenues opened up by the Web 2.0, are currently at the centre of the discipline and will continue to be so in the near future.

The boom in the formation of volunteer translation communities has also fostered the development of novel kinds of translation platforms, tools and services to accommodate the various types of collaboration. The development of these tools or platforms represents a key element in the potential success of any crowdsourcing effort (DePalma and Kelly 2011). These new technologies normally incorporate collaborative translation memory with terminology-management capabilities as well as translation-management tools that focus on textual chunking (Filip 2012b). The different types of tools can be subdivided between open-source technologies, crowdsourcing tools and outsourced crowdsourcing services. Open-source technologies encompass a wide range of tools, such as content management systems (Drupal, Wordpress, Movable type) or terminology-management systems (Termwiki, Omegawiki). Recently there has been a boom in the development of platforms for collaborative translation and crowdsourcing, which in turn can be divided between pure platforms and those that are mixed with MT post-editing, such as Tradubi[6] or Yakushite.net. Pure platforms have been the object of research with efforts such as Transbey (Bey *et al.* 2006) or the platform created in Canada by Désilets (2007). Additionally, as we have seen, a number of services offer their technologies to provide crowdsourced[7] or professional translation services, such as Gengo, Speaklike or Getlocalization. Many of these services either offer volunteer services or involve payments of small amounts to participants in the fashion of Mechanical Turk – Amazon's online marketplace designed to pay people small sums of money to perform Human Intelligence Tasks (or HITs): tasks that are difficult for computers but easy for people (Zaidan and Callison-Burch 2011).

MACHINE TRANSLATION AND POST-EDITING

The use of Human-Assisted Machine Translation (HAMT) is currently the other trend that looks like having the biggest impact on web localization. When discussing the role of MT in web localization, it is necessary to separate two main methods: first, the use of online MT engines to automatically localize websites entirely, and, second, the HAMT model in which translation experts participate to achieve high localization quality by post-editing the output from MT systems. As García (2009, 2011, 2012) indicates, the future of web localizers' tasks seems bound to move away from the triple combination of management, translating textual segments with TM, and quality control towards an HAMT model that focuses on: (1) management, (2) pre- and post-editing of web texts with TM-assisted MT and (3) quality control.

Two distinct types of architecture are popular in web systems (Hutchins and Somers 1992): the earlier rule-based MT with services, such as Babelfish supported by Systrans technology, and the later statistically based MT which relies on massive online corpora, such as Google Translate. The former systems are based on the application of 'morphological, syntactic and/or semantic rules to the analysis of a source-language text and synthesis of a target language text' (Quah 2006: 70–1). These models assume that translation entails a process of analysis and representation of the meaning of any source text to produce the equivalent in the target language. Interlingua and transfer systems are the two types of approaches in this area (Hutchins 2005), although only the latter are currently available on the market. This architecture, mainly represented by Systrans, Lucy, Apertium and Babelfish online, is less popular than the newer statistics- and example-based ones, even though some open-source initiatives such as Apertium are widely popular. Statistical MT is based on data provided by massive corpora of parallel and monolingual texts, and the translation is extracted using specific statistical methods. It is currently the most popular model in web-based fully automated MT systems. It includes approaches at the word, phrase and syntax level – with phrase models being the ones currently in the market, used by Google, Microsoft Bing or SDL Language Weaver. Google's translation engine is a prime example of this database-at-phrase-level approach. The system is constantly and simultaneously enriched by new translations that feed the parallel corpus, and by the feedback of users who are offered the possibility of uploading their own translation memories or their translations, or even post-editing the output of the translation directly.[8] Thus, new data-driven architectures are continually being improved through feedback and intervention from users, in what could be defined as a crowdsourced approach to improving MT systems. Some services such as Microsoft Translator offer a widget for Free Online MT (FOMT) that websites can incorporate in order to let the community improve the final quality of the automatic web localization, a convergence of crowdsourcing and MT foreseeable for the future.

Of all the possible uses of FOMT, the most popular is localizing web pages or web content (Austermühl 2011; Gaspari 2007). The objectives are mostly assimilation or informational purposes: that is, to quickly obtain the gist of the information that would not otherwise be available through commercial localization (Hutchins 2005). Its popularity is demonstrated by the fact that these engines get over 50 million hits a day and over 50% of users are speakers of languages other than English from around the world (DePalma and Kelly 2009; Och 2012). Despite its widespread use, FOMT cannot be considered a standard business model in the localization industry, even though it has been successfully applied in very restricted text types and contexts, such as Microsoft online knowledge base. In such very restricted cases, research has found users tend to rate machine-translated articles similarly to, or even more highly than, those translated by humans (Gerber 2008).

Within the overall effect of MT in web localization, the phenomenon having an increasing impact is the shift towards HAMT models, in which technical writers pre-edit source texts and translators post-edit the output of MT engines. This implies gains of time and efficiency in localizing websites and user-generated content. It was towards the end of the last decade that some corporations decided that MT output would help rather than distract translators and, consequently, started to implement TM-assisted MT systems (García 2009: 207). Nowadays, 40% of localization companies post-edit MT output for web localization purposes according to a 2009 survey by

TAUS Data Association, which perhaps indicates a future in which most processes may be performed this way. One of the main reasons for doing so is the time and budget savings that industry specialists say can amount to 60 to 80% compared to human translation of specific pre-edited texts. These potential benefits mean that, in future, localizers will probably not work from scratch on complete source texts, nor even use a segment-based process with TM, but will repair MT output: quite a dull process, due to the repetitive nature of MT errors. They will also be required to point out repetitive errors so that developers can fix them in the system (Hearne and Way 2011). Nevertheless, it is rather reassuring to know that localization and translation experts are still at the core of this new post-editing model; post-editing needs to be done by translators or experts with knowledge of the source language and transfer skills (Hutchins 2005).

The efficiency post-editing can provide is enhanced if texts are specifically prepared for this process. Normally, MT can process three types of text: 'raw', pre-edited, or texts prepared using controlled language systems, an approach widely used in specific industries (Hutchins 2005). The MT engine can then be a domain-specific one or a sublanguage-one, and specific terminology databases might be applied. The pre-editing of source texts entails a principle somewhat similar to the internationalization paradigm advocated by Pym (2010), in which web texts are not only processed to simplify the syntactic structures and range of terminology, but also to control the cultural, creative and metaphorical issues in source texts, so rendering them supposedly 'culture-neutral' and unambiguous. This is geared towards facilitating the task of MT systems and for those who have English as a second language. The texts can subsequently be processed and leveraged with TM systems, in what is known as MT-assisted TM: matches in the TM

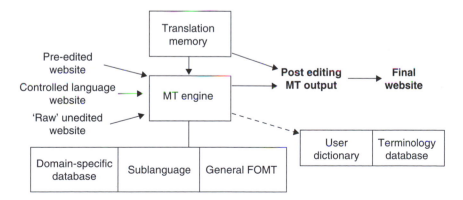

Figure 8.1 The cycle of human-aided MT for web localization. Adapted from Hutchins (2005: 4)

are leveraged or reused, and the new segments are processed by the MT engine. The output might be subsequently post-edited or not, and this post-editing can also be performed to some extent semi-automatically (Kuhn *et al* 2010).

There has been a considerable amount of research on post-editing translations in general (i.e. Krings 2001), some of it specifically with regard to MT post-editing (i.e. Allen 2003; O'Brien 2006, 2011; Fiederer and O'Brien 2009; Guerberof 2009; García 2011). However, so far no research has been carried out particularly on post-editing translations in web localization. Post-edited texts have been found to be rated as just as accurate and clear as human-translated ones, but not as highly rated in regard to style (Fiederer and O'Brien 2009). In some cases they have also been found to some extent more useful or relevant for translators than fuzzy matches from TMs (Plitt and Masselot 2010). If we consider this shift towards post-editing models as inevitable, it should also be mentioned that translators resist moving to the post-editing model, as it is less satisfying and more stressful than working with the source text from scratch (Wallis 2008). This shift will obviously come at the expense of great adjustments in the training and daily practice of web localizers (García 2009). Despite claims of efficiency and savings, the cognitive effort involved in repairing MT-translated texts has also been found to be similar to that of processing a source text from scratch (O'Brien 2006). Therefore, it is of great interest to research how the new model will impact the daily tasks of professional localizers globally. This gradual shift is currently being analysed by scholars, with journals such as *Tradumática* dedicating special issues to this trend. The most discussed issue in MT research is quality: translation quality appears more often as the topic of research in MT publications than in TS ones. As we saw in Chapter 5, MT quality can be a somewhat elastic concept, and it depends on several variables: source processing, engine preparation, engine type (rule-based, statistical, or some kind of hybrid), and language-pair combination.

Finally, the use of MT in web-mediated communications, not necessarily in web localization, should also be mentioned. This occurs in web chats or instant translation of user-generated content when the predetermined language of the user does not match that of the content. For example, as we have seen, Facebook gives the option of translating postings or comments when the language used does not match the preferred locale. We can clearly see the impact of MT in Web 2.0 interactive and social environments, with more and more information being constantly and automatically translated as well as customized to the user's language needs. Similarly, other exciting developments in MT, in combination with crowdsourcing, let users take pictures with smart phones and have the linguistic content translated – for example, Speaklike or PicTranslator. As we see, the possibilities are endless.

UNCERTAIN PERSPECTIVES

We could not end this chapter without considering the unpredictable nature of technological advances and their potential impact on web localization. Web localization is 'being determined by new technologies' (Munday 2008: 194), and therefore the unpredictable nature of new technologies will continue to determine the evolution of web localization as we know it. Technologies have shaped societies since antiquity (Cronin 2010, 2013), and web localization will continue to be caught between the technological developments that hasten communication globally and the need to make a variety of content available to larger audiences with different cultures and languages. The TAUS Data Association organization sees the future of translation as determined by unlimited potentials: unlimited languages, unlimited content, and multidirectional continuous translation. Also, as the meteoric rise of social networking sites shows, new genres will continue to appear, merge and develop, probably combining different platforms, such as smart phones, tablets, websites, etc. As the imaginative Don Quixote told his companion Sancho Panza, 'Thou hast seen nothing yet': the possibilities of the future are endless. It looks as if the web localization revolution has just started, and we should brace ourselves for new and exciting developments.

SUMMARY

This chapter has examined important questions related to the continuing evolution of web localization in the context of constant technological developments. The key issues analysed have been professionalization in the field in light of crowdsourcing and volunteer translation practices, as well as the impact of MT in the localization of both websites and user-generated content. We have reviewed how crowdsourcing practices that started with web localization have expanded to cover all types of translation content and how they do not necessarily represent a threat to localization as a profession. We have also argued that web localization processes are moving towards MT-assisted Translation Memory models in which post-editing rather than translation from scratch is the norm. The chapter ended with a brief review of how the unpredictability of technological developments will continue to challenge practitioners and translation scholars alike.

FURTHER READING

For a concise review of the global impact of technology on Translation Studies, see Cronin 2013 and O'Hagan's (2012b) entry in the *Routledge Handbook of Translation Studies*. The special issue of *Linguistica Antverpiensia* on crowdsourcing also edited by O'Hagan (2011) offers a comprehensive account of all issues related to this phenomenon from industry and academic experts, including quality, ethical and management aspects and case studies. See the chapter by DePalma and Kelly (2011) for best practices in management crowdsourcing efforts, and the European Commission (2012) report for an institutional view on this phenomenon. There is a large number of publications that cover all aspects of Machine Translation. See the articles of García (2009, 2010, 2011, 2012) or Guerberof (2009) for a TS perspective, as well as Quah's (2006) monograph on translation and technology, especially chapters 2 and 3. See Pym (2012) on how MT post-editing is changing translation training. Translation technology is a fast-evolving area, and industry-oriented journals such as *Multilingual* or websites such as John Yunker's Global by Design website (http://www.globalbydesign.com/), Common sense Advisory (http://www.commonsenseadvisory.com/) and especially the new TAUS Data Association website (www.translationautomation. com) offer great insights into current developments.

NOTES

CHAPTER 1

1 Internet active websites according to Netcraft in March 2012: http://news.netcraft.com/.

2 As an example, IDC Research predicted that for 2007, 22.7% of the market share in the translation industry would be for web localization and just 12.8% for software localization.

3 Applications and content that are available via the browser and not tied necessarily to any particular computer or device.

4 The initial more static nature of HTML content favoured a higher involvement of regular translators in web localization processes. For example, in a 2005 survey by Reinke 55% of British translators claimed to regularly translate HTML content, due to the widespread use of tag-editing translation memory software, such as Trados TagEditor (Reinke 2005).

5 As an example, the following segment that Facebook presents to volunteer translators incorporates a number of variables that closely resemble software localization strings: '{name 1}, {name 2} and {n-more-friends} like {target}'s {=deal} {deal title} on your Wall'. Translating this string requires an understanding of programming in terms of how to handle software variables during localization processes.

6 http://www.internetworldstats.com/stats.htm.

7 The *Microsoft Press Computer Dictionary* defined software localization as the process of altering a program so that it is appropriate for the area in which it is used (Microsoft Press 1994).

8 According to Microsoft Corporation (2003), the technical conventions are mostly related to: time, currency formatting, casing, sorting and string comparison, number formatting, addresses, paper size, telephone numbers, units of measure.

9 This can be seen in the Unicode Common Locale Data Repository: http://cldr.unicode.org/.

10 ISO 639 *Codes for the representation of names of languages.*

11 ISO 3166 *Codes for the representation of names of countries.*

12 Microsoft offers a complete list of locales at http://msdn.microsoft.com/en-us/library/oh88fahh(v=vs.85).aspx, or the Unicode consortium offers the Unicode Common Locale Date Repository at: http://cldr.unicode.org/.

13 LISA ceased operating in 2011.

14 The physical component would not apply to web localization *per se*, as it refers to actual physical modifications, such as changing a plug type in a product or placing the wheel on the right side of a car (LISA 2007: 7).

15   Hypertexts also exist in printed form, for example phone books, instruction manuals, etc. (Foltz 1996).

CHAPTER 2

1   In this case, 'text' refers to the entire website, and internationalization primarily focuses on development efforts, coding or recoding a website to remove any particular language/locale biases. 'Text' is not used here as a linguistic and communicative notion.

2   This is different from the notion of equivalence derived from early linguistic approaches to translation (Nord 1997).

3   While software localization is typically restricted to a main code base such as Java or .Net.

4   Once these errors have been detected a 'we will deal with this later' attitude normally prevails in industry settings.

5   Descriptions and dimensions for each country can be found at http://geert-hofstede.com/dimensions.html.

6   This dimension is based on the works of Hall (1976).

7   Nowadays, a GMS that is good for multilingual website deployment will allow the creation of global templates that can be used across all languages, as well as allowing customizations for certain language/locales. A good GMS allows for a core set of general information plus deviations from the 'main' site for locale-specific info (like local job listings, news feeds and contact information).

8   http://www.useit.com/alertbox/20030825.html.

9   Reading is nevertheless considered a dynamic and interactive act in which readers cognitively interact with the interpretation of any text.

10   In a sense, these texts represent what functionalists refer to as 'offers of information' (Reiss and Vermeer 1984). Receivers can accept these offers or not. For example, usability studies refer to the case of 'banner blindness' or 'pop-up blindness': the fact that users grow accustomed to ignoring moving or flashing text boxes on the periphery of the main text.

CHAPTER 3

1   Some authors criticize the linguistic approach that confines the maximum unit of translation to the text, offering the culture as the ultimate unit of translation (Bassnett and Lefevere 1990).

2   The fact that hypertexts represent units of production and presentation, in the context of constant updates to websites, is to some extent similar to the definition of hypertexts in Information Management as 'Information Objects' (Hofmann and Mehnert 2000). Web texts are defined as a collection of information identified as a unit, defined by its communicative purpose, the user they address, the company or product they represent, the information provided (in a specific format and for a specific audience, and advertising restrictions) (Hofman and Mehnert 2000).

3   According to Bowker, whenever a new way of working is introduced there will inevitably be effects on both the process and the product (Bowker 2006).

4   Some research groups, such as the TRACE group in the Universitat Autonoma of Barcelona, have focused on the impact of CAT tools on translated texts: http://grupsderecerca.uab.cat/tradumatica/es/content/trace-traducci%C3%B3n-asistida-calidad-y-evaluaci%C3%B3n.

5   Even though, with hypertexts, developers can change or enlarge them at any time.

6   Breadcrumb navigation refers to the navigation path within a website that appears on top of the main content of each page, such as 'Home>About us>Our Mission> Volunteer opportunities'.

7   De Beaugrande and Dressler define coherence as 'the ways in which the components of the TEXTUAL WORLD, i.e. the configuration of CONCEPTS and RELATIONS which underline the surface text, are mutually accessible and relevant' (1981: 4).

8   The author defines cognitive overhead as 'the additional effort and concentration necessary to maintain several tasks or trails at one time' (Conklin 1987: 40).
9   See Jiménez-Crespo (2009e) for a review on accessible navigation.
10 Such as the Avral Tramigo tool for localizing Macromedia Flash animations.

CHAPTER 4

1   For example, in Stubbs's (1996: 11) seminal book on Corpus Linguistics he indicated: 'some authors distinguish between text type and genre. I will not'. Similarly, from the Corpus-Based TS perspective, Laviosa writes 'The terms subject domain, subject field, text category and text genre are used interchangeably in this study. I have deliberately chosen to avoid the words "genre" and "type"' (1998: 566).
2   Initially Reiss (1976) included the notion of an 'audio media' type to cover those texts represented in written mode but intended to be perceived by the recipient via other media, such as operas. However, in a later publication Reiss adopted the notion of a 'multimedia' text type to include those texts expressed through a combination of media, such as comic books.
3   Swales (1990: 24–7) defines a 'discourse community' thus:

    1.   A discourse community has a broadly agreed set of common public goals.
    2.   A discourse community has mechanisms of intercommunication among its members.
    3.   A discourse community uses its participatory mechanisms primarily to provide information and feedback.
    4.   A discourse community utilizes and hence possesses one or more genres in the communicative furtherance of its aims.
    5.   In addition to owning genres, a discourse community has a threshold level of members with a suitable degree of relevant content and discourse expertise.

4   Some TS scholars have used several terms to refer to this concept such as *textsorte* or 'class of text' (Reiss and Vermeer 1984; Göpferich 1995a) or text form (Bell 1991).
5   More information can be found in the websites of GENTT <www.gentt.uji.es> or GITRAD <www.gitrad.uji.es>.
6   This notion has a parallel in the functionalist proposal of Reiss and Vermeer (1984) of 'complex texts': texts that can incorporate instances of other texts.
7   The concept of 'norm' can be defined as 'the translation of general values or ideas shared by a group – as to what is conventionally right and wrong, adequate and inadequate – into performance instructions appropriate for and applicable to particular situations, specifying what is prescribed and forbidden, as well as what is tolerated and permitted in a certain behavioral dimension' (Toury 1998: 14).
8   Hatim and Mason write: 'within a given language and across languages, the various forms of a given type may not be equally available to all users – a factor we may refer to as text type deficit' (1997: 133).
9   These notions are inspired in the theoretical framework of cognitive 'schemata' (Rumelhart 1980).

CHAPTER 5

1   ASTM F2575-06 Standard Guide for Quality Assurance in Translation.
2   Nevertheless, it is assumed that a process should be in place to minimize and effectively correct those errors.
3   WWW Accessibility Initiative: http://www.w3.org/WAI/. A study by Tercedor and Jiménez-Crespo (2008) reported that only a third of websites localized into Spanish from the largest US companies included processed basic accessibility content, such as translations of alternative text to images.

4   The Austrian Önorm has now been renamed ASI (Austrian Standard Institute).
5   http://www.etsi.org/website/newsandevents/2011_07_isg_lis.aspx.
6   Translation problems are also associated with translation strategies. From a cognitive perspective a translation strategy is defined as 'a potentially conscious procedure for the solution of a problem which an individual is faced with when translating a text segment from one language to another' (Löscher 1991: 76).
7   This has also been framed in terms of absolute and functional errors (Gouadec 1998).
8   Gouadec's taxonomy of errors includes 300 lexical and 375 syntactic ones.
9   In the case of the SAE J2450 automotive industry scale, error impact varies from minimal to potentially leading to a car accident and death (Wright 2006).
10 Hallidayian systemic-functionalism for House and argumentation theory for Williams.
11 The North American ASTM quality standard is nevertheless firmly grounded on functionalist principles.
12 First of all, the comparable corpus includes both a translated and non-translated collection of texts. This corpus allows us to observe patterns in non-translated texts in the same genre and text type in order to produce more natural-sounding translations. The second component, a quality corpus, is a small hand-picked corpus consisting of texts selected primarily for their conceptual content. The next component is a quantity corpus, an extensive collection of carefully selected texts in the same domain, genre, text type, etc. Finally, Bowker proposes a section called inappropriate corpus, a corpus that contains 'inappropriate' parallel texts, that is, texts that are very similar to the original text but include different web genres or subgenres.
13 A collocation can be defined as a co-occurrence of two or more words within a given span (distance from each other), while colligations are co-occurrences between specific words and grammatical classes, or interrelations of grammatical categories (Tognini-Bonelli 2001: 74). Collocations are therefore related to lexical or semantic relations, while colligations are co-occurrences of words and grammatical classes.
14 To some extent, this approach parallels failure mode and effects (FMEA) risk analysis.
15 Some services provided by companies, such as Nielsen Netratings, quantitatively measure in seconds how long visitors spend on any page and website.

CHAPTER 6

1   These beginnings mirror the first in the 1970s and 1980s stages of interpreting and audiovisual translation research, the two other areas that are consistently proposed as distinct branches within Translation Studies (Munday 2012).
2   Including those underlying the models and theories applied.
3   Gile also indicates that it adds to the spread of paradigms, and might further weaken the status of TS research as an autonomous discipline.
4   This goal has been the object of much debate, and as a result scholars propose conceptualizing translation phenomena in probabilistic rather than absolute terms (Toury 2004; Chesterman 2000).
5   Holmes included as medium-restricted written and oral translation, as well as human vs. machine translation. In this regard, the label 'medium' was used more as a classificatory aid or heuristic device – a way of expressing how contents are transmitted differently – than according to the strict sense of the term (Cronin 2010).
6   One of the proposed general tendencies of translation, conventionalization (Kenny 2001), was found not to appear in web localization, thus challenging the inclusion of this tendency as part of a possible general theory of translation (Jiménez-Crespo 2009a).
7   As pointed out by Rabadán (2010), addressing non-scholars adds another layer of complexity to research carried out in this branch.
8   Or in the case of functionalist theories, might acknowledge it just for specific cases as required by the translation function (Nord 1997).

9   Theoretical localization models should not be confused with the professional notion of work-flow models that attempt to streamline localization.

10   BITRA, Bibliography of Interpreting and Translation, http://aplicacionesua.cpd.ua.es/tra_int/usu/buscar.asp?idioma=en.

11   'Representativity' embodies the main criterion required for corpora, and it can be defined as to guarantee that the corpus represents the textual population intended by means of sampling.

12   It also functions as an app for the Firefox browser: http://mac.softpedia.com/get/Internet-Utilities/WaybackFox.shtml.

13   http://www.httrack.com/.

CHAPTER 7

1   The diverse approaches to the teaching of localization can be also seen in the different settings in which it takes place, specialized courses in undergraduate four-year programmes, or translation MAs, localization-specific MAs (such as the ones at the Monterey Institute of International Studies in California, the Localization Research Centre in Limerick, Ireland or the Masters in Translation technology and localization at the Universitat Autonoma of Barcelona or the Universitat Jaume I in Spain), two-year community college certifications in the USA, etc.

2   Esselink (2001: 5) indicates that localization engineers need to have 'knowledge of programming languages, development environments, user interface design guidelines, localization and translation tools, language characteristics, and translation challenges . . . the job of localization engineer is ideal for those who like to fiddle around with tools, are keen on solving problems, and love to communicate with developers and translators alike.'

3   This could be to some extent the foundation for industry-centred training efforts, as specialists and professionals intuitively centre their teaching on the most common problems found in their profession.

4   Among several other terms used in the discipline, this notion has also been referred to as 'translatorial competence' (Toury 1995), 'translator competence' (Kiraly 1995).

5   http://corpus.leeds.ac.uk/mellange/ecolore_tmx_corpus.html.

6   http:// ecolomedia.uni-saarland.de/.

CHAPTER 8

1   On the other hand, Nida's approach was hailed as the first approach to quality evaluation that was not based on assessing some sort of equivalence to a source text.

2   TDA TAUS (http://www.tausdata.org/), Linguee (www.Linguee.com), Webitext (www.webitext.com), Mymemory (www.mymemory.translated.net).

3   Tim Berners-Lee, the inventor of the WWW, also regards the Web 1.0 as an entirely dynamic, interactive model, as it was intended from the start as a collaboration platform. He refers to the WWW, including the Web 2.0, as 'ReadWriteWeb'.

4   In some areas, such as Free and Open Software (FOSS), localizations have mostly been done by amateurs.

5   Mostly to languages of lesser diffusion.

6   Tradubi, like many other new projects, was discontinued.

7   Examples of community translation tools include, but are not limited to: CrowdIn (http://crowdin.net/), CrowdSight (http://www.welocalize.com) or LingoTek (http://www.lingotek.com).

8   These systems offer users the option to 'click to edit' or 'contribute to a better translation' thus improving future MT performance.

REFERENCES

Adkisson, H. (2002) 'Identifying De-Facto Standards for E-commerce Websites', unpublished MS thesis, University of Washington.

Agost, R. (1999) *Traducción y doblaje: Palabras, voces e imágenes*, Barcelona: Ariel.

Alcina, A. (2008) 'Translation Technologies: Scope, Tools and Resources', *Target*, 20: 79–102.

Alcina, A., V. Soler and J. Granell (2008) 'Translation Technology Skills Acquisition', *Perspectives*, 15: 203–44.

Allen, J. (2003) 'Post-editing', in H. Somers (ed.) *Computers and Translation: A Translators Guide*, Amsterdam-Philadelphia: John Benjamins, pp. 297–317.

Altanero, T. (2006) 'The localization job market in academe', in A. Pym, A. Perekrestenko and B. Starink (eds) *Translation Technology and its Teaching*, Tarragona: Intercultural Studies Group, pp. 31–6.

Alvstad, C., A. Hild and E. Tiselius (eds) (2011) *Methods and Strategies of Process Research: Integrative approaches in Translation Studies*, Amsterdam-Philadelphia: John Benjamins.

Anastasiou, D. and R. Schäler (2009) 'Translating Vital Information: Localisation, Internationalisation, and Globalisation', *Synthèses*, 3: 11–25.

Angelelli, C. (2005) 'Healthcare Interpreting Education: Are We Putting the Cart Before the Horse?', *ATA Chronicle*, 34: 33–8, 55.

Angelelli, C. and H. Jacobson (eds) (2009) *Testing and Assessment in Translation and Interpreting Studies*, Amsterdam-Philadelphia: John Benjamins.

Archibald, J. (ed.) (2004) *La Localisation: Problématique de la formation*, Montreal: Linguatec Editeur.

Askehave, I. and A. E. Nielsen (2005) 'Digital Genres: A Challenge to Traditional Genre Theory', *Information Technology and People*, 18: 120–41.

ASTM International (2006) *F2575-06 Standard Guide for Quality Assurance in Translation*, West Conshohocken PA: ASTM International.

Austermühl, F. (2006) 'Training Translators to Localize', in A. Pym, A. Perekrestenko and B. Starink (eds) *Translation Technology and its Teaching*, Tarragona: Intercultural Studies Group, pp. 69–81.

—— (2007) 'Translators in the Language Industry: From Localization to Marginalization', in A. Holderbaum and K. Brenner (eds) *Gebundener Sprachgebrauch in der Übersetzungswissenschaft*, Trier: Wissenschaftlicher Verlag Trier, pp. 39–51.

—— (2011) 'On Clouds and Crowds: Current Developments in Translation Technology', *T21N-Translation in Transition*, 9. Online. Available HTTP: <www.t21n.com/homepage/articles/T21N-2011-09-Austermuehl.pdf> (accessed 10 July 2012).

Austermühl, F. and C. Mirwald (2010) 'Images of Translators in Localization Discourse', in F. Austermühl and J. Kornelius (eds) *Learning Theories and Practice in Translation Studies*, Trier: Wissenschaftlicher Verlag Trier, pp. 99–138.

Baker, M. (1995) 'Corpora in Translation Studies: An Overview and Some Suggestions for Future Research', *Target*, 7: 223–43.

—— (2011) *In other Words: A Coursebook on Translation*, 2nd ed., New York-London: Routledge.

Baker, M. and G. Saldanha (eds) (2008) *Routledge Encyclopedia of Translation Studies*, New York-London: Routledge.

Baroni, M. and M. Ueyama (2006) 'Building General- and Special-purpose Corpora by Web Crawling', Proceedings of the 13th NIJL International Symposium, *Language Corpora: Their Compilation and Application*, Tokyo, pp. 31–40.

Barthes, R. (1977) *Image – Music – Text*, New York: Hill & Wang.

Bass, S. (2006) 'Quality in the Real World', in K. Dunne (ed.) *Perspectives on Localization*, Amsterdam-Philadelphia: John Benjamins, pp. 69–84.

Bassnett, S. and A. Lefevere (1990) *Translation, History and Culture*, London-New York: Pinter Publishers.

Bastin, G. (2008) 'Adaptation' in M. Baker and G. Saldanha (eds) *Routledge Encyclopedia of Translation Studies*, London-New York: Routledge, pp. 5–8.

Bateman, J. (2008) *Multimodality and Genre: A Foundation for the Systematic Analysis of Multimodal Documents*, Basingstoke: Palgrave MacMillan.

Bazerman, C. (1994) 'Systems of Genres and the Enactment of Social Intentions', in A. Freedman and P. Medway (eds) *Genre and the New Rhetoric*, London: Taylor and Francis, pp. 79–101.

Beaugrande, R. de (1978) *Factors in a Theory of Poetic Translating*, Amsterdam: Rodopi.

Beaugrande, R. de and W. Dressler (1981) *Introduction to Text Linguistics*, London: Longman.

Bédard, C. (2000) 'Mémoire de traduction cherche traducteur de phrases', *Traduire*, 186: 41–9.

Beeby, A., P. Rodríguez Inés and P. Sánchez-Gijón (eds) (2009) *Corpus Use and Translating*, Amsterdam-Philadelphia: John Benjamins.

Bell, R. T. (1991) *Translation and Translating: Theory and Practice*, London: Longman.

Berkenkotter, C. and T. Huckin (1995) *Genre Knowledge in Disciplinary Communications: Cognition, Culture, Power*, Hillsdale NJ: Lawrence Erlbaum.

Bernardini, S. (2004) 'The Theory Behind the Practice. Translator Training or Translator Education?', in K. Malmkjaer (ed.) *Translation in Undergraduate Degree Programmes*, Amsterdam-Philadelphia: John Benjamins, pp. 17–29.

Berners-Lee, T. (2000) *Weaving the Web: The Past, Present and Future of the World Wide Web by its Inventor*, London: Texere.

Berners-Lee, T., *et al.* (1992) 'World Wide Web: The Information Universe', *Electronic Networking*, 2(1): 52–8.

Bey, Y., C. Boitet and K. Kageura (2006) 'The TRANSBey Prototype: An Online Collaborative Wiki-based CAT Environment for Volunteer Translators', in E. Yuste Rodrigo (ed.) *Proceedings of the Third International Workshop on Language Resources for Translation Work, Research & Training (LR4Trans-III)*, Paris: ELRA, pp. 49–54.

Bey, Y., K. Kageura and C. Boitet (2008) 'BEYTrans: A Wiki-based environment for helping online volunteer translators', in E. Yuste Rodrigo (ed.) *Topics in Language Resources for Translation and Localisation*, Amsterdam-Philadelphia: John Benjamins, pp. 139–54.

Bhatia, V. K. (1993) *Analysing Genre: Language Use in Professional Settings*, London: Longman.

—— (1997) 'Genre-mixing in Academic Introductions', *English for Specific Purposes*, 16: 181–95.

—— (2002) 'Applied Genre Analysis: A Multi-Perspective Model', *Ibérica*, 4: 3–19.

—— (2008) 'Genre Analysis, ESP and Professional Practice', *English for Specific Purposes*, 27: 161–74.

Biau Gil, J. R. and A. Pym (2006) 'Technology and Translation (A Pedagogical Overview)', in A. Pym, A. Perekrestenko and B. Starink (eds) *Translation Technology and its Teaching*, Tarragona: Intercultural Studies Group, pp. 5–19.

Biber, D. (1988) *Variations across Speech and Writing*, Cambridge: Cambridge University Press.

Biber, D. (1989) 'A Typology of English Texts', *Linguistics*, 27: 3–43.

—— (1993) 'Representativeness in Corpus Design', *Literary and Linguistic Computing*, 8: 243–57.

Biber, D. and J. Kurjian (2004) 'Towards a Taxonomy of Web Registers and Text Types: A Multidimensional Analysis', *Language and Computers – Corpus Linguistics and the Web*, 23: 109–31.

Bly, R. (2002) *The Online Copywriter's Handbook*, New York: McGraw-Hill.

Bolaños, A. (2004) 'Propuesta metodológica para la didáctica de la localización de sitios Web' [A methodological proposal for the teaching of localization of websites]', in S. Bravo Utrera (ed.) *Traducción, lenguas, literaturas. Sociedad del conocimiento. Enfoques desde y hacia la cultura*, Las Palmas: Universidad de Las Palmas, pp. 22–45.

Bolaños, A., *et al.* (2005) 'Analysing Digital Genres: Function and Functionality in Corporate Websites of Computer Hardware', *Ibérica*, 9: 123–47.

Borja, A. (2000) *El texto jurídico inglés y su traducción al español*, Barcelona: Ariel.

Borja, A., I. García Izquierdo and V. Montalt (2009) 'Research Methodology in Specialized Genres for Translation Purposes', *The Interpreter and Translator Trainer*, 3: 57–77.

Börjel, J. (2007) 'Language-specific Quality Issues in a Real World Localization Process', unpublished MS Thesis, Linköpings Universitet, Sweden.

Bortoli, M. de and J. M. Maroto (2009) 'Usability and Website Localization', in G. Anderman and J. Díaz Cintas (eds) *Audiovisual Translation. Language Transfer on the Screen*, Basingstoke: Palgrave McMillan, pp. 186–96.

Bouffard, P. and P. Caignon (2006) 'Localisation et variation linguistique: Vers une géolinguistique de l espace virtuel francophone', *Meta*, 51: 806–23

Bourdieu, P. (1972) *Esquisse d'une théorie de la pratique précédé de trois études d'ethnologie kabyle*, Geneva: Droz.

Bowker, L. (1998) 'Using Specialised Monolingual Native-Language Corpora as a Translation Resource: A Pilot Study', *Meta*, 43: 331–51.

—— (2001) 'Towards a Methodology for a Corpus-Based Approach to Translation Evaluation', *Meta*, 46: 345–64.

—— (2002) *Computer-Aided Translation Technology: A Practical Introduction*, Ottawa: University of Ottawa Press.

—— (2006) 'Translation Memory and Text', in L. Bowker (ed.) *Lexicography, Terminology and Translation*, Ottawa: University of Ottawa Press, pp. 174–87.

Bowker, L. and Barlow, M. (2008) 'A Comparative Evaluation of Bilingual Concordancers and Translation Memory Systems', in E. Yuste Rodrigo (ed.) *Topics in Language Resources for Translation and Localization*, Amsterdam-Philadelphia: John Benjamins, pp. 1–22.

Brink, T., D. Gergle and S. D. Wood (2002) *Usability for the Web*, San Francisco: Morgan Kauffman.

Brooks, D. (2000) 'What Price Globalization? Managing Costs at Microsoft', in R.C. Sprung (ed.) *Translating into Success*, Amsterdam-Philadelphia: John Benjamins, pp. 42–59.

Bryman, A. (2004) *Social Research Methods*, 2nd ed., Oxford: Oxford University Press.

Bublitz, W. (2005) 'The User as "Cyberego": Text, Hypertext and Coherence', in L. Moessner (eds) *Anglistentag 2004 Aachen: Proceedings*, Wissenschaftlicher Verlag Trier, pp. 311–24.

Budin, G. (2005) 'Localization', in K. Brown (ed.) *Encyclopedia of Language and Linguistics*, London: Elsevier, pp. 290–1.

—— (2008) 'Global Content Management: Challenges and Opportunities for Creating and Using Digital Translation Resources', in E. Yuste Rodrigo (ed.) *Topics in Language Resources for Translation and Localization*, Amsterdam-Philadelphia: John Benjamins, pp. 121–34.

Bühler, K. (1965/1934) *Sprachtheorie*, Stuttgart: G. Fischer.

Cadieux, P. and B. Esselink (2002) 'Feeling GILTy – Defining the Terms Globalization, Internationalization, Localization and Translation', *Language International*, June: 22–5.

Chandler, H. (2005) *The Game Localization Handbook*, Hingham MA: Charles River Media.

Chandler, H. and S. O'Malley Deming (2011) *The Game Localization Handbook*, 2nd ed., Burlington MA: Jones & Bartlett Learning.

Cheng, S. (2000) 'Globalizing an E-commerce Website', in R. C. Sprung (ed.) *Translating into Success*, Amsterdam-Philadelphia: John Benjamins, pp. 29–41.

Chesterman, A. (2000) 'A Causal Model for Translation Studies', in M. Olohan (ed.) *Intercultural Faultlines. Research Models in Translation Studies I: Textual and Cognitive Aspects*, Manchester: St Jerome, pp. 15–27.

—— (2001) 'Empirical Research Methods in Translation Studies', Proceedings from Erikoiskielet ja käännösteoria VAKKI-symposiumi XX 27: 9–22.

—— (2002) 'On the Interdisciplinarity of Translation Studies', *Logos*, 3: 1–9.

—— (2004) 'Beyond the Particular', in A. Mauranen and P. Kujamäki (eds) *Translation Universals. Do they Exist?* Amsterdam-Philadelphia: Benjamins, pp. 33–49.

Chesterman, A. and E. Wagner (2002) *Can Theory Help Translators? A Dialogue between the Ivory Tower and the Wordface*, Manchester: St Jerome.

Chomsky, N. (1965) *Aspects of the Theory of Syntax*, Cambridge: MIT Press.

Codina, L. (2003) 'Hiperdocumentos: Composición, estructura y evaluación', in J. Díaz Noci and R. Salaverría Aliaga (eds) *Manual de redacción ciberperiodística*, Barcelona: Ariel Comunicación, pp. 141–94.

Colina, S. (2008) 'Translation Quality Evaluation: Empirical Evidence from a Functionalist Approach', *The Translator*, 14: 97–134.

—— (2009) 'Further Evidence for a Functionalist Approach to Translation Quality Evaluation', *Target*, 21: 235–64.

Collombat, I. (2009) 'La didactique de l'erreur dans l'apprentissage de la traduction', *Jostrans*, 12: 37–54.

Conklin, J. (1987) 'Hypertext: An introduction and survey', *Computer*, 20: 17–41.

Corte, N. (2000) 'Web Site Localization and Internationalization: A Case Study', unpublished MA thesis, City College, United Kingdom.

Cronin, M. (2003) *Translation and Globalisation*, London-New York: Routledge.

—— (2010) 'The translation crowd', *Tradumàtica*, 8. Online. Available HTTP: <http://www.fti.uab.es/tradumatica/revista/num8/articles/04/04central.htm> (accessed 10 July 2012).

—— (2013) *Translation in the Digital Age*. New York-London: Routledge.

Crowston, K. (2010) 'Internet Genres', *Encyclopedia of Library and Information Sciences*, 3rd ed., vol. I, New York-London: Routledge, pp. 2983–95.

Crowston, K. and M. Williams (1997) 'Reproduced and Emergent Genres of Communication on the World Wide Web', Proceedings of the XXX Annual Hawaii International Conference on System Sciences, Maui, Hawaii. Los Alamitos, CA: IEEE-Computer Society, pp. 30–39.

—— (1999) 'The Effects of Linking on Genres of Web Documents', Proceedings of the XXXIII Annual Hawaii International Conference on System Sciences, Kilea, Hawaii, Los Alamitos: IEEE-Computer Society.

Crystal, D. (2001) *Language and the Internet*, Cambridge: Cambridge University Press.

—— (2011) *Internet Linguistics*, London: Routledge.

Cyr, D. and T. Haizley (2004) 'Localization of Web Design: An Empirical Comparison of German, Japanese, and United States Web Site Characteristics', *Journal of the American Society for Information Science and Technology*, 55: 1199–208.

Delisle, J. (1980) *L'Analyse du discours comme méthode de traduction*, Cahiers de Traductologie 2, Ottawa: Editions de l'Université d'Ottawa.

—— (1993) *La traduction raisonnée*, Ottawa: Presses de l'Université d'Ottawa.

—— (2005) *L'Enseignement pratique de la traduction*, Beirut-Ottawa: Presses de l'Université d'Ottawa.

DePalma, D. and N. Kelly (2009) 'The Business Case for Machine Translation'. Online. Available HTTP: <http://www.mt-archive.info/MTS-2009-DePalma-ppt.pdf> (accessed 10 July 2012).

—— (2011) 'Project Management for Crowdsourced Translation: How User-Translated Content Projects Work in Real Life', in K. Dunne and E. Dunne (eds) *Translation and Localization Project Management: The Art of the Possible*, Amsterdam-Philadelphia: John Benjamins, pp. 379–408.

Depraetere, I. (ed.) (2011) *Perspectives on Translation Quality*, Berlin-Boston: De Gruyter Mouton.

Désilets, A. (2007) 'Translation Wikified: How Will Massive Online Collaboration Impact the World of Translation?' *Proceedings of Translating and the Computer 29*, London: ASLIB.

Désilets, A. and J. van der Meer (2011) 'Co-creating a Repository of Best-Practices for Collaborative Translators', *Linguistica Antverpiensia*, 10: 11–27.

Desjardins, R. (2011) 'Facebook Me!: Arguing in Favour of Using Social Networking as a Tool for Translator Training', *Linguistica Antverpiensia*, 10: 154–75.

Devitt, A. (2008) *Writing Genres*, Carbondale IL: Southern Illinois University Press.

Díaz Cintas, J. and P. Muñoz Sánchez (2006) 'Fansubs: Audiovisual Translation in an Amateur Environment', *Jostrans*, 6: 37–52.

Díaz Cintas, J. and A. Remael (2007) *Audiovisual Translation: Subtitling (Translation practices Explained)*. Manchester: St Jerome.

Díaz Fouçes, O. (2004) 'Localizaçao de páginas da Internet na Formaçao de Tradutores', *Confluéncias – Revista de Traduçao Científica e Técnica*, 1. Online. Available HTTP: <http://confluencias.net/n1/fouces.pdf> (accessed 10 July 2012).

Diéguez Morales, M. I. (2008) 'Análisis terminológico de sitios web localizados del inglés al español: Uso de técnicas de amplificación y elisión', *Tradumática*, 6. Online. Available HTTP: <http://ddd.uab.cat/pub/tradumatica/15787559n6a9.pdf> (accessed 10 July 2012).

Diéguez Morales, M.I. and R. Lazo Rodríguez (2011) 'El español en Internet: Aciertos y errores en sitios web localizados del inglés', *Onomázein*, 24: 299–326.

DiFranco, C. (2003) 'Localization Skills for Translators: Localizability Requirements for Clients', *ATA Chronicle*. Online. Available HTTP: <http://www.abroadlink.com/Articles/Localization%20Skills%20for%20Translators-Localizability%20Requirements%20for%20Clients.pdf> (accessed 10 July 2012).

Dillon, A. and B. A. Gushrowski (2000) 'Genres and the Web: Is the Personal Home Page the First Uniquely Digital Genre?', *Journal of the American Society for Information Science*, 5: 202–5.

DIN 2345 (1998) *Übersetzungsaufträge*. Berlin: Beuth.

Drugan, J. (2011) 'Translation Ethics Wikified: How do Professional Codes of Ethics and Practice Apply to Non-professionally Produced Translation', *Linguistica Antverpiensia*, 10: 97–111.

Dunne, K. (2006a) 'A Copernican Revolution', in K. Dunne (ed.) *Perspectives on Localization*, Amsterdam-Philadelphia: John Benjamins, pp. 1–11.

—— (2006b) 'Putting the Cart Behind the Horse: Rethinking Localization Quality Management', in K. Dunne (ed.) *Perspectives on Localization*, Amsterdam: John Benjamins, pp. 95–117.

—— (2009) 'Assessing Software Localization: For A Valid Approach', in C. Angelelli and H. Jacobson (eds) *Testing and Assessment in Translation and Interpreting Studies*, Amsterdam: John Benjamins, pp. 185–222.

—— (2011) 'Managing the Fourth Dimension: Time and Schedule in Translation and Localization Projects', in K. Dunne and E. Dunne (eds) (2011) *Translation and Localization Management*, Amsterdam-Philadelphia: John Benjamins, pp. 119–52.

Dunne, K. and E. Dunne (eds) (2011) *Translation and Localization Management*, Amsterdam-Philadelphia: John Benjamins.

Engebretsen, M. (2000) 'Hypernews and Coherence', *Journal of Digital Information*, 1: 12–19.

Englund Dimitrova, B. (2005) *Expertise and Explicitation in the Translation Process*, Amsterdam-Philadelphia: John Benjamins.

Erickson, T. (1999) 'Rhyme and Punishment: The Creation and Enforcement of Conventions in an On-line Participatory Limerick Genre', *Proceedings of the 32nd Annual Hawaii International Conference on System Sciences, Hawaii*. Los Alamitos CA: IEEE Press.

Ericsson, K. A. (2000) 'Expertise in Interpreting: An Expert-performance Perspective', *Interpreting*, 5: 189–222.

—— (2006) 'Introduction', in K. A. Ericsson, *et al.* (eds) *The Cambridge Handbook of Expertise and Expert Performance*, Cambridge: Cambridge University Press, pp. 3–19.

Esselink, B. (2001) *A Practical Guide to Localization*, Amsterdam-Philadelphia: John Benjamins.

—— (2002) 'Localization Engineering: The Dream Job?', *Tradumática*, 1. Online. Available HTTP: <http://www.fti.uab.es/tradumatica/revista/articles/besselink/besselink.PDF> (accessed 10 July 2012).

—— (2006) 'The Evolution of Localization', in A. Pym, A. Perekrestenko and B. Starink (eds) *Translation Technology and its Teaching*, Tarragona: Intercultural Studies Group, pp. 21–30.

European Commission (2012) 'Crowdsourcing Translation', Studies on Multilingualism and Translation. Online. Available HTTP: <http://ec.europa.eu/dgs/translation/publications/studies/crowdsourcing_translation_en.pdf> (accessed 10 September 2012).

Fernández Costales, A. (2008) 'Translation 2.0. The Localization of Institutional Websites Under the Scope of Functionalist Approaches', in D. de Crom (ed.) *Translation and the (Trans)formation of Identities: Selected Papers of the CETRA Research Seminar in Translation Studies 2008*. Online. Available HTTP: <http://www.kuleuven.be/cetra/papers/papers.html> (accessed 10 July 2012).

—— (2011) '2.0 Facing the Challenges of the Global Era', Proceedings from Tralogy. Online. Available HTTP: <http://lodel.irevues.inist.fr/tralogy/index.php?id=120> (accessed 10 July 2012).

—— (2012) 'The Internationalization of Institutional Websites: The Case of Universities in the European Union', in A. Pym and D. Orrego-Carmona (eds) *Translation Research Projects 4*, Tarragona: Intercultural Studies Group. Online. HTTP: <http://isg.urv.es/publicity/isg/publications/trp_4_2012/index.htm>.

Ferreira-Alves, F. (2010) 'Brave New Wor(l)ds: Translation, Standardization and the Reshaping of a Professional Profile in the Language Industry', *T21N – Translation in Transition*, 8. Online. Available HTTP: <http://www.t21n.com/homepage/articles/T21N-2010-06-Ferreira-Alves.pdf> (accessed 10 July 2012).

Fiederer, R. and S. O'Brien (2009) 'Quality and Machine Translation: A Realistic Objective?', *Jostrans*, 11: 52–74.

Filip, D. (2012a) 'The Localization Standards Ecosystem', *Multilingual*, 127 (3): 29–37.

—— (2012b) 'Using Business Process Management and Modelling to Analyse the Role of Human Translators and Reviewers in Bitext Management Workflows', paper presented at the conference IATIS 2012, June 30th, Belfast, UK.

Filip, D., D. Lewis and F. Sasaki (2012) 'The Multilingual Web', Proceedings of the 21st World Wide Web Conference WWW 2012, Lyon, France, ACM proceedings. Online. Available HTTP: <http://www.cngl.ie/drupal/sites/default/files/papers3/fp26-filip.pdf> (accessed 10 July 2012).

Fletcher, W. H. (2007) 'Concordancing the Web: Promise and Problems, Tools and Techniques', in H. N. Nesselhauf and C. Biewer (eds) *Corpus Linguistics and the Web*, Amsterdam: Rodopi, pp. 25–46.

—— (2011) 'Corpus Analysis of the World Wide Web', in C.A. Chapelle (ed.) *Encyclopedia of Applied Linguistics*, London: Wiley-Blackwell. Available HTTP: <http://webascorpus.org/Corpus_Analysis_of_the_World_Wide_Web.pdf> (accessed 10 July 2012).

Folaron, D. (2006) 'A Discipline Coming of Age in the Digital Age: Perspectives on Localization', in K. Dunne (ed.) *Perspectives on Localization*, Amsterdam-Philadelphia: John Benjamins, pp. 195–222.

—— (2010) 'Web and translation', in Y. Gambier and L. van Doorslaer (eds) *Handbook of Translation Studies*, Amsterdam-Philadelphia: John Benjamins, pp. 446–50.

Foltz, P. W. (1996) 'Comprehension, Coherence and Strategies in Hypertext and Linear Text', in J. F. Rouet *et al.* (eds) *Hypertext and Cognition*, New Jersey: Lawrence Erlbaum, pp. 109–36.

Forcada, M. L. (2011) 'Apertium: A Free/Open-source Platform for Rule-based Machine Translation', *Machine Translation*, 25: 127–44.

Fritz, G. (1998) 'Coherence in hypertext', in W. Bublitz, U. Lenk and E. Ventola (eds) *Coherence in Spoken and Written Discourse: How to Create it and How to Describe it*, Amsterdam: John Benjamins, pp. 221–34.

GALA (2011) 'What is localization?'. Online. Available HTTP: <http://www.gala-global.org/what-localization> (accessed 10 July 2012).

Gambier, Y. and L. van Doorslaer (ed.) (2010) *Handbook of Translation Studies*, Amsterdam-Philadelphia: John Benjamins.

Gambier, Y. and H. Gottlieb (eds) (2004) *(Multi) Media Translation: Concepts, Practices, and Research*, Amsterdam-Philadelphia: John Benjamins.

Gamero, S. (2001) *La traducción técnica*, Barcelona: Ariel.

García, I. (2008a) 'Translating and Revising for Localisation: What Do We Know? What Do We Need to Know', *Machine Translation*, 16: 49–60.

García, I. (2008b) 'The proper place of professionals (and non-professionals and machines) in web translation', *Tradumática*, 8. Online. Available HTTP:http://www.fti.uab.cat/tradumatica/revista/num8/sumari.htm (accessed 10 July 2012).

—— (2009) 'Beyond Translation Memory: Computers and the Professional Translator', *Jostrans*, 12: 199–214.

—— (2010) 'Is machine translation ready yet?', *Target*, 15: 7–21.

—— (2011) 'Translating by Post-editing: Is It the Way Forward?', *Journal of Machine Translation* 25: 217–37.

—— (2012) 'Machines, Translations and Memories: Language Transfer in the Web Browser', *Perspectives* 20: 451–61.

García Izquierdo, I. (ed.) (2005) *El género textual y la traducción: Reflexiones teóricas y aplicaciones pedagógicas*, Berne: Peter Lang.

—— (2007) 'Los géneros y las lenguas de especialidad', in E. Alcaraz, *et al.* (eds) *Las lenguas profesionales y académicas*, Barcelona: Ariel, pp. 119–25.

García Izquierdo, I. and V. Montalt (2002) 'Translating into textual genres', *Linguistica Antverpiensia*, 1: 135–43.

Gaspari, F. (2007) 'The Role of MT in Web Translation', unpublished doctoral dissertation, University of Manchester.

Gaspari, F. and J. Hutchins (2007) 'Online and Free! Ten Years of Online Machine Translation: Origins, Developments, Current Use and Future Prospects', proceedings of MT Summit XI, Copenhagen, Denmark, pp. 199–206.

Gentzler, E. (2001) *Contemporary Translation Theories*, Bristol: Multilingual Matters.

Gerber, L. (2008) 'Recipes for Success With Machine Translation, Part 1', *Clientside News*, 8: 15–17.

Gibb, F. and I. Matthaiakis (2007) 'A Framework for Assessing Web Site Localisation', *The Electronic Library*, 25: 664–78.

Gile, D. (1998) 'Observational Studies and Experimental Studies in the Investigation of Conference Interpreting', *Target* 10: 69–93.

—— (2004) 'Response to Invited Papers', in C. Schäffner (ed.) *Translation Research and Interpreting Research*, Bristol: Multilingual Matters, pp. 124–7.

—— (2010) 'Why Translation Studies Matters: A Pragmatist's Viewpoint', in D. Gile, G. Hansen and N. K. Pokorn (eds) *Why Translation Studies Matter*, Amsterdam: John Benjamins, pp. 251–61.

Giltrow, J. and D. Stein (2008) *Genres on the Internet*, Amsterdam-Philadelphia: John Benjamins.

Gläser, R. (1990) *Fachtextsorten im Englischen*, Tübingen: Gunter Narr.

González Davies, M. (2004) *Multiple Voices in the Translation Classroom*, Amsterdam-Philadelphia. John Benjamins.

—— (2005) 'Minding the Process, Improving the Product: Alternatives to Traditional Translator Training', in M. Tennent (ed.) *Training for the New Millennium: Pedagogies for Translation and Interpreting*, Amsterdam-Philadelphia: John Benjamins, pp. 67–82.

Göpferich, S. (1995a) *Textsorten in Naturwissenschaften und Technik: Pragmatische Typologie – Kontrastierung – Translation*, Tübingen: Gunter Narr.

—— (1995b) 'A Pragmatic Classification of LSP Texts In Science and Technology', *Target*, 7: 305–26.

—— (2009) 'Towards a Model of Translation Competence and its Acquisition: The Longitudinal Study TransComp', in S. Göpferich *et al.* (eds) *Behind the Mind: Methods, Models and Results in Translation Process Research*, Copenhagen: Samfundslitteratur 2009, pp. 12–37.

Göpferich, S. and R. Jääskeläinen (2009) 'Process Research into the Development of Translation Competence: Where are We, and Where do We Need to Go?', *Across Languages and Cultures* 10: 169–91.

Göpferich, S., *et al.* (2011) 'Exploring Translation Competence Acquisition: Criteria of Analysis Put to the Test', in S. O'Brien (ed.) *Cognitive Explorations in Translation*, London: Continuum, pp. 57–85.

Gouadec, D. (1998) 'Comprendre, évaluer, prévenir: Pratique, enseignement et recherche face à l'erreur et à la faute en traduction', *TTR*, 2: 35–54.

—— (2003) 'Le bagage spécifique du locateur/localizateur. La vrai "nouvel profil" requis', *Meta*, 28: 526–45.

—— (2007) *Translation as a Profession*, Amsterdam-Philadelphia: John Benjamins.

—— (2010) 'Quality in Translation', in Y. Gambier and L. van Doorslaer (eds) *Handbook of Translation Studies*, Amsterdam-Philadelphia: John Benjamins, pp. 270–5.

Guerberof, A. (2009) 'Productivity and Quality in MT post-editing', Proceedings of MT Summit XII, Ontario, Canada.

Hall, E. (1976) *Beyond Culture*, Garden City NY: Anchor Press.

Halliday, M. A. K. and R. Hasan (1976) *Cohesion in English*, London: Longman.

Halliday, M. A. K. and J. R. Martin (1993) *Writing Science: Literacy and Discursive Power*, London and Washington, DC: Falmer Press.

Halverson, S. (1999) 'Conceptual Work and the "Translation" Concept', *Target*, 11: 1–31.

—— (2003) 'The Cognitive Basis of Translation Universals', *Target*, 15: 197–241.

—— (2009) 'Elements of Doctoral Training', *The Interpreter and the Translator Trainer*, 3: 70–106.

—— (2010) 'Translation', in Y. Gambier and L. van Doorslaer (eds) *Handbook of Translation Studies*, Amsterdam-Philadelphia: John Benjamins, pp. 378–84.

Hanks, W. F. (1996) *Language and Communicative Practices: Critical Essays in Anthropology*, Boulder CO-Oxford: Westview Press.

Harris, B. (1977) 'The Importance of Natural Translation', *Working Papers on Bilingualism*, 12: 96–114.

Harris, B. and B. Sherwood (1978) 'Translating as an Innate Skill', in D. Gerver and H. W. Sinaiko (eds) *Language Interpretation and Communication*, New York: Plenum Press, pp. 155–70.

Hartley, T. (2009) 'Technology and Translation', in J. Munday (ed.) *The Routledge Companion to Translation Studies*, London-New York: Routledge, pp. 106–27.

Hartmann, R. (1980) *Contrastive Textology: Comparative discourse analysis in Applied Linguistics*, Heidelberg: Groos.

Hatim, B. and I. Mason (1990) *Discourse and the Translator*, London-New York: Longman.

—— (1997) *The Translator as Communicator*, London: Routledge.

Hatim, B. and J. Munday (2004) *Translation: An Advanced Resource Book*, London: Routledge.

Hearne, M. and A. Way (2011) 'Statistical Machine Translation: A Guide for Linguists and Translators', *Language and Linguistics Compass*, 5: 205–26.

Hermans, T. (1999) *Translation Systems. Descriptive and System-oriented Approaches Explained*, Manchester: St Jerome.

Herring, S. (2010) 'Web Content Analysis: Expanding the Paradigm', in J. Hunsinger, M. Allen and L. Kastrup (eds) *The International Handbook of Internet Research*, Dordrecht: Springer, pp. 233–50.

Herring, S., *et al.* (2004) 'Bridging the Gap: A Genre Analysis of Weblogs', *Proceedings from the XXXVIII Annual Hawaii International Conference on Systems Sciences*, Los Alamitos CA: IEEE Computer Society Press.

Heyn, M. (1998) 'Translation Memories: Insights and Prospects', in L. Bowker, *et al.* (eds) *Unity in Diversity? Current Trends in Translation Studies*, Manchester: St Jerome, pp. 123–36.

Hoey, M. (2005) *Lexical Priming. A New Theory of Words and Language*, London: Routledge.

Hofmann, C. and T. Mehnert (2000) 'Multilingual information management at Schneider Automation', in R. Sprung (ed.) *Translating into Success*, Amsterdam-Philadelphia: John Benjamins, pp. 59–69.

Hofstede, G. (1991) *Cultures and Organizations: Software of the Mind*, London: McGraw-Hill.

Holmes, J. S. (1988/2000) 'The Name and Nature of Translation Studies', in L. Venuti (ed.) *The Translation Studies Reader*, London: Routledge, pp. 172–85.

Holz-Mänttäri, J. (1984) *Translatorisches Handeln: Theorie und Methode*, Helsinki: Suomalainen Tiedeakatemia.

Hönig, H. G. (1987) 'Wer macht die Fehler?', in J. Albrecht, H.W. Drescher *et al.* (eds) *Translation und interkulturelle Kommunikation*, Frankfurt: Lang, pp. 37–45.

—— (1995) *Konstruktives Übersetzen* (Studien zur Translation 1), Tübingen: Stauffenburg.

—— (1998) 'Positions, Power and Practice: Functionalist Approaches and Translation Quality Assessment', in C. Schäffner (ed.) *Translation and Quality*, Bristol: Multilingual Matters, pp. 6–34.

House, J. (1997) *Translation Quality Assessment: A Model Revisited*, Tübingen: Gunter Narr.

——— (2008) 'Translation quality', in M. Baker and G. Saldanha (eds) *Routledge Encyclopedia of Translation Studies*, Amsterdam-Philadelphia: John Benjamins.

Howe, J. (2006) 'The Rise of Crowdsourcing', *Wired* 14(6). Online. Available HTTP: <http://www.wired.com/wired/archive/14.06/crowds.html> (accessed 10 July 2012).

——— (2008) *Crowdsourcing: Why the Power of Crowd is Driving the Future of Business*, London: Random House.

Hunsinger, J., M. Allen and L. Kastrup (eds) (2010) *The International Handbook of Internet Research*, Dordrecht: Springer.

Hurtado, A. (1999) *Enseñar a traducir: Metodología en la enseñanza de traductores e intérpretes*, Madrid: Edelsa.

——— (2001) *Traducción y traductología: Introducción a la traductología*, Madrid: Cátedra.

Hutchins, J. (2005) 'Current Commercial Machine Translation Systems and Computer-based Translation Tools: System Types and their Uses', *International Journal of Translation*, 17: 5–38. Online. Available HTTP: <http://www.hutchinsweb.me.uk/IJT-2005.pdf.> (accessed 10 July 2012).

Hutchins, J. and H. Somers (1992) *An Introduction to Machine Translation*, London: Academic Press.

Inghilleri, M. (2005) 'Mediating Zones of Uncertainty: Interpreter Agency, the Interpreting Habitus and Political Asylum Adjudication', *The Translator*, 11: 69–85.

InternetWorldStats (2012) Internet Usage Statistics. Available HTTP: <http://www.internetworld-stats.com/stats.htm> (accessed 10 July 2012).

Jääskeläinen, R. (2010) 'Are All Professionals Experts?', *Translation and Cognition*, 6: 213–27.

Jääskeläinen, R., P. Kujamaki and M. Jukka (2011) 'Towards Professionalism – Or Against It?: Dealing with the Changing World in Translation Research and Translation Education', *Across Languages and Cultures*, 12 (2): 143–56.

Jakobsen, A. (2005) 'Investigating Expert Translators' Processing Knowledge', in H.V. Dam, J. Engberg and H. Gerzymisch-Arbogast (eds) *Knowledge Systems and Translation*, Berlin-New York: Mouton de Gruyter, pp. 173–89.

Jakobson, R. (1960) 'Closing Statement: Linguistics and Poetics', in T. Sebeok (ed.) *Style in Language*, Cambridge MA: MIT Press, pp. 350–77.

Janoschka, A. (2003) *Web Advertising*, Amsterdam-Philadelphia: John Benjamins.

Jeney, C. (2007) *Writing for the Web: A Practical Guide*, Columbus: Pearson Prentice Hall.

Jiangbo, H. and T. Ying (2010) 'Study of the translation errors in the light of the Skopostheorie. Samples from the websites of some tourist attractions in China', *Babel*, 56: 35–46.

Jiménez-Crespo, M.A. (2008a) 'El proceso de localización web: Estudio contrastivo de un corpus comparable del género sitio web corporativo', unpublished PhD dissertation, University of Granada.

——— (2008b) 'Caracterización del género "sitio web corporativo" español: Análisis descriptivo con fines traductológicos', in M. Fernández Sánchez and R. Muñoz Martín(eds) *Aproximaciones cognitivas al estudio de la traducción e interpretación*, Granada: Comares, pp. 259–300.

——— (2008c) 'Web Texts in Translation Training', in M. Garant (ed.) *Current Trends in Translation Teaching and Learning*, Helsinki: Helsinki University Translation Studies Department Publication IV, pp. 14–39.

——— (2008d) 'Web Genres in Localization: A Spanish Corpus Study', *Localization Focus – The International Journal of Localization*, 6: 2–13.

——— (2009a) 'Conventions in Localization: A Corpus Study of Original vs. Translated Web Texts', *Jostrans*, 12: 79–102.

——— (2009b) 'The Effect of Translation Memory Tools in Translated Web Texts: Evidence from a Comparative Product-based Study', *Linguistica Antverpiensia*, 8: 213–32.

——— (2009c) 'El uso de corpus textuales en localización', *Tradumática*, 7. Online. Available HTTP: <http://ddd.uab.cat/pub/tradumatica/15787559n7a5.pdf> (accessed 10 July 2012).

——— (2009d) 'The Evaluation of Pragmatic and Functionalist Aspects In Localization: Towards a Holistic Approach to Quality Assurance', *The Journal of Internationalization and Localization*, 1: 60–93.

—— (2009e) 'Navegación Web accesible', in M. Tercedor (ed.) *Inclusión y accesibilidad desde el diseño y la presentación de materiales multimedia*, Granada: Editorial Tragacanto, pp. 187–206.

—— (2010a) 'The Intersection of Localization and Translation: A Corpus Study of Spanish Original and Localized Web Forms', *TIS: Translation and Interpreting Studies*, 5: 186–207.

—— (2010b) 'Web Internationalization Strategies and Translation Quality: Researching the Case of "International' Spanish"', *Localization Focus – The International Journal of Localization*, 8: 13–25.

—— (2011a) 'A Corpus-based Error Typology: Towards a More Objective Approach to Measuring Quality in Localization', *Perspectives*, 19: 315–38.

—— (2011b) 'The Future of Universal Tendencies In Translation: Explicitation in Web Localization', *Target*, 23: 3–25.

—— (2011c) 'To Adapt or Not to Adapt in Web Localization: A Contrastive Genre-based Study of Original and Localized Legal Sections in Corporate Websites', *Jostrans*, 15: 2–27.

—— (2011d) 'From Many One: Novel Approaches to Translation Quality in a Social Network Era', *Linguistica Antverpiensia*, 10: 112–31.

—— (2011e) 'Localization and Writing for a New Medium: A Review of Digital Style Guides', *Tradumática*, 8. Online. Available HTTP: <www.fti.uab.es/tradumatica/revista/num8/articles/08/08.pdf> (accessed 10 July 2012).

—— (2012a) '"Loss" or "Lost" in Translation: A Contrastive Genre Study of Original and Localised Non-profit US Websites', *Jostrans*, 17: 136–63.

—— (2012b) 'Web Localization in US Non-profit Websites: A Descriptive Study of Localization Strategies', in I. García Izquierdo (ed.) *Iberian Studies on Translation and Interpreting*, Oxford: Peter Lang.

—— (2013) 'Do Translation Crowdsourcing and Corpus Use Have the Same Goal? A Comparable Corpus Study of Facebook and Non-translated Social Networking Sites', *TIS: Journal of Translation and Interpreting Studies*, 8:1.

Jiménez-Crespo, M.A. and M. Tercedor (2010) 'Theoretical and Methodological Issues in Web Corpus Design and Analysis', *International Journal of Translation*, 22: 37–57.

—— (2012) 'Applying Corpus Data to Define Needs in Localization Training', *Meta*, 58.

Johansson, S. (1998) 'On the Role of Corpora in Cross-linguistic Research', in S. Johansson and S. Oksefjell (eds) *Corpora and Cross-linguistic Research: Theory, Method and Case Studies*, Amsterdam-New York: Rodopi, pp. 3–24.

Jucker, A. H. (2003) 'Mass media Communication at the Beginning of the Twenty-first Century', *Journal of Historical Pragmatics*, 4: 129–48.

—— (2005) 'Hypertext Research: Some Basic Concepts', in L. Moessner (ed.) *Anglistentag 2004 Aachen: Proceedings*, Trier: Wissenschaftlicher Verlag Trier, pp. 285–95.

Kade, O. (1968) *Zufall und Gesetzmässigkeit in der Übersetzung*, Leipzig: Verlag Enziklopädie.

Kageura, K., *et al.* (2011) 'Has Translation Gone Online and Collaborative?: An Experience from Minna no Hon'yaku', *Linguistica Antverpiensia*, 10: 45–74.

Karlgren, J. (2011) 'Conventions and Mutual Expectations — Understanding Sources for Web Genres', in A. Mehler, S. Sharoff and M. Santini (eds) *Genres on the Web*, New York: Springer, pp. 33–46.

Karsch, B. I. (2009) 'Profile of a Terminologist in Localization Environments', *Journal of Internationalization and Localization*, 1: 122–48.

Katan, D. (1999) *Translating Cultures: An Introduction for Translators, Interpreters and Mediators*, Manchester: St Jerome.

—— (2009) 'Translation as intercultural communication', in J. Munday (ed.) *The Routledge Companion to Translation Studies*, London-New York: Routledge, pp. 74–92.

Kelly, D. (2005) *Handbook for Translation Trainers*, Manchester: St Jerome.

—— (2008) 'Training the Trainers: Towards a Description of Translator Trainer Competence and Training Needs Analysis', *TTR*, 21: 99–125.

—— (2010) 'Translation Didactics', in Y. Gambier and L. van Doorslaer (eds) *Handbook of Translation Studies*, Amsterdam-Philadelphia: John Benjamins, pp. 389–97.

Kelly, N. (2009) 'Freelance Translators Clash with LinkedIn Over Crowdsourced Translation'. Online. Available HTTP: <http://www.commonsenseadvisory.com/Default.aspx?Contenttype=A rticleDetAD&tabID=63&Aid=591&moduleId=391> (accessed 10 July 2012).

Kelly, N., R. Ray and D. DePalma (2011) 'From Crawling to Sprinting: Community Translation Goes Mainstream', *Linguistica Antverpiensia*, 10: 45–76.

Kennedy, A. and M. Shepherd (2005) 'Automatic Identification of Home Pages on the Web', *Proceedings of the XXXVIII Annual Hawaii International Conference on System Sciences, Maui, Hawaii*. Los Alamitos CA: IEEE-Computer Society, p. 99c.

Kenny, D. (2001) *Lexis and Creativity in Translation*, Manchester: St Jerome.

Kersten, G. E., M. A. Kersten and W. Rakowski (2001) 'Software and Culture: Beyond the Internationalization of the Interface', *Journal of Global Information Management*, 10: 86–101.

Kintsch, W. and T. Van Dijk (1978) 'Toward a model of text comprehension and production', *Psychological Review*, 85: 363–94.

Kiraly, D. (1995) *Pathways to Translation: Pedagogy and Process*, Kent OH: Kent State University Press.

—— (2000) *A Social Constructivist Approach to Translator Education – Empowerment from Theory to Practice*, Manchester: St Jerome.

Kress, G. (1985) *Linguistic Processes in Sociocultural Practice*, Geelong: Deakin University Press.

—— (1993) 'Genre as social process', in B. Cope and M. Kalantzis (eds) *The Powers of Literacy: A Genre Approach to Teaching Writing*, London: Falmer Press, pp. 22–37.

Krings, H. (2001) *Repairing Texts: Empirical Investigations of Machine Translation Postediting Processes*, Kent OH: Kent State University Press.

Krug, S. (2006) *Don't Make Me Think: Common-sense Approach to Web Usability*, Berkeley CA: New Riders.

Kruger, A. and J. Munday (2011) *Corpus-Based Translation Studies: Research and Applications*, London: Continuum.

Kuhn, P., *et al.* (2010) 'Automatic Post-Editing', *MultiLingual*, 21(2): 43–6.

Kuhn, T. S. (1962) *The Structure of Scientific Revolutions*, 1st ed., Chicago IL: University of Chicago Press.

Kussmaul, P. (1995) *Training the Translator*, Amsterdam-Philadelphia: John Benjamins.

Labov, W. (1973) 'The Boundaries of Words and their Meanings', in C. J. Bailey and R.W. Shuy (eds) *New Ways of Analyzing Variation in English*, Washington: Georgetown University Press, pp. 340–73.

Lakoff, G. and M. Johnson (1980) *Metaphors We Live By*, Chicago IL: University of Chicago Press.

Landow, G. (1992) *Hypertext: The Convergence of Contemporary Critical Theory and Technology*, Baltimore: John Hopkins University Press.

Larose, R. (1998) 'Méthodologie de l'évaluation des traductions', *Meta*, 43: 163–86.

Laviosa, S. (1998) 'The English Comparable Corpus: A Resource and a Methodology', in L. Bowker, M. Cronin, D. Kenny and J. Pearson (eds) *Unity in Diversity: Current Trends in Translation Studies*, Manchester: St Jerome, pp. 101–12.

—— (2002) *Corpus-based Translation Studies*, Amsterdam: Rodopi.

Levitina, N. (2011) 'Requirement Collection: The Foundation of Scope and Scope Management in Localization Projects', in K. Dunne and E. Dunne (eds) *Translation and Localization Management*, Amsterdam-Philadelphia: John Benjamins, pp. 95–118.

Lewis, K. D. (1969) *Convention. A Philosophical Study*, Cambridge, MA: Harvard University Press.

Lindemann, C. and L. Littig (2011) 'Classification of Web Sites at the Supergenre Level', in A. Mehler, S. Sharoff and M. Santini (eds) *Genres on the Web*, New York: Springer, pp. 211–36.

Lingo (2004) *Guide to Translation and Globalization*, Portland OR: Lingo Systems.

LISA (2003) *Localization Industry Primer*, Debora Fry (ed.), Geneva: Localization Industry Standards Association.

—— (2004) *Localization Industry Primer*, 2nd ed., Geneva: Localization Industry Standards Association.

—— (2006) LISA *Best Practice Guide: Managing Global Content. Global Content Management and Global Translation Management Systems*, 2nd ed., Geneva: Localization Industry Standards Association.

—— (2007) *LISA Globalization Industry Primer*, Romainmôtier, Switzerland: Localization Industry Standards Association.

Liu, C., *et al.* (1997) 'Web Sites of the Fortune 500: Facing Customers Through Home Pages', *Information & Management*, 31: 335–45.

Lockwood, R. (1999) 'You Snooze, You Lose', *Language International*, 11: 12–16.

—— (2000) 'Machine Translation and Controlled Authoring at Caterpillar', in R. Sprung (ed.) *Translating into Success*, Amsterdam-Philadelphia: John Benjamins, pp. 187–202.

Lockwood, R. and K. Scott (2000) *A Writer's Guide to the Internet*, London: Allison and Busby.

Lommel, A., S. Gladkoff and H. Fenstermacher (2011) *Standards: A Broad View*, GALA Whitepaper. Online. Available HTTP: <http://www.gala-global.org/files/webfm/GALA-Standards-A-Broad-View-WhitePaper.pdf> (accessed 10 July 2012).

Longacre, R. (1983) *The Grammar of Discourse*, New York: Plenum.

Lörcher, W. (1991) *Translation Performance, Translation Process, and Translation Strategies*, Tübingen: Gunter Narr.

Lynch, C. (2006) 'GMS Technology Making the Localization Business Case', in K. Dunne (ed.) *Perspectives on Localization*, Amsterdam-Philadelphia: John Benjamins, pp. 37–46.

Macklovitch, E. and G. Russell (2000) 'What's Been Forgotten in Translation Memory', in J. White (ed.) *Envisioning Translation Memory in the Information Future: Proceedings of the AMTA 2000*, Berlin: Springer, pp. 137–46.

Mahadi, T., H. Vaezian and M. Akbari (2010) *Corpora in Translation: A Practical Guide*, Bern-New York: Peter Lang.

Malmkjær, M. and K. Windle (eds) (2011) *Oxford Handbook of Translation Studies*, Oxford: Oxford University Press

Mangiron, C. and M. O'Hagan (2006) 'Game Localization: Unleashing Imagination With "Restricted" Translation', *Jostrans*, 6: 10–21.

Marco, J. (2009) 'Training Translation Researchers: An Approach Based on Models and Best Practice', *The Interpreter and Translator Trainer*, 3: 13–35.

Martin, J. R. (1985) *Factual Writing, Exploring and Challenging Social Reality*, Geelong: Dunkin University Press.

—— (1995) 'Text and Clause: Fractal Resonance', *Text*, 15: 5–42.

Martínez, N. and A. Hurtado (2001) 'Assessment in Translation Studies: Research Needs', *Meta*, 47: 272–87.

Mata, M. (2005) 'Localización y traducción de contenido web', in D. Reineke (ed.) *Traducción y Localización*, La Palmas de Gran Canaria: Anroart Ediciones, pp. 187–252.

Mayor Serrano, Blanca (2007) 'La importancia de la tipología textual pragmática para la formación de traductores médicos', *Panace@*, 9 (26): 124–37. Online. Available HTTP: <www.tremedica.org/panacea/Indice-General/n26_tribuna-Serrano.pdf> (accessed 10 July 2012).

Mayoral, R. (1997) 'Sincronización y traducción subordinada: De la traducción audiovisual a la localización de software y su integración en la traducción de productos multimedia', in R. Mayoral and A. Tejada (eds) Proceedings of the First Symposium on Multimedia Localization, Granada: Departamento de Lingüística Aplicada a la Traducción e Interpretación.

Mazur, I. (2007) 'The Metalanguage of Localization: Theory and Practice', *Target*, 19: 337–57.

McDonough Dolmaya, J. (2006a) 'Beavers, Maple Leaves and Maple Trees. A Study of National Symbols on Localized and Domestic Websites', *Localization Focus*, 5: 7–14.

—— (2006b) 'Hiding Difference: On the Localization of Websites', *The Translator*, 12: 85–103.

—— (2010) '(Re)imagining Canada: Projecting Canada to Canadians Through Localized Websites', *Translation Studies*, 3: 302–17.

—— (2011) 'The Ethics of Crowdsourcing', *Linguistica Antverpiensia*, 10: 75–96.

—— (2012) 'Analyzing the Crowdsourcing Model and Its Impact on Public Perceptions of Translation', *The Translator* 18(2): 167–91.

Mehler, A., Sharoff, S. and M. Santini (2011) *Genres on the Web: Empirical Studies*, New York: Springer.

MeLLANGE (2006) *Error typology*. Online. Available HTTP: <http://corpus.leeds.ac.uk/mellange/images/mellange_error_typology_en.jpg> (accessed 10 July 2012).

Microsoft Corporation (2003) *Developing International Software*, Redmond WA: Microsoft Corporation.

Microsoft Press (1994) *Microsoft Press Computer Dictionary*, Redmond WA: Microsoft Press.

Miller, C.R. (1984) 'Genre as Social Action', *Quarterly Journal of Speech*, 70: 151–67.

Miller, C.R. and D. Shepherd (2004) 'Blogging as Social Action: A Genre Analysis of the Weblog', in L. G. Gurak *et al.* (eds) *Into the Blogosphere: Rhetoric, Community, and Culture of Weblogs.* Online. Available HTTP: <http://blog.lib.umn.edu/blogosphere/> (accessed 10 July 2012).

Montalt, V. and M. Davies (2006) *Medical Translation Step by Step*, Manchester: St Jerome.

Montalt, V. P. Ezpeleta and I. García Izquierdo (2008) 'The Acquisition of Translation Competence Through Textual Genre', *Translation Journal*, 12. Online. Available HTTP: <http://translation-journal.net/journal/46competence.htm> (accessed 10 July 2012).

Mossop, B. (2006) 'How Computerization Has Changed Translation', *Meta*, 51: 777–93.

Müller, E. (2005) 'Step-by-step Localization', *Multilingual*, 75 (16): 16–18.

Munday, J. (ed.) (2008) *The Routledge Companion to Translation Studies*, New York-London: Routledge.

—— (2012) *Introducing Translation Studies*, 3rd ed., New York-London: Routledge.

Muñoz Martín, R. (1995) *Lingüística para traducir*, Barcelona: Teide.

—— (2009) 'Expertise and Environment in Translation', *Mutatis Mutandis*, 2(1): 24–37.

Muñoz Sánchez, P. (2009) 'Video Game Localisation for Fans by Fans: The Case of Romhacking', *Journal of Internationalization and Localization*, 1: 168–85.

Munro, R. (2010) 'Crowdsourced Translation for Emergency Response in Haiti: The Global Collaboration of Local Knowledge', AMTA Workshop on Collaborative Crowdsourcing for Translation. Online. Available HTTP: <http://www.mt-archive.info/AMTA-2010-Munro.pdf> (accessed 10 July 2012).

Musale, S. (2001) 'Localization in the Wireless World: What to Look Out For When Localizing Small-Screen Software Products', *Language International*, 13: 37–40.

Myers, G. (1990) *Writing for Biology*, Madison WI: University of Wisconsin Press.

Nelson, T. (1993) *Literary Machines*, Sausalito CA: Mindful Press.

Neubert, A. (1996) 'Textlinguistics of Translation: The Textual Approach to Translation', in M. Gaddis Rose (ed.) *Translation Horizons: Beyond the Boundaries of 'Translation Spectrum'*, Translation Perspectives 9, Binghamton NY: State University of New York Center for Research in Translation, pp. 87–106.

—— (2000) 'Competence in Language, in Languages, and in Translation', in C. Schäffner and B. Adab (eds) *Developing Translation Competence*, Amsterdam-Philadelphia: John Benjamins, pp. 3–18.

Neubert, A. and M. Shreve (1992) *Translation as Text*, Kent OH: Kent State University Press.

Neuert, S. (2007) 'Translating Websites', Proceedings of the LSP Translation Scenarios (MuTra) conference, Vienna. Online. Available HTTP: <www.euroconferences.info/proceedings/. . ./2007_Nauert_Sandra.pdf> (accessed 10 July 2012).

Neunzig, W. (2011) 'Empirical Studies in Translation: Methodological and Epistemological Questions', *TTR: Etudes sur le texte et ses transformations* 24: 15–39.

Nida, E. (1964) *Towards a Science of Translation*, Leiden: Brill.

Nida, E. and C. Taber (1969) *The Theory and Practice of Translation*, Leiden: Brill.

Nielsen, J. (2001) *Designing Web Usability: The Practice of Simplicity*, Indianapolis IN: New Riders.

—— (2003) 'Usability 101: Introduction to Usability'. Online. Available HTTP: <http://www.useit.com/alertbox/20030825.html> (accessed 10 July 2012).

—— (2004) 'The need for Web design standards'. Online. Available HTTP: <http://www.useit.com/alertbox/20040913.html> (accessed 10 July 2012).

Nielsen, J. and H. Loranger (2006) *Prioritizing Web Usability*, Indianapolis IN: News Riders.

Nielsen, J. and K. Pernice (2010) *Eyetracking Web Usability*, Berkeley: New Riders.

Nielsen, J. and M. Tahir (2002) *Homepage Usability: 50 Websites Deconstructed*, Indianapolis IN: New Riders.

Nobs, M. (2006) *La traducción de folletos turísticos: ¿Qué calidad demandan los turistas?*, Granada: Comares.

Nord, C. (1991) *Text Analysis in Translation*, Amsterdam-Atlanta: Rodopi.

—— (1996) 'El error en la traducción: Categorías y evaluación', in A. Hurtado (ed.) *La enseñanza de la traducción*, Castelló: Universitat Jaume I, pp. 91–107.

—— (1997) *Functionalist Approaches Explained*, Manchester: St Jerome.

—— (2003) 'El análisis contrastivo y cultural en la clase de lengua', *Quaderns, Revista de Traducció*, 10: 23–39.

—— (2005) 'Training Functional Translators', in M. Tennent (ed.) *Training for the New Millennium. Pedagogies for Translation and Interpreting*, Amsterdam-Philadelphia: John Benjamins, pp. 209–24.

Nwogu, K.N. (1997) 'The Research Paper: Structure and Functions', *ESP* 16: 119–38.

O'Brien, S. (2006) 'Pauses as Indicators of Cognitive Effort in Post-Editing Machine Translation Output', *Across Languages and Cultures*, 7: 1–21.

—— (2011) 'Towards Predicting Post-Editing Productivity', *Machine Translation*, 25: 197–215.

—— (2012) 'Towards a Dynamic Quality Evaluation Model for Translation', *Jostrans*, 17: 55–77.

O'Hagan, M. (2007) 'An Empirical Investigation of Temporal and Technical Post-Editing Effort', *TIS*, 2: 83–136.

—— (2008) 'Fan Translation Networks: An Accidental Translator Training Environment?', in J. Kearns (ed.) *Translator and Interpreter Training: Issues, Methods and Debates*, London-New York: Continuum, pp. 159–83

—— (2009) 'Evolution of User-generated Translation: Fansubs, Translation Hacking and Crowdsourcing', *Journal of Internationalization and Localization*, 1: 94–121.

—— (2011) 'Introduction: Community Translation: Translation as a Social Activity and its Possible Consequences in the Advent of Web 2.0 and Beyond', *Linguistica Antverpiensia*, 10: 1–10.

—— (2012a) 'Translation as the New Game in the Digital Era', *Translation Spaces*, 1: 123–41.

—— (2012b) 'The Impact of New Technologies on Translation Studies: A Technological Turn?', in C. Millan-Varela and F. Bartrina (eds) *Routledge Handbook of Translation Studies*, London: Routledge, pp. 503–18.

O'Hagan, M. and D. Ashworth (2003) *Translation-mediated Communication in a Digital World: Facing the Challenges of Globalization and Localization*, Bristol: Multilingual Matters.

O'Hagan, M. and C. Mangiron (2013) *Game Localization: Translating for the Global Digital Entertainment Industry*. Amsterdam-Philadelphia: John Benjamins.

Och, F. (2012) 'Breaking Down the Language Barrier – Six Years In', Official Google Blog. Online. Available HTTP: <http://googleblog.blogspot.com.au/2012/04/breaking-down-language-barriersix-years.html> (accessed 10 July 2012).

Olohan, M. (2004) *Introducing Corpora in Translation Studies*, London: Routledge.

ÖNORM D 1200 (2000) *Translation and Interpretation Services, Translation Services. Requirements of the Service and the Provision of the Service*, Vienna: Österreichisches Normungsinstitut.

Orozco, M. (2004) 'The Clue to Common Research in Translation and Interpreting: Methodology', in C. Schäffner (ed.) *Translation Research and Interpreting Research. Traditions, Gaps and Synergies*, Bristol: Multilingual Matters, pp. 98–103.

Orozco, M. and A. Hurtado (2002) 'Measuring Translation Competence Acquisition', *Meta*, 47: 375–402.

Ørsted, J. (2001) 'Quality and Efficiency: Incompatible Elements in Translation Practice?', *Meta*, 46: 438–47.

PACTE (2000) 'Exploratory Texts in a Study of Translation Competence', *Conference Interpretation and Translation* 4: 41–69.

—— (2001) 'La competencia traductora y su adquisición', *Quaderns, Revista de Traducció*, 6: 39–45.

—— (2003) 'Building a Translation Competence Model', in F. Alves (ed.) *Triangulating Translation*, Amsterdam-Philadelphia: John Benjamins, pp. 43–66.

—— (2005) 'Investigating Translation Competence: Conceptual and Methodological Issues', *Meta*, 50: 609–19.

—— (2009) 'Results of the Validation of the PACTE Translation Competence Model: Acceptability and Decision-making', *Across Languages and Cultures*, 10(2): 207–30.

PACTE (2011) 'Results of the Validation of the PACTE Translation Competence Model: Translation Project and Dynamic Translation Index', in S. O'Brien (ed.) *IATIS Yearbook 2010*, London: Continuum, pp. 317–43.

Paltridge, B. (1997) *Genre, Fames and Writing in Research Settings*, Amsterdam-Philadelphia: John Benjamins.

Paolillo, J.C., J. Warren and B. Kunz (2007) 'Social Network and Genre Emergence in Amateur Flash Multimedia', Proceedings 40th Hawaii International Conference on System Sciences, Los Alamitos CA: IEEE Press.

Payne, G. and J. Payne (2004) *Key Concepts in Social Research*, London: Sage Publications.

Pedrola, M. (2009) 'Multimodality and Translation in Embassy Websites: A Comparative Approach', unpublished doctoral dissertation, Università Cattolica del Sacro Cuore, Italy.

Perrino, S. (2009) 'User-generated Translation: The Future of Translation in a Web 2.0 Environment', *Jostrans*, 11: 55–78.

Petras, R. (2011) 'Localizing with Community Translation', *Multilingual*, October-November: 40–41.

Pierini, P. (2006) 'Quality in Web Translation: An Investigation into UK and Italian Tourism Web Sites', *Jostrans*, 8: 85–103.

Plitt, M. and F. Masselot (2010) 'A Productivity Test of Statistical Machine Translation. Post-editing in a Typical Localisation Context', *Prague Bulletin of Mathematical Linguistics* 93: 7–16.

Posteguillo, S., *et al.* (eds) (2007) *The Texture of Internet: Netlinguistics in Progress*, Newcastle: Cambridge Scholars Publishing.

Presas, M. (1996) 'Problemas de traducció i competencia traductora', unpublished doctoral dissertation, Universitat Autonoma de Barcelona.

Price, J. and L. Price (2002) *Hot Text: Web Writing That Works*, Berkeley CA: News Riders.

Pym, A. (1992) 'Translation Error Analysis and the Interference with Language Teaching', in C. Dollerup and A. Loddegaard (eds) *The Teaching of Translation*, Amsterdam: John Benjamins, pp. 279–88.

—— (2003a) 'Redefining Translation Competence in an Electronic Age: In Defence of a Minimalist Approach', *Meta*, 48: 481–97.

—— (2003b) 'What Localization Models Can Learn From Translation Theory', *The LISA Newsletter: Globalization Insider*, 12.

—— (2004a) *The Moving Text: Localization, Translation and Distribution*, Amsterdam-Philadelphia: John Benjamins.

—— (2004b) 'Localization from the Perspective of Translation Studies: Overlaps in the Digital Divide?', paper presented at the conference SCALLA 2004, Kathmandu. Online. Available HTTP: <http://www.elda.org/en/proj/scalla/SCALLA2004/Pymv2.pdf> (accessed 10 July 2012).

—— (2004c) 'Localization and the Training of Linguistic Mediators for the Third Millennium', *FORUM – International Journal of Interpretation and Translation*, 2: 125–35.

—— (2005) 'Localization: On its Nature, Virtues and Dangers', *Synaps*, 17: 17–25.

—— (2006) 'Localization, Training, and the Threat of Fragmentation'. Online. Available HTTP: <http://www.tinet.org/~apym/on-line/translation.html> (accessed 10 July 2012).

—— (2010) *Exploring Translation Theories*, London: Routledge.

—— (2011a) 'What Technology Does to Translating', *Translation & Interpreting*, 3: 1–9.

—— (2011b) 'Translation Research Terms – A Tentative Glossary for Moments of Perplexity and Dispute', in A. Pym (ed.) *Translation Research Projects 3*, Tarragona: Intercultural Studies Group, pp. 75–99.

—— (2012) 'Translation Skill-sets in a Machine-translation Age'. Online. Available HTTP: <http://usuaris.tinet.cat/apym/on-line/training/2012_competence_pym.pdf> (accessed 10 July 2012).

Pym, A. and K. Windle (2011a) 'Website localization', in K. Malmkjaer and K. Windle (eds) *The Oxford Handbook of Translation Studies*, Oxford: Oxford University Press, pp. 410–24.

—— (2011b) 'Training translators', in K. Malmkjaer and K. Windle (eds) *The Oxford Handbook of Translation Studies*, Oxford and New York: Oxford University Press.

Quah, C.K. (2006) *Translation and Technology*, Basingstoke-New York: Palgrave MacMillan.

Quirion, M. (2003) 'La formation en localisation à l'université: Pour quoi faire?', *Meta*, 48: 546–58.

Rabadán, R. (2008) 'Refining the Idea of "Applied Extensions"', in A. Pym, M. Shlesinger and D. Simeoni (eds), *Beyond Descriptive Translation Studies*, Amsterdam-Philadelphia, John Benjamins, pp. 103–17.

—— (2010) 'Applied Translation Studies', in Y. Gambier and L. van Doorslaer (eds) *Handbook of Translation Studies*, Amsterdam-Philadelphia: John Benjamins, pp. 7–11.

Remael, A. (2010) 'Audiovisual translation', in Y. Gambier and L. van Doorslaer (eds) *Handbook of Translation Studies*, Amsterdam-Philadelphia: John Benjamins, pp. 12–17.

Ray, R. and N. Kelly (2011) *Crowdsourced Translation: Best Practices for Implementation*, Lowell MA: Common Sense Advisory.

Rehm, G. (2002) 'Towards Automatic Web Genre Identification: A Corpus-Based Approach in the Domain of Academia by Example of the Academic's Personal Homepage', Proceedings from the XXXV Hawaii International Conference on System Sciences (HICSS-35) Big Island, Hawaii, Los Alamitos CA: IEEE.

Reid, I. (ed.) (1987) *The Place of Genre in Learning*, Geelong: Deakin University.

Reineke, D. (ed.) (2005) *Traducción y Localización*, Las Palmas de Gran Canaria: Anroart Ediciones.

Reineke, D. and Sánchez, E. (2005) 'Perfil laboral y formación de traductores: Una encuesta a proveedores de servicios', in D. Reineke (ed.) *Traducción y Localización*, La Palmas de Gran Canaria: Anroart Ediciones, pp. 347–62.

Reinke, U. (2005) 'Using eCoLoRe Materials in Translator Training. Some Experiences from a Teacher's Viewpoint. Resources and Tools for e-Learning in Translation and Localisation', Proceedings of the eCoLoRe/MeLLANGE Workshop, Leeds, 21–23 March. Online. Available HTTP: <http://ecolore.leeds.ac.uk/downloads/workshop/eCoLoRe-MeLLANGE_workshop_proceedings.zip> (accessed 10 July 2012).

Reiss, K. (1971) *Möglichkeiten und Grenzen der Übersetzungskritik*, Munich: Hueber.

—— (1976) *Texttyp und Übersetzungsmethode. Der operative Text*, Kronberg: Scriptor Verlag.

Reiss, K. and J. H. Vermeer (1984) *Grundlegung einer Allgemeinen Translationstheorie*, Tübingen: Niemeyer.

Renau, M.L. (2004) 'La página web de la industria cerámico-azulejera: Un estudio descriptivo y su aplicación a la enseñanza del ingles para la informática', unpublished doctoral dissertation, Castelló: Universitat Jaume I.

Risku, H. (1998) *Translatorische Kompetenz*, Tübingen: Stauffenburg.

Robbins, S. and A. Stylianou (2003) 'Global Corporate Web Sites: An Empirical Investigation of Content and Design', *Information & Management*, 40: 205–12.

Rothe-Neves, R. (2002) 'Translation Quality Assessment for Research Purposes: An Empirical Approach', *Cadernos de Tradução: O processo de Tradução*, 2: 113–31.

Rumelhart, D. E. (1980) 'On evaluation of story grammars', *Cognitive Science*, 4: 313–16.

Sager, J. (1989) 'Quality and Standards: The Evaluation of Translations', in C. Picken (ed.) *The Translator's Handbook*, London: ASLIB, pp. 91–102.

Sandrini, P. (2005) 'Website Localization and Translation', MuTra – Multidimensional Translation Conference Proceedings: Challenges of Multidimensional Translation, Saarbrücken.

—— (2008) 'Localization', in H. Gerzymisch-Arbogast *et al.* (eds) *Key Issues in LSP Translation*, Amsterdam-Philadelphia: John Benjamins.

Santini, M. (2007) 'Automatic Identification of Genre in Web Pages', unpublished doctoral dissertation, University of Brighton.

Santini, M. and S. Sharoff (2009) 'Web Genre Benchmark Under Construction', *Journal for Language Technology and Computational Linguistics (JLCL)* 25: 129–45.

Santini, M., *et al.* (2011) 'Riding the Rough Waves of Genres on the Web: Concepts and Research Questions', in A. Mehler, S. Sharoff and M. Santini (eds) *Genres on the Web*, New York: Springer, pp. 3–29.

Saussure, F. de (1916) *Cours de Linguistique General*, Paris: Payot.

Scarpa, F., M. T. Musacchio and G. Palumbo (2009) 'A Foot in Both Camps: Redressing the Balance Between the "Pure" and Applied Branches of Translation Studies', *Interpreting &*

Translation, 1: 32–43. Online. Available HTTP: <http://trans-int.org/index.php/transint/article/view/49/51> (accessed 10 July 2012).

Schäler, R. (2001) 'Learning to Localize in Limerick', *Language International*, 13: 22–6.

—— (2002) 'The Cultural Dimension in Software Localization', *Localization Focus*, 1 (2): 5–9.

—— (2005) 'The Irish model in localization', Paper presented at LISA Forum Cairo 2005: *Perspectives from the Middle East and Africa*, 5–8. December 2005.

—— (2007) 'Translators and Localization: Education and Training in the Context of the Global Initiative for Local Computing (GILC)', *The Interpreter and Translator Trainer*, 1: 119–35.

—— (2008a) 'Localization', in M. Baker and S. Saldanha (eds) *Encyclopedia of Translation Studies*, London: Routledge, pp. 156–61.

—— (2008b) 'Linguistic Resources and Localization', in E. Yuste Rodrigo (ed.) *Topics in Language Resources for Translation and Localization*, Amsterdam-Philadelphia: John Benjamins, pp. 194–214.

—— (2008c) 'Reverse Localization', *Localization Focus – The International Journal of Localisation*, 6: 39–49.

—— (2010) 'Localization and Translation', in Y. Gambier and L. van Doorslaer (eds) *Handbook of Translation Studies*, Amsterdam-Philadelphia: John Benjamins, pp. 209–14.

Schmitz, K. D. (2007) 'Indeterminacy of Terms and Icons in Software Localization', in B. Antia (ed.) *Indeterminacy in LSP and Terminology: Studies in Honour of Heribert Picht*, Amsterdam-Philadelphia: John Benjamins, pp. 49–58.

Séguinot, C. (1989) 'The Translation Process: An Experimental Study', in C. Séguinot (ed.) *The Translation Process*, Toronto: HG Publications, pp. 21–53.

Shepherd, M. and C. Watters (1998) 'The Evolution of Cybergenres', in R. Sprague (ed.) *Proceedings of the XXXI Hawaii International Conference on System Sciences*, Los Alamitos CA: IEEE-Computer Society, 97–109.

—— (1999) 'The Functionality Attribute of Cybergenres', *Proceedings of the XXXII Hawaii International Conference on System Sciences, Maui, Hawaii*, Los Alamitos CA: IEEE-Computer Society.

Shepherd, M., C. Watters and A. Kennedy (2004) 'Cybergenre: Automatic Identification of Home Pages on the Web', *Journal of Web Engineering*, 3: 236–51.

Shimoata, S., *et al.* (2001) 'Collaborative Translation Environment on the Web', *Proceedings of the MT Summit 8*, pp. 331–34. Online. Available HTTP: <www.mt-archive.info/MTS-2001-Shimohata.pdf> (accessed 10 July 2012).

Shirky, C. (2010) *Cognitive Surplus: Creativity and Generosity in a Connected Age*, New York: Penguin Press.

Shreve, G. M. (2006a) 'Translation and Expertise: The Deliberate Practice', *Journal of Translation Studies*, 9: 27–42.

—— (2006b) 'Corpus Enhancement and Localization', in K. Dunne (ed.) *Perspectives on Localization*, Amsterdam-Philadelphia: John Benjamins, pp. 309–31.

Shreve, G. and E. Angelone (eds) (2010) *Translation and Cognition*, Amsterdam-Philadelphia: John Benjamins Publishing.

Shreve, G. and B. Diamond (1997) 'Cognitive Processes in Translation and Interpreting: Critical Issues', in J. H. Danks *et al.* (eds) *Cognitive Processes in Translation and Interpreting*, Thousand Oaks CA: Sage Publications, pp. 233–51.

Sikes, R. (2011) 'Rethinking the Role of the Localization Manager', in K. Dunne and E. Dunne (eds) *Translation and Localization Management*, Amsterdam-Philadelphia: John Benjamins, pp. 235–54.

Singh, N., O. Furrer and O. Massimiliano (2004) 'To Localize or to Standardize on the Web: Empirical Evidence from Italy, India, Netherlands, Switzerland and Spain', *Multinational Business Review*, 12: 69–88.

Singh, N., K. Lehnert and K. Bostick (2012) 'Global Social Media Usage: Insights Into Reaching Consumers Worldwide', Thunderbird International Business Review, 54: 683–70.

Singh, N. and A. Pereira (2005) *The Culturally Customized Website: Customizing Websites for the Global Marketplace*, Oxford: Elsevier.

Singh, N., D. Tory and L. Wright (2009) 'A Diagnostic Framework for Measuring Website Localization', *Thunderbird International Business Review*, 51: 281–95.

Snell-Hornby, M. (1988) *Translation Studies: An Integrated Approach*, Amsterdam-Philadelphia: John Benjamins.

—— (1996) *Translation und Text: Ausgewählte Vorträge*, Vienna: Vienna University Press.

—— (2006) *The Turns of Translation Studies*, Amsterdam-Philadelphia: John Benjamins.

Snell-Hornby, M., F. Pöchhacker and K. Kaindl (eds) (1994) *Translation Studies: An Interdiscipline*, Amsterdam-Philadelphia: John Benjamins.

Spilka, I. V. (1984) 'Analyse de traduction', in A. Thomas and J. Flamand (eds) *La traduction: l'universitaire et le praticien*, Ottawa: Éditions de l'Université d'Ottawa, pp. 72–81.

Sprung, R. C. (ed.) (2000) *Translating into Success: Cutting-edge Strategies for Going Multilingual in a Global Age*, Amsterdam-Philadelphia: John Benjamins.

Spyridakis, J. H. (2000) 'Guidelines for Authoring Comprehensible Web Pages and Evaluating Their Success', *Technical Communication*, 47: 359–82.

Stejskal, J. (2009) 'Ask Not What the Crowd Can Do for You, But What You Can Do for the Crowd', *ATA Chronicle*, August, 2009.

Storrer, A. (2002) 'Coherence in Text and Hypertext', *Document Design*, 3: 157–68.

Stubbs, M. (1996) *Text and Corpus Analysis: Computer-assisted Studies of Language and Culture*, London: Blackwell.

Sun, S. and G. Shreve (2012) 'Reconfiguring Translation Studies', *Translation Spaces*, 1. Online. Available HTTP: http://sanjun.org/ReconfiguringTS.html (accessed 10 September 2012).

Swales, J. (1990) *Genre Analysis: English in Academic and Research Settings*, Cambridge: Cambridge University Press.

—— (2004) *Research Genres: Explorations and Applications*, Cambridge: Cambridge University Press.

Swales, J.M. and C. Feak (2000) *English in Today's Research World: A Writer's Guide*, Michigan: Michigan University Press.

Symmonds, N. (2002) *Internationalization and Localization Using Microsoft.Net*, Berkeley CA: Apress.

TAUS (2012) *Dynamic Quality Framework Report*, Online, HTTP: <https://tauslabs.com/dynamic-quality/about-dqf>.

Teich, E. (2003) *Cross-Linguistic Variation in System and Text: A Methodology for the Investigation of Translations and Comparable Texts*, Berlin: Mouton de Gruyter.

Tercedor, M. (2005) 'Aspectos culturales en la localización de productos multimedia', *Quaderns, Revista de Traducció*, 12: 151–60.

—— (2010) 'Translating Web Multimodalities: Towards Inclusive Web Localization', *Tradumática*, 9. Online. Available HTTP: <http://www.fti.uab.cat/tradumatica/revista/num8/articles/09/9central.htm> (accessed 10 July 2012).

Tercedor, M. and M.A. Jiménez-Crespo (2008) 'Accesibilidad web, imágenes y traducción técnica' in C. Jiménez and A. Rodríguez (eds) *Accesibilidad a los medios audiovisuales para personas con discapacidad*, Madrid: Real Patronato de Discapacidad, pp. 123–8.

Tirkkonen-Condit, S. (1989) 'Professional Versus Non-professional Translation: A Think-aloud Protocol Study', in C. Séguinot (ed.) *The Translation Process*, Toronto: HG Publications, pp. 87–98.

—— (1992) 'The Interaction of World Knowledge and Linguistic Knowledge in the Processes of Translation: A Think-aloud Protocol Study', in B. Lewandowska-Tomaszczyk and M. Thelen (eds) *Translation and Meaning, Part 2*, Maastricht: Rijkshogeschool Maastricht, pp. 433–40.

Tirkkonen-Condit, S. and Jääskeläinen, R. (eds) (2010) *Tapping and Mapping the Processes of Translation and Interpreting*, Amsterdam-Philadelphia: John Benjamins.

Todorov, T. (1990) *Genres in Discourse*, Cambridge: Cambridge University Press.

Tognini-Bonelli, E. (2001) *Corpus Linguistics at Work*, Amsterdam-Philadelphia: John Benjamins.

Torres-Hostench, O. *et al.* (2010) 'TRACE: Measuring the impact of CAT tools on translated texts', in L. Gea *et al.* (eds) *Linguistic and Translation Studies in Scientific Communication*, London: Peter Lang, pp. 255–76.

Torresi, I. (2010) *Translating Promotional and Advertising Texts*, Manchester: St Jerome.

Toury, G. (1995) *Descriptive Translation Studies and Beyond*, Amsterdam-Philadelphia: John Benjamins.

—— (1998) 'A Handful of Paragraphs on Translation and Norms', *Current Issues in Language and Society*, 5: 10–32.

—— (2004) 'Probabilistic Explanations in Translation Studies. Welcome As They Are, Would They Qualify As Universals?' in A. Mauranen and P. Kujamäki (eds) *Translation Universals: Do they Exist?*, Amsterdam-Philadelphia: John Benjamins, pp. 15–32.

Trosborg, A. (1997) 'Text Typology: Register, Genre and Text Type', in A. Trosborg (ed.) *Text Typology and Translation*, Amsterdam-Philadelphia: John Benjamins, pp. 3–23.

Tymoczko, M. (2005) 'Trajectories of Research in Translation Studies', *Meta* 50: 1082–97.

Tyrkkö, J. (2007) 'Making sense of digital textuality', *European Journal of English Studies*, 11: 147–61.

—— (2011) 'Fuzzy coHerence: Making Sense of Continuity in Hypertext Narratives', unpublished PhD dissertation. University of Helsinki.

Ulrych, M. and S. Anselmi (2008) 'Applied Translation Studies and Beyond: A Socio-historical Perspective on a Changing Discipline', in G. Iamartino, M.L. Maggioni and R. Facchinetti (eds) *Thou Sittest at Another Boke . . . English Studies in Honour of Domenico Pezzini*, Monza: Polimetrica International Scientific Publisher, pp. 145–70.

Uren, E., R. Howard and T. Perinotti (1993) *Software Internationalization and Localization: An Introduction*, New York: Van Nostrand-Reinhold.

Van Dijk, T. A. (1988) *News as Discourse*, Hillsdale NJ: Lawrence Erlbaum Associates.

Van Dijk, T. A. and W. Kintsch (1983) *Strategies of Discourse Comprehension*, New York: Academic Press.

Vandepitte, S. (2008) 'Remapping Translation Studies: Towards a Translation Studies Ontology', *Meta*, 53: 569–88.

Vaughan, M. and V. Dillon (2006) 'Why Structure and Genre Matter for Users of Digital Information: A Longitudinal Experiment with Readers of a Web-based Newspaper', *International Journal of Human Computer Studies*, 64: 502–25.

Venuti, L. (1995) *The Translator Invisibility: A History of Translation*, New York-London: Routledge.

Waddington, C. (2001) 'Different Methods of Evaluating Student Translation: The Question of Validity', *Meta* 46: 312–25.

Wallis, J. (2008) 'Interactive Translation vs. Pre-translation in TMs: A Pilot Study', *Meta*, 53: 623–9.

Werlich, E. (1975) *Typologie der Texte*, Heidelberg: Quelle & Meyer.

Williams, J. and A. Chesterman (2002) *The Map. A Beginner's Guide to Doing Research in Translation Studies*, Manchester: St Jerome.

Williams, M. (2004) *Translation Quality Assessment*, Ottawa: Ottawa University Press.

Wilss, W. (1992) *Übersetzungsfertigkeit: Annäherungen an einen komplexen übersetzungspraktischen Begriff*, Tübingen: Gunter Narr.

Wolf, M. (2007) 'Introduction: The Emergence of a Sociology of Translation', in M. Wolf and A. Fukari (eds) *Constructing a Sociology of Translation*, Amsterdam-Philadelphia: John Benjamins, pp. 1–36.

—— (2010) 'Translation "Going Social"? Challenges to the (Ivory) Tower of Babel', *MonTI*, 2: 29–46.

Wright, S. (2004) 'Localization Competence for Translation and Project Management', in E. Fleischmann, P. Schmitt and G. Wotjak (eds) *Translationskompetenz*, Tübingen: Stauffenburg, pp. 581–95.

—— (2006) 'Language Industry Standards', in K. Dunne (ed.) *Perspectives on Localization*, Amsterdam-Philadelphia: John Benjamins, pp. 241–78.

Wright, S. E. and G. Budin (2001) *Handbook of Terminology Management*, Amsterdam-Philadelphia: John Benjamins.

Wu, X. (2010) 'Recreation Through Translation: Examining China's Online Volunteer Translators', Paper presented at Translation and the Humanities Conference, University of Illinois, Urbana-Champaign, October 14–16, 2010.

Yates, J. and W. Orlikowski (1992) 'Genres of Organizational Communication: A Structural Approach to Studying Communications and Media', *Academy of Management Review*, 17: 299–326.

Yunker, J. (2003) *Beyond Borders: Web Globalization Strategies*, Indianapolis IN: New Riders.

—— (2010) *The Art of the Global Gateway: Strategies for Successful Multilingual Navigation*, Ashland OR: Byte Level Books.

Zabalbeascoa, P. (2008) 'The Nature of Audiovisual Text and its Parameters', in J. Díaz Cintas (ed.) *The Didactics of Audiovisual Translation*, Amsterdam-Philadelphia: John Benjamins, pp. 21–38.

Zaidan, O. and C. Callison-Burch (2011) 'Crowdsourcing Translation: Professional Quality from Non-Professionals', *Proceedings of the 49th Annual Meeting of the Association for Computational Linguistics: Human Language Technologies,* Portland OR: Association for Computational Linguistics, pp. 1220–9.

Zanettin, F. (1998) 'Bilingual comparable corpora and the training of translators', *Meta*, 43: 616–30.

Zanettin, F., S. Bernardini and D. Stewart (eds) (2003) *Corpora in Translator Education*, Manchester: St Jerome.

Zatlin, P. (2005) *Theatrical Translation and Film Adaptation: A Practitioner's View*, Bristol: Multilingual Matters.

INDEX

Italicized and bold page numbers refer to figures and tables respectively. Page numbers followed by 'n' refer to notes.

www.routledge.com/linguistics

3rd Edition
The Translation Studies Reader

Edited by **Lawrence Venuti**

The Translation Studies Reader provides a definitive survey of the most important and influential developments in translation theory and research, with an emphasis on twentieth-century developments. With introductory essays prefacing each section, the book places a wide range of seminal and innovative readings within their thematic, cultural and historical contexts.

The third edition of this classic reader has been fully revised and updated and adds a new section: 2000 and beyond, which includes five new readings. These new readings bring the *Reader* up to date with recent developments in the field and include articles on translation and world literature and translation and the internet.

2012: 246 x 174 mm: 560pp
ISBN: 978-0-415-61347-7 (hbk)
ISBN: 978-0-415-61348-4 (pbk)